BLESSED CHARLES OF AUSTRIA

BLESSED CHARLES OF AUSTRIA

A Holy Emperor and His Legacy

CHARLES A. COULOMBE

TAN Books
Gastonia, North Carolina

Cover design by Caroline Green

Cover image: Emperor Charles I of Austria, in uniform, (b/w photo) © SZ Photo / Scherl / Bridgeman Images

Library of Congress Control Number: 2020931190

ISBN: 978-1-5051-1328-0

Kindle ISBN: 978-1-5051-1330-3

EPUB ISBN: 978-1-5051-1329-7

Published in the United States by
TAN Books
PO Box 269
Gastonia, NC 28053
www.TANBooks.com

Printed in the United States of America

To the memory of His Imperial and Royal Highness
Archduke Otto von Habsburg,
this book is respectfully dedicated

CONTENTS

FOREWORD

When the Catholic Church elevates somebody to being blessed, he becomes an example to follow for all Christendom. At first glance, the question might arise, what makes Emperor Karl (Charles)[1] an example to copy? I'm very grateful to Charles Coulombe for undertaking a work to get a better understanding of the personality of Blessed Emperor Karl, his character, but also the very complex political situation in and through which he lived.

Having a grandfather who has been designated by the Catholic Church to the status of blessed gives you the possibility, but also the responsibility, to take a very personal look at his personality. Although I did not meet him, I had the good fortune to still have met several persons who knew him personally, and they were wonderful witnesses to give me a very vivid description of his character.

Thinking about Blessed Emperor Karl, three principal roles of the man present themselves: the soldier, the politician, and the family man. The most astounding fact is that Emperor Karl excelled in all three areas. "Excelling" does not mean that he was successful in his endeavors but rather that he approached all of his roles with the best intent and carried out his duties under the influence of and guided by religious

1 He is known as both Karl and Charles.

values. One of his guidelines was to seek God's will in all and everything he was undertaking and to strive to fulfill it in the best possible way.

As a soldier, he had vast experience of the front. Actually, he was the only head of state in the First World War who had this firsthand knowledge of what soldiers had to go through when they were sent to war. This definitely had a great impact on his decision-making process, especially his constant search for peace. But it was also influential in his conduct of the war. He was often accused regarding the use of chemical weapons during the war. The archives tell a different story: whenever possible, he stopped the use of that weapon. But since the militarily more dominant German "Bündnispartner" considered the use of gas as essential for success in war, Karl was not able to implement his will on every part of the frontline.

As a politician, he was also definitely much more able than the war propaganda admitted. He did not have the same apparatus at his disposal as did his predecessor as crown prince. Franz Ferdinand had a sizeable staff to plan for the future and prepare policy for the upcoming decades. Archduke Karl did not have this luxury but communicated frequently with Franz Ferdinand to get an understanding of his plans. Furthermore, when Karl came to power, WWI had already proceeded in a way where a victory was almost impossible. Although the German warmongers and their Austrian partners did still believe in a victorious peace, Emperor Karl was realistic enough to understand that, with the United States joining the war effort of the entente, a victory was impossible. He also understood very well that centralization could never be a solution for political problems. His "Manifesto to my peoples" is clear proof that he saw the principle of subsidiarity as a leitmotif for a supranational order—that is, that it should rightfully be an animating principle determining European politics also in our days. On the social side, his efforts for widows and orphans of the war, as well as in healthcare questions, was unique for the time and remained unparalleled in the rest of the world, often for decades.

Regarding the family man Karl, I was able to learn a huge amount from my grandmother, Empress Zita. He used every free moment in his very busy schedule to spend time with his family and to provide them with information into the affairs of state and of the war. It was very moving to hear, that he always said that the happiest time of his life was during his military positioning in Kolomea in today's Ukraine, since it was there that he had the most time to spend with his young family, just expecting their first child.

On closer examination, Emperor Charles does not match the picture painted of him by the war propaganda. He was definitely not weak; he understood the perils of the situation and was trying to use all political and even family links to find a peaceful solution to the war. When it would have meant to continue the conflict and create more victims, as during the effort to regain power in Hungary, he chose to accept personal losses of power rather than to see more bloodshed. He was a true humanitarian.

From his life, we can learn that it is not necessarily the results or the achievements that count but the will to try to do what is right. And if the rewards don't come immediately, there is no need to despair; if we live rightly, we can trust in God's promise that they will come later in the form of heavenly blessings.

Archduke Karl von Habsburg

PREFACE

October 3, 2004 saw what appeared to many to be a very strange thing: Emperor-King Charles of Austria-Hungary, last Habsburg to rule in Central Europe and wartime foe of the United States, was raised to the altars of the Church as a blessed by St. John Paul II. But odd as this appeared, the real story of the "Peace Emperor" and his just as remarkable wife reads like a combination of suspense thriller, Greek tragedy, and hagiography. The inheritor of a tradition of Catholic monarchy dating back to the Roman Empire, Blessed Charles struggled to update it sufficiently to survive in the modern world. A brave soldier coming to the throne during a war whose start he had no part in, he risked everything to bring the bloody conflict to an end. Betrayed on all sides by allies, enemies, and subjects, his deep devotion to the Blessed Sacrament, the Sacred Heart, and the Virgin Mary helped him to avoid hating those who wronged him. Devoted to his wife and children, Charles succeeded with the help of his loving empress in leading a good Catholic family life despite everything. In a life filled with signs and miracles before and after, Blessed Charles managed to combine deep piety with intense practicality. After his death, his wife and children continued his work—she is herself a candidate for beatification. The growth of devotion to the couple is a saga in itself—and a strange one given the times in which we are living.

Over one hundred years since the end of World War I, the twentieth century's rejection of the religious and political values that built Western civilization have brought us to the point where abortion is—for many in public and private life—a sacred right; in more recent years, acceptance of gender confusion has joined freedom of infanticide as a measure of refined behavior. In a word, the formerly Christian world has given itself over to its lowest vices. What has it gained in return? Ever increasing hatred between classes, races, and the sexes; falling standards of every sort, to include personal civility; and the implosion of both family life and the birthrate. Our technology has vastly grown over the past decades and brought us many choice gifts—which we often misuse. Moreover, where once we were able to produce leaders of magnitude—and, love them or hate them, Churchill, de Gaulle, Eisenhower, and the rest who won the Second World War certainly qualified—we seem unable to do so today. What is true of political life is also true of culture, the arts, and all else.

From our vantage point, then, the idea that such a couple as Blessed Emperor Charles and his empress, Servant of God Zita, could have found themselves, however briefly, at the apex of what was still a great power seems utterly fantastic. In their piety, bravery, and good cheer, they seem like figures out of the stories of King Arthur and Charlemagne, characters from the pages of *Lord of the Rings* and *The Chronicles of Narnia*. But they are not; the "Peace Emperor" died a little less than a century ago, and his enchanting consort only in

1988. Rather than the days when knights were bold, the imperial couple found themselves in a world of poison gas and U-boats; their foes were not Saladin or Suleiman the Magnificent but Georges Clemenceau and Woodrow Wilson. They may indeed have had the heroic hearts of crusaders, but they were very much people of our time.

This may well account, among other things, for their increasing popularity—not only in their former realms but in the United States. The inspiration they offer for those struggling to maintain their sanity and personal values in a world seemingly gone mad is enormous. Are we faced with economic problems? They lost everything. Are outward problems putting pressure on our marriages? Whatever they may be, they pale in comparison with what these star-crossed but devoted lovers endured. Do we worry about the future of our children? Having lost everything, they still put the love and education of their sons and daughters first; as a young widow, Zita had to face a politically hostile world and still see her eight young ones prepared for the roles Providence had given them. Betrayed by enemies, allies, and often enough their own sworn ministers and soldiers, they never became bitter, never gave in to hatred; indeed, Charles offered up his miseries for the welfare of his peoples. They both maintained their devout faith to the end. So it is that in negotiating the perils of this present life, we may look—strange as it may seem—to Charles and Zita as sure and certain guides for our perplexity. As we shall see, that guidance was and is deeply rooted in realities that time has not been able to destroy—truths at once ancient and new.

Exciting as their lives were, and inspiring as the study of their sanctity is, to understand them for who and what they were, we are going to have to look into the background that produced them—and here we face a lot of material that really *is* foreign to us, in time and space. For we must understand the imperial idea that Charles was heir to, the ideals of Catholic monarchy which both he and his wife were raised in, and the specific traditions that produced them both. To be sure, we shall be presenting the very highest ideals of each topic—and admittedly, since the time of Christ, most rulers who have attempted them have fallen short. While on the one hand, these aspirations are far higher than anything we expect of our current political leadership, on the other, a fair number of monarchs have indeed managed to realize them (hence the fairly large number of royal saints). Charles and Zita are certainly fitting members of that company.

The other topic we shall have to examine before we part ways with the imperial pair is their continuing legacy—both religious and political. Here, too, we are on uncertain ground for modern Americans, not least because we have had the mantra of "Separation of Church and State" drilled into us. Now, that is not to say either that all who pray for Charles and Zita's intercession are monarchists, nor that the many who would see part, at least, of Charles's political ideas come to fruition in Central Europe or the mother continent as a whole are devout Catholics. But just as there was a lively interplay between these two aspects in their lives, so too with their legacy. Moreover, there are the ongoing careers of their descendants to note briefly. But beyond all of those endeavors, there is one more we shall have to look at. There are nine shrines to Blessed Emperor Charles in the United States, and the American branch of the Emperor Charles League of Prayer keeps expanding. Why, in the country arguably most responsible for the final catastrophe that overtook his life, does he have so many clients? It is a question we shall take up last.

Given that the centennial of Blessed Emperor Charles's tragically early death shall be coming up in 2022, we shall include in appendices not only a bibliography of books and websites but a gazetteer of websites of places associated with the imperial pair. It has been an exciting journey discovering their past and present, and it is my dearest hope that you shall enjoy the reading of it as much as I have the writing.

Charles A. Coulombe
Trumau, Lower Austria
29 May 2019
Feast of Blessed Constantine XI
Restoration Day

ACKNOWLEDGMENTS

As with every book I have ever written, I am all too aware that this work is in many ways a community effort. So let us deal with the departed first: my parents, Guy and Patricia Coulombe, who first regaled me with stories of the Habsburgs, and Scott MacMillan, who first broached to me some years ago the idea of doing a documentary about Blessed Emperor Charles. Amongst the living, in no real order (save vaguely chronological), Stephan Baron von Hoeller-Bertram for stories about the dynasty and the Old Monarchy as I was growing up; HI&RH the Archduke Karl von Habsburg, for his kind foreword; the Archdukes Georg and Michael and Archduchesses Maria Theresia and Annie-Claire von Habsburg, Eva Demmerle, Ralf Siebenburger, Florian Gaberzig, Albert Petho, Peter Count von Stolberg, Peter Uhel, Peter Szasz, Matej Cadil, Rainhard Kloucek, Thomas Spanring, Alvin-Mario Fantini, Jan Tretiak, the Brothers Mateffy, Martin Horvatic, my comrades in the Josefina, Starhemberg, and Maximiliana Landsmanschaften, the Koruna Cesky, the Kraljevina Hrvatska, and all the rest of my many friends in Vienna, Budapest, Prague, Bratislava, Zagreb, and elsewhere in the Old Empire, whose advice, insight, and support were so crucial; those involved in promoting the Causes: Fr. Wolfgang Buchmüller, O.Cist, of the

Austrian friends of Empress Zita and Fr. Marion Gruber, O.Cist., international head of the Emperor Charles Prayer League, as well as his colleagues in charge of the League in various countries: Suzanne Pearson in the United States, Milan Novak in Czechia, Fr. Stanley Zlnay in Slovakia, and Marcin Kula in Poland; those who extended such incredibly kind hospitality to me: HI&RH Nikolaus, Duke von Hohenberg at Schloss Artstetten, Micaela and Christina Blazek at Schloss Wartholz, Gerald Oitzinger at Schloss Eckartsau; Brigadier Gottfried Neuberger at Schloss Schwarzau, and HI&RH Archduke Alexander von Habsburg at Schloss Persenbeug; John Moorehouse, my editor at TAN Books; and, of course, the faculty, administration, and my fellow students at Trumau, who have been such a great "family-away-from-home." They all deserve a share of whatever good there may be in this book.

Book One

THE INHERITANCE

CHAPTER 1

THE IMPERIAL IDEA

Regard also our most devout Emperor N., and since Thou knowest, O God, the desires of his heart, grant by the ineffable grace of Thy goodness and mercy, that he may enjoy with all his people the tranquillity of perpetual peace and heavenly victory.

—HOLY SATURDAY EXSULTET

Empire has come to have a bad connotation in what passes for modern thought. For many people today, it conjures up pictures of absolute and arbitrary rulers, forcing conquered peoples to accept whatever pops into their debauched minds. While there have been such characters in history—and some have ruled empires—very few who claimed to be Christians were remotely like that. Indeed, in our time, when freely elected governments—and not so freely-elected judiciaries—claim the right to redefine against centuries of history and tradition, to say nothing of the will of the people, not only the nature of marriage but of humanity itself, it could be argued that we moderns tolerate far more absolute and arbitrary rule than did our ancestors.

That aside, it should be remembered that there are empires and there are empires. The Spanish, Portuguese, French,

British, Dutch, and other colonial empires that had the effect of transforming European civilization into the global one we have today were one sort. Whatever else may be said about them, it is highly unlikely that you would be reading these words had they not existed. The French Empire of the two Napoleons was a centralized nation state that went continental, while the Second Reich of the Hohenzollerns and even the Third Reich of Hitler were more of the same, just with a different nation as a basis (and a wildly evil ideology backing the last named). The Soviet Empire, like the American, pretended that it wasn't one (though possessing an infinitely more malevolent ruling idea than its competitor). None of these are useful in understanding the imperial idea of which Blessed Emperor Charles was the last living incarnation, to date.

For him, as for his predecessors, it described a supranational entity that, for the most part successfully, carried on what to us must seem a great paradox. For such an entity, on the one hand, encompassed many diverse regions jealous of their local liberties—subsidiarity, as we would say today—with an emperor whose authority (as opposed to power) was supreme. That authority, derived from God and the Church and hallowed by tradition, was exercised by that emperor over each of his provinces and peoples according to their own laws. This was the imperial idea that Blessed Charles inherited, and to understand him, we must understand it.

The word emperor comes from the Latin imperator, meaning "one who orders" or perhaps "commands." His doing so was called imperium. This word came into use as the Roman Republic was making its transition back into a monarchy under the nephew of Julius Caesar, Caesar Augustus. As a sop to the ingrained republicanism of the Romans, this term was used rather than king (rex, from Latin regere, "to rule"). The last of the Roman kings had been overthrown while away on a military campaign in 509 BC, and the Senate and people of the city had been boasting about it ever since. Of course, as the first century BC wound down, Rome came increasingly under the control of dictators; the last of whom, the above-named Julius Caesar, was famously murdered on the ides of March, 44 BC. After a decade or more of civil wars, Augustus found himself as sole ruler of Rome, emperor. In time, the family name Caesar would become an imperial title—so much so that it gave the word for emperor to German (kaiser), Russian (tsar), and Hindustani (kaisar). Thus it was that Augustus found himself master not only of Rome and Italy but an agglomeration of directly and indirectly ruled provinces, colonies, and protectorates around the Mediterranean. During the course of a census ordered for his jumbled dominions by this first emperor, a newlywed couple, both senior members of a dispossessed local royal line, had to make their way from their residence of Nazareth to their ancestral home of Bethlehem.

But if the Romans had been the first to introduce the title of emperor and empire to describe such a large collection of territories—many of which continued to be ruled by native princes while others had varying degrees of connection to the given supreme ruler—they had not originated the concept. Around forty years after Rome deposed its last king, a Middle Asian people called the Persians erupted from the Iranian plateau. First becoming known to history as subjects of the Assyrians back during the ninth century BC when the Assyrians were overthrown by their subject peoples—the Egyptians, Babylonians, Lydians, and Medes—between 616 and 609 BC, the Persians simply took the last-named as their new masters. But by 552, under the Achaemenid dynasty, the Persian had turned the tables and conquered their former overlords. Very rapidly they overran the other states that had carved up the Assyrian inheritance, and the Persians ruled from Egypt and Asia Minor to the Indus Valley.

But where their various preceding states had attempted to rule their subjects of various races directly, the Persians preferred to retain the services of locals called satraps, often members of the former Royal family, to govern their provinces under them. This system of indirect rule was their greatest single contribution to statecraft, and it allowed the formation of the largest governmental unit the planet had yet seen. But the central authorities could hire and fire local satraps. Since the word *emperor* had not yet been invented, the sovereign had to content himself with the title *shahanshah*, "king of kings," which he quite literally was. Moreover, his court was conducted with gorgeous ritual. So it was that ancient Persia was the actual birth of the imperial idea: a collection of ethnically and often religiously diverse peoples nevertheless held together by shared political loyalties.

But along the western coast of the recently conquered Asia Minor were a group of city states that were part of the Hellenic world—Greece, Southern Italy, and to some extent half-barbarian Macedonia. As we know, this was the land that first gave us Homer, and then endless amounts of poetry, plays, and philosophy; what it lacked in political unity and effectiveness, it made up for in intellectual and artistic creativity and power. Indeed, Greek philosophy, symbolized by the Acropolis of Athens, is seen as one of the "three mountains" upon which our Western—now global—civilization rests. But each city-state was jealous of its independence, which made it very difficult to unite against the Persian menace. In 499, there began two decades of strife between Persia and Greece, including such exciting occurrences as the Battle of Thermopylae. Yet despite Greek disorganization, they had managed to defeat the mightiest empire the world had ever seen.

Impressive as that demonstration was—and as impressive also as was the rise of such philosophers as Socrates, Plato, and Aristotle—internal rivalries and warfare between Athens, Sparta, and other of the city-states led to intense weakness of them all, in the face of the growing power of Macedonia. In 346 BC, Philip II, king of Macedonia, asserted his rule over Athens and most of the rest of Greece. In the decade that he ruled over the peninsula, he hired Aristotle to act as tutor to his son, Alexander. But in 336, Philip was assassinated, and Alexander took up his father's sporadic fighting with the Persians.

To say that Alexander the Great, as he has been called ever since, was successful at warfare is an incredible understatement. By the time he had been ten years on the throne, he had conquered all of the Persian Empire and was invading India. Only his exhausted and homesick troops' insistence led him to give up his endless campaigning and return, not to Macedonia, but to his new capital of Babylon. There he died in 323. But he had not been idle; taking over the Persian machinery of native governors, he also established twenty cities named Alexandria after himself across his huge territories—the most famous is the one in Egypt. These colonies were settled by Greeks, who brought their own religion and culture and absorbed some or much of what was already there. The syncretic culture that emerged from these efforts is dubbed "Hellenistic." Such cultural mixing was also evident at Alexander's own court, where Persian ritual replaced much of Macedonian. In return, Greek came to be spoken throughout his empire—even after his death, when three generals took over the lion's share of his conquests: Antigonus took Greece and Macedonia, to Ptolemy fell Egypt, and Seleucus the remainder. It was against his descendant that the Maccabees revolted in 167 BC. Under the Assyrians, Babylonians, and Persians, the Hebrews had kept themselves to themselves—save when carried off into exile (from which the ten northern tribes of Israel seemed not to have returned). But the Hellenistic era saw them adopting Greek and spreading their religious ideas even among the gentiles.

The increasingly frail successors of Alexander's generals were no match for the rising power of Rome; by the time Caesar was murdered, the Romans controlled a huge swath of southern Europe, northern Africa, and the modern Near East, including their domination over Palestine under its native rulers—not the House of David, to be sure; the Maccabees died out, and Herod the Great married their last female members. Greek and Latin were both taught, and the Roman roads and coinage made trade and movement far easier. Roman law also added an organic source for these things and created a blueprint for administration. This is the reason it is said that Rome's Capitol Hill—where her laws were made—is the second "mount" upon which our culture rests.

So things stood when "a decree went out from Caesar Augustus that all the world should be enrolled" (Lk 2:1). As noted, the newlywed couple—Mary and Joseph—came to Bethlehem, and she gave birth. Her Son was, of course, the Prince of Peace and King of kings. From thenceforward began his career of preaching, which would take him all over Palestine and find him in company with twelve apostles and seventy disciples. At length, after three years of active ministry, Jesus's time on earth culminated in the Last Supper and the crucifixion. This is why Calvary or Golgotha is referred to as the third mountain underlying Western civilization. But little did Tiberius Caesar then expect that those events would utterly transform both his empire and the world.

In the Cenacle, Christ, heir to the Davidic kingship, met with his disciples for the Last Supper and first Mass. There emerged the Holy Eucharist, the Blessed Sacrament—transubstantiated by him in the dish or cup immortalized later as the "Holy Grail" of song and story. His apostles were constituted as a priesthood, but his disciples as a whole became part of a communion united to his kingship and his Mystical Body. This is why it can be said that the Last Supper also saw the birth of Christian monarchy—symbolized by Christ's washing of the feet and repeated by so many sovereigns since then. But the Eucharistic action initiated at the Last Supper was completed by the sacrifice on the cross the following day; an action which has also been seen as the birth of

Christian chivalry or knighthood. This is because Christ's self-sacrifice was taken as a prototype of what the knight, or the king, should be willing to do for God and his people. It was an example Blessed Charles would often have cause to remember.

Of course, in the immediate, after Emperor Nero outlawed the Church in AD 67, it was an example that every pope and many of his followers would have to follow, from St. Peter on. Yet despite persecution, the Church continued to grow, dioceses to be established, and souls to be saved. The Roman roads allowed relatively quick and safe travel throughout the empire from Britain to Egypt, and Catholic missionaries took full advantage to spread the Gospel in every Roman province and across the frontiers. But what was their response toward the emperors who were intent on wiping them out? That counselled by their founder: prayer. The Church Father Tertullian, in his *Apology* (AD 197), devoted four chapters, 30 to 34, to the Christian practice of praying for the emperor at Mass. Reasserting the fact that members of the Church would never accept him as divine, he declared that they were in fact the most loyal subjects he had: "Without ceasing, for all our emperors we offer prayer. We pray for life prolonged; for security to the empire; for protection to the imperial house; for brave armies, a faithful senate, a virtuous people, the world at rest, whatever, as man or Cæsar, an emperor would wish."[1] Indeed, the earliest liturgical texts we have indicate just these sorts of prayers. The sons of the Church did not just pray for the emperor's armies, however;

---

1 Tertullian, *Apology*, ch. 30.

they joined them. And while loyal soldiers and true, they would not worship him, thus the proliferation of countless martyred soldiers saints, as with saints George, Maurice, and Sebastian. They were indeed the emperor's good servants, but God's first.

In three centuries, all of this activity bore fruit. In the early fourth century, Armenia, Georgia, and Ethiopia became officially Christian; this would mark their national cultures (and their monarchies) ever after. Very famously, after his vision at the Milvian Bridge and subsequent victory, Constantine the Great legalized the Church with the Edict of Milan in 313. He subsidized the journeys of his mother, the empress St. Helena, to the Holy Land, where she identified the major sites connected with Our Lord's life and recovered various relics—most notably the true cross. There are two different traditions regarding his personal conversion: one that it took place in Rome shortly after his victory, the other that he was received into the Church on his deathbed. Whichever might be the case, one thing is certain: he was the first Christian emperor. Understanding him and the role he created for himself is key to understanding all the rest who would follow, down to and including Blessed Charles himself.

It is important to note that, in a real sense, Constantine was the first European: born in Nis, Serbia, his mother was a Briton, from York or Colchester (both cities claim her), and he would spend time there. He had a palace in Trier, Germany, lived at times in Rome, and most famously built Constantinople. The Church was to feel the benefit of his wide-ranging largesse: at Rome, he built the first versions of St. Peter's, St. John Lateran, and Santa Croce, to name a few; at Constantinople, Hagia Sophia and Holy Apostles; in the Holy Land, the emperor erected the first versions of Jerusalem's Holy Sepulchre and Bethlehem's Basilica of the Nativity; and scores of other churches around the empire. Constantine, although merely tolerating Christianity as far as the law was concerned, tightened up the marriage laws in particular to bring them closer to Church teaching. But his greatest intervention on behalf of the Church was to convoke the Council of Nicaea in order to end the Arian heresy, from which emerged the Nicene Creed. The following seven councils were likewise convoked by emperors, although their acts required papal approval to take effect. From the ninth council, Lateran I, on they were almost all convoked by popes, although up to and including Trent, with imperial participation. The one glaring exception was the Council of Constance in 1414; due to the existence of three claimants to the papacy, Emperor Sigismund called the council in a successful bid to end the chaos.

At any rate, Constantine set the example of care toward the Church that remained a requirement of the imperial office until Blessed Charles's time. For this, he is considered by Eastern Christians—both Catholic and Orthodox—as a saint and is venerated as such with his mother, St. Helen, on May 21. The liturgical prayer on his feast runs, "Having seen the figure of the Cross in the heavens, and like Paul not having received his call from men, O Lord, Your apostle among rulers, the Emperor Constantine, has been set by Your hand as ruler over the Imperial City that he preserved in peace for many years, through the prayers of the Theotokos, O only lover of mankind." While not on the general calendar of saints in the Latin Rite, he is honored as a saint in a number of localities in Sicily, Sardinia, southern Italy, and at least one village in Tyrol! Needless to say, Latin Catholics are free to venerate anyone who is so approved for their Eastern Catholic brethren.

Although Constantine left both the empire and the Church in far better shape than he had found them, and though he had favored Catholicism over Judaism and all the pagan cults, the machinery of governance remained essentially pagan, with state-supported temples and so on. This would not end until 380 when Emperor Theodosius the Great proclaimed the Edict of Thessalonica:

> It is our desire that all the various nations which are subject to our Clemency and Moderation, should continue to profess that religion which was delivered to the Romans by the divine Apostle Peter, as it has been preserved by faithful tradition, and which is now professed by the Pontiff Damasus and by Peter, Bishop of Alexandria, a man of apostolic holiness. According to the apostolic teaching and the doctrine of the Gospel, let us believe in the one deity of the Father, the Son and the Holy Spirit, in equal majesty and in a holy Trinity. We authorize the followers of this law to assume the title of Catholic Christians; but as for the others, since, in our judgment they are foolish madmen, we decree that they shall be branded with the ignominious name of heretics, and shall not presume to give to their conventicles the name of churches.

> They will suffer in the first place the chastisement of the divine condemnation and in the second the punishment of our authority which in accordance with the will of Heaven we shall decide to inflict.

Not only did this measure signal an end to imperial sponsorship of Arianism (one of Constantine's sons was Arian, with horrible results), but Theodosius also took the opportunity to close down all pagan temples and institutions that had depended upon the imperial government. More important than these measures was Theodosius's decision regarding Roman citizenship. Up to this time, citizens were a minority, and their status envied—we remember how much St. Paul valued his. But Theodosius the Great decreed that, henceforth, Baptism not only inserted the recipient into the Church but made him a Roman citizen as well. In time, this brought about a situation where Church and empire were considered two facets of the same body—the *Res Publica Christiana*—and pope and emperor seen as joint heads of the same body. Interestingly, despite his insistence on papal headship of the Church and acceptance of a severe rebuke by St. Ambrose, he is considered a saint by the Orthodox but not by Catholics of any rite.

Theodosius was the last emperor to rule a united Roman Empire. Hard-pressed from within and without, and given the stresses and strains under which the ruler of an empire must labor, he decided to leave the Western half of the empire to his son Honorius and the Eastern half to his other son, Arcadius. But it cannot be repeated too strongly that this was not considered a division of the empire. There might be two emperors, but they were considered partners in a single jurisdiction. When barbarians invaded Italy and threatened Rome, Honorius and his court decamped for Ravenna, a much more secure locale surrounded by swamps. This left the pope as the highest ranking official in the Eternal City and marked the beginning of the providential rise of the Papal States.

The German tribes swooped in and annexed chunks of imperial territory; this process continued until, in 476, the last emperor in the west, Romulus Augustulus, was deposed. This is the date we usually think of as the fall of the Roman Empire. But Odoacer, the Germanic mercenary who did the deposing and made himself king, did not look at it that way, and neither did the Roman citizens he ruled, nor Theodoric, the Ostrogothic king who in turn overthrew him. For Odoacer had sent the imperial diadem back to Constantinople, saying that there was now only one emperor once again. He, Theodoric, and the kings of the Visigoths who seized Spain and southern France, as well as the other Germanic tribes, all believed themselves to be somehow subject to that emperor, and part of the empire; they were baptized after all. This was even true of the Arian tribes.

One of the tribes that had taken advantage of the collapse of Roman government to settle on Roman territory, while claiming allegiance to the emperor, was the Franks. In 481, a fifteen-year-old boy inherited their throne. In the next few years, he added to his ancestral domains in what is now northeast France by snuffing out the last remnant of Roman rule around Paris and pushing the Visigoths out of France and over the Pyrenees. Married to a Christian Burgundian princess named St. Clotilde, he agreed to convert, like Constantine, to his wife's religion if he won a battle. Victorious, he allowed himself to be baptized and crowned at Reims in 496. This, the baptism of Clovis, is considered to be the beginning of France; it was certainly the beginning of the Franks as a great power.

In the meantime, although the Eastern emperors had kept their realms intact, some felt more displeased with their nominal headship of the West than others. Justinian I (525–567) felt it more than most. An energetic ruler at home (he rebuilt Hagia Sophia into what we know today, as well as founded the great monastery on Mont Sinai), he wished to restore the empire to its greatest extent. He failed, but his troops did reconquer all of Italy, North Africa, and southern Spain. His was a contradictory attitude toward the Church; he honored several popes, had himself crowned by one (as his father had been), and put the papal supremacy into his law code, but he also seized and imprisoned a pontiff. At any rate, he is another emperor whom the Orthodox consider a saint, although Catholics do not.

His rule, however, was the Byzantine high-water mark. After his death, yet another Germanic tribe, the Lombards, invaded Italy, seized the interior, and confined the Byzantines to the coastal cities, including Rome. But defending Rome from the Lombards for the good of the pope and the Church became one of the empire's ongoing responsibilities. This became much harder with the rise of Islam; when the Muslims conquered the Holy Land, Syria, Egypt, and North Africa in the 600s, successive emperors became too busy preserving what was left to deal with Rome's needs.

Meanwhile, the Muslim threat grew, as they seized North Africa and rolled into Spain in the 700s. Pouring over the Pyrenees, they invaded France, but were halted in 732 at the Battle of Tours by the Frankish chieftain Charles Martel. Ever plagued by the Lombards, the popes had found an alternative protector to the preoccupied Eastern emperors (some of whom succumbed to the iconoclastic heresy). Charles's son Pepin brought an army down to Rome to drive off the Lombard; in return, the pope sanctioned the deposition of Clovis's descendants and crowned Pepin king, thus began the Carolingian dynasty. When Pepin died, his son Charles succeeded him. He too proved himself a great defender of the papacy, so much so that on Christmas day, 800, Pope St. Leo III revived the empire in the West and crowned him emperor. We know him today as Blessed Charlemagne.

We think of Charlemagne as the first Holy Roman emperor, and certainly he is always counted as Emperor Charles I, but he is also considered to be Charles I of France; both the holy Roman emperors and the kings of France considered him their progenitor. Had it not been for the transition into the Austrian Empire (about which more shortly), our Charles Habsburg would have been Charles VIII. As with Caesar, the neighbors were so impressed with Charlemagne that the various Slavic and Magyar words for king (*kral*, *kiral*) are derived from Charles; even the Norse name Magnus comes from Charlemagne. This shifting of the imperial office from the Romans to the Franks was called the *Translatio Imperii*.

There were a number of similarities between the first Charles and the eighth, who is the subject of this book. As ruler of what are now France, northmost Spain, Germany, the Low Countries, most of Italy, Czechia, and various adjoining areas, Charlemagne had to deal with as dizzying an array of peoples as did his last successor; as with him, the earlier Charles had to act as common father. The two both saw their position as essentially a religious one, which is what in the end raised both to the altars; they are both blesseds. Of course, any number of calumnies have been launched against Charlemagne; about these, Dom Gueranger comments in his coverage of the earlier emperor's feast (January 28) in The Liturgical Year: "We affirm, with the great Bossuet, that the morals of Charlemagne were without reproach, and that the contrary-opinion, which is based on certain vague and contradictory expressions of a few writers of the Middle-Ages, has only gained ground by Protestant influence."[2] Moreover, "The honor of the Church herself is at stake in this question, and it is the duty of every Catholic to suspect the imputations cast on the name of Charlemagne as calumnies."[3] According to Father Alban Butler in his Lives of the Saints, "This prince was not less worthy of our admiration in the quality of a legislator than in that of a conqueror; and in the midst of his marches and victories, he gave the utmost attention to the wise government of his dominions, and to everything that could promote the happiness of his people, the exaltation of the church, and the advancement of piety and every branch of sacred and useful learning."[4] Although not in the Roman Martyrology,

---

2 Volume III, "Christmas," Bk. 2, pp. 468–69.

3 Gueranger, *The Liturgical Year*, p. 470.

4 Rev. Alban Butler (1711–73). Volume I: January, *The Lives of the Saints*, 1866.

Blessed Charlemagne's feast is still celebrated on January 28 at Aachen, Frankfurt, and elsewhere.

Blessed Charlemagne's elevation to the purple was not immediately recognized by his putative colleague at Constantinople. Indeed, that colleague was the widowed Empress Irene, who briefly considered marrying the new Western emperor and reuniting the thrones. We can't know what would have happened, of course, but that did not. Not only were East and West to remain separate, but after Charlemagne's death, his son was unable to keep the empire united. France separated from the rest of the empire, which itself fragmented. The German branch became extinct in the male line in 911, while in France they were replaced by their cousins the Capets, forerunners of the later Bourbon dynasty. The imperial title became a plaything of various Italian noble houses, as indeed did the papacy. This unpleasant state of affairs was put an end to by the Saxon king Otto I, who ascended the throne in 936. A series of campaigns against Germans, Magyars, and Italians led directly to his coronation as emperor at Rome in 963 and his ending the thick corruption of the papacy. Otto and his wife, St. Adelaide, were very friendly with the Byzantine emperors of the time, and so secured a Byzantine princess, Theophanu (herself now a candidate for beatification), for their son. At his father's death in 973, Otto II ascended the throne, only to die ten years later at age twenty-eight, leaving his three-year-old son to become Emperor Otto III. Half German, half-Byzantine, with a friendly pope, Sylvester II, this third Otto, when he aged, had a very clear vision for reuniting all of the Roman Empire, East and West. He was directly responsible for bringing Poland, Czechia, and Hungary into the system of Europe. Despite such a full reign, he died very young in 1002, at the age of twenty-one. He was succeeded by his cousin, St. Henry II. The new emperor (as his future canonization would show) was very pious, as was his consort, St. Cunigunda, so much so that the imperial couple had a "Josephite"—that is to say, celibate—marriage. As a result, they were childless when the emperor died in 1024. The Ottonian dynasty thus died out, and the nobles elected Conrad II, of the Salian House, to succeed Henry.

While by this time the emperors held sway only over a small portion of the continent, they were believed to hold some intangible authority over all Western Christendom—even as the Russians, Bulgars, and Serbs claimed to somehow be subject to the emperor at Constantinople—even when they were at war with him. This may seem odd to us, but it is important to remember that just as Europe was a jumble of near-independent kingdoms, so too was each of those kingdoms a jumble of dukedoms, provinces, et cetera. Viscount Bryce puts the ideological situation well in his *The Holy Roman Empire*:

> The Pope, as God's vicar in matters spiritual, is to lead men to eternal life; the Emperor, as vicar in matters temporal, must so control them in their dealings with one another that they may be able to pursue undisturbed the spiritual life, and thereby attain the same supreme and common end of everlasting happiness. In the view of this object his chief duty is to maintain peace in the world, while towards the Church

> his position is that of Advocate, a title borrowed from the practice adopted by churches and monasteries of choosing some powerful baron to protect their lands and lead their tenants in war. The functions of Advocacy are twofold: at home to make the Christian people obedient to the priesthood, and to execute their decrees upon heretics and sinners; abroad to propagate the faith among the heathen, not sparing to use carnal weapons."[5]

However much the facts may have changed, the imperial idea remained what it had been under Theodosius I.

Under the first two Salian emperors, the relationship between emperor and pope was cordial, but in 1075, open hostility emerged between Emperor Henry IV and Pope St. Gregory VII over the investiture question, which would be fought in other countries with their monarchs as well. In a world when most bishops also had to be feudal lords, to whom ought they be loyal? The dispute would be resolved to a degree, but it continued to fester. Another event that occurred during the Salian rule was the Great Schism between Rome and Constantinople in 1054. Where before there was an uneasy sort of mutual recognition between the emperors, the feud between their respective prelates pried them apart as well. Nevertheless, in 1095, at a local Church council held in Piacenza to condemn Henry, emissaries from Byzantine Emperor Alexius I Comnenus arrived to beg Blessed Pope Urban II to send aid to the faltering Eastern empire—both

---

5 James Bryce, *The Holy Roman Empire* (MacMillan and Co., 1871), p. 106.

to shore up the Byzantines and rescue the Christians of the Holy Land—who in addition to being oppressed had had to watch the Holy Sepulchre be destroyed. The pope duly proclaimed the First Crusade two years later. In this first and most successful of these conflicts, whenever the Byzantines and crusaders cooperated effectively, they were victorious; when they did not, they were not.

The Crusades had as big an effect on the imperial idea and monarchy in general in Europe as they did on anything else. For one thing, these remote ancestors of the multinational peacekeeping missions with which we are familiar marked the first time that there had been anything like an attempt for Christendom to react collectively to outside aggression as a body. Chivalry became an international body, despite being deeply rooted in each European nation. The concept of the Crusade widened as time went on to include the expeditions against the Moors in Spain and the pagans in the Baltic. In time, "the Crusade" was seen as an ongoing thing to which all monarchs and nobles were expected to contribute, either in person or through financial support. At the accession of the first Hohenstaufen emperor, Conrad III, in 1128, he was in a dispute with the papacy. In 1146, he joined with the French king Louis VII for the Second Crusade, designed to restore territories just seized in Palestine by the Muslims. The attempt was something of a failure; nevertheless, his nephew, Frederick I, called Barbarossa, resolved to try again. In 1187, the crusaders suffered a horrible defeat, and Jerusalem fell to the Muslims. Pope Gregory VIII preached a new crusade in 1190, and he and Barbarossa, who had had their quarrels, nevertheless patched things up for the greater good. Richard the Lionheart of England and Philip Augustus of France also signed up, but Barbarossa, as emperor, was titular head of the Third Crusade. Unfortunately, he died en route, and the French and English kings started quarrelling. It was not a very edifying thing, and the Crusade failed. Barbarossa's son, Henry VI, reigned a scant eight years; his son, Frederick II, was a minor. Although Pope Innocent III was the boy's godfather, the new emperor grew up with an ambivalent attitude toward the papacy.

In the meantime, a real catastrophe had occurred: the Fourth Crusade went renegade and seized and sacked Constantinople. They made one of their commanders a Latin emperor in place of the imperial family, one member of which set up a rival imperial seat at Nicaea. Bad as this was, when Frederick II was of age, he quarreled with successive popes and went so far as to go on Crusade while excommunicated. Nevertheless, through negotiation rather than warfare, he recovered Jerusalem. Even so, the war between his supporters and those of the popes eventuated in pushing imperial rule out of Italy entirely. He and then his son and successor continued to fight, but the death of the latter ended the House of Hohenstaufen and began the Great Interregnum: from 1250 to 1273, there would be no emperor in the West. Anarchy would reign supreme in Germany, and fairly close to it elsewhere as well.

There were, moreover, two emperors in the east: the papally-backed one in Constantinople and the Byzantine, Michael VIII Palaeologos. In 1263, Michael reconquered Constantinople and placed the Greek Orthodox patriarch back in his place. But eleven years later, he sent emissaries to the Second Council of Lyons for the express purpose of ending the Schism and uniting Christendom against the Turks. Despite initial success, the union was resisted by many in both East and West and died soon after. Things in the east continued to decline, and over a century and a half later at the Council of Florence, Michael's descendant, Emperor John VIII Palaeologos, renewed the union. Unfortunately, this did not bring the hoped-for Western aid; his brother and successor, Blessed Emperor Constantine XI, died fighting the Turks when the city fell in 1453. Ironically, this last Constantine's mother was also named Helen. Another irony was that sixteen years later, Pope Paul II negotiated the marriage of Blessed Constantine's niece to the grand duke of Moscow. From this time on, the grand dukes called themselves tsars, claiming to be the heirs of the Byzantine emperors and asserting that Moscow was the third Rome: "The Old Rome fell to the barbarians, and Constantinople, the New Rome, to the Turks; Moscow is the New Rome, and there shall not be a fourth!"

All of that was in the future, however, when the Great Interregnum in the West was finally ended with the election of Swiss nobleman and supporter of Frederick II, Rudolf von Habsburg. He was the first of his family to ascend the imperial throne, but he would not be the last. From 1438 until the putative dissolution of the empire in 1806, all but one of the Holy Roman emperors would be Habsburgs. As we shall see, in those centuries, and especially after the so-called Reformation, the empire would be ever less universal and ever more a vehicle for the Habsburgs—and shaped by them. Nevertheless, when Francis II, last to hold the title of Holy

Roman emperor (having created an "Empire of Austria" as an escape hatch should it be necessary), abdicated in 1806, he still bore the titles of "Advocate of the Christian Church, Vicar of Christ, Imperial head of the faithful, Leader of the Christian army, and Protector of Palestine, of general councils, of the Catholic faith."[6] Alongside the double eagle (also used by the Russian tsars for the same reason), symbol of their claim to continuity with the Christian Roman Empire, these titles were reminders of their office's once universal mandate.

Although the abdication of Francis II was held to be the end of the Holy Roman Empire, it did not end the deep desire on the part of many—in and out of power—to seek a multinational grouping of some kind that would fulfill the same function as the holy empire was intended to do. Thus, after Napoleon's defeat, Tsar Alexander I (who certainly saw himself as an imperial heir) proposed the Holy Alliance that would bind all Christian European rulers together; for a short while, the system of European Congresses provided some stability, until the collapse of the Restoration settlement in 1830. Not too surprisingly, after the carnage of World War I, the League of Nations was invented, and, since the Second World War, successive popes' enthusiastic embrace of both the EU and the UN can perhaps be seen as an unconscious yearning for an emperor.

In addition to their imperial legacy, much of what the Habsburgs inherited (and which came down, however briefly, to Blessed Charles, and molded him) was common

---

6 Ibid., p. 202.

to European Catholic monarchy in general. It is to that which we must now turn our attention.

Chapter 2

SACRED MONARCHY

O Lord, save N. our King.
R. And hear us in the day when we call upon Thee.
Let us pray.
We beseech Thee, almighty God, that Thy servant N. our King, who has been called by Thy mercy to rule over this kingdom, may also receive from Thee an increase of all virtues. Fittingly adorned with these, may he be able to shun all evildoing, (in time of war: to conquer his enemies) and, finally, being well pleasing before Thee, together with his consort and the royal family, attain unto Thee who art the Way, the Truth and the Life. Through Christ Our Lord.
R. Amen.

—Prayer for the King after Mass

If Blessed Charles was very conscious of what being an emperor entailed, in being at once the strong right hand of the Church and father equally of a multitude of peoples, he was also very much aware of the sacred character his office shared with other monarchies. From whence came this character other than the generally blessed nature of political authority in Catholic teaching? First and foremost, from his coronation.

Monarchies have never been secular. They have differed from each other in countless ways down through the millennia, but one thing always remained intact: every monarchy of whatever religion depended upon what its people considered divine to sanction its authority. In some cases, as in the pre-Constantinian Roman Empire, that meant worshipping the ruler directly. In the Far East, the emperor of Japan was considered to be the descendant of the Sun goddess, and he and his brother emperors in China and Vietnam functioned as high priests of the national cult.

With Christian monarchs, it was different; even the emperor himself was no more than the temporal equivalent of the pope, who was also a vicar of the invisible Godhead. Nevertheless, his office had to receive divine sanction, as mediated through the Church; in this sense, a monarch was a sort of chief layman. From early days—as far back as the Egyptians—rulers had worn some sort of special headgear and wielded a rod of command. Constantine the Great wore a Persian style diadem; this would in time develop into the sort of crown with which we are familiar. Celtic and Germanic tribes would elevate their chiefs on shields and acclaim them. Later Roman emperors found themselves acclaimed in similar fashion by their Germanic troops, and then crowned. With the baptism of the Frankish king Clovis, we find the first anointing to accompany the rite.

In short order, the Christian coronation service spread throughout Europe. It always had these three elements, whatever else might change: crowning, anointing (with oil of catechumens, save for France, England, Scotland, Sicily, and Jerusalem, whose bishops all used Holy Chrism to crown the king), and acclamation by the chief people of the realm. This ceremony was considered highly sacred, a sort of eighth sacrament. The new ruler took solemn oaths to uphold his realm's laws and the rights of the Church. The crown jewels bestowed upon the new monarch would often include a ring, betokening his "marriage" to his realm—it was considered to be life-long. As with both the consecration of bishops and the marriage of a couple, the union of emperor or king with empire or kingdom was held to be deep and intimate, and as both Matrimony and Holy Orders draw particular graces for married or clerical life down from heaven upon their recipients, so too with the coronation. In many countries, spurs were included as well to show that the sovereign was also the chief of the country's knighthood. In some lands, dubbing knights was a regular part of the ceremony. The crown and sceptre each had their own symbolism, as did the orb, a round object topped by a cross, symbolizing Christ's kingship over the world.

Before these regalia were placed on him, however, the new monarch swore an oath. Like many other such elements of the rite, it varied from place to place, but the version of the coronation ceremony in the Roman Pontificale is representative:

> I, N., with God's consent the future King N., profess and promise in the presence of God and his Angels to bring about and maintain law, justice and peace, as far as I am able to do so, in the Church of God and in the

> nation subject to me, having a fitting respect for the mercy of God, as best I can devise in accordance with the counsel of my faithful subjects. I will also give due and canonical honor to the Bishops of the Churches of God and preserve inviolate those things which have been conferred upon and rendered to the Churches by Emperors and Kings. I will give fitting honor to my Abbots, Counts, and Vassals in accordance with the counsel of my faithful subjects.

The ceremony was generally performed by the highest-ranking bishop of the given country; in the case of the Byzantine and Holy Roman emperors, this was done by the patriarch of Constantinople or the pope. The location where it took place often became the holiest in the country, such as Reims Cathedral in France or England's Westminster Abbey. Indeed, the ruler was, by virtue of this rite, considered to be neither a priest nor a layman, but in some manner, both. Thus in many coronation ceremonials, the new sovereign was dressed like a priest, with stole and cope. Many authorities considered the coronation equivalent to ordination to the subdiaconate.

Nor was this all. In many countries, his new *persona mixta* status allowed him to be enrolled as an honorary canon in various churches—and in Rome! The Holy Roman emperor was thus made a canon of St. Peter's, and the kings of Spain, France, and England of St. Mary Major, St. John Lateran, and St. Paul-Outside-the-Walls respectively. So, too, they often had close connections with local abbeys and other places; certain shrines, for example, would be particularly dear to each respective royal house. Most of these families had at least one canonized predecessor or relation, and devotion to these ancestral saints was also an important part of each such clan's ethos.

In addition, each monarch had a staff of priests to look after the spiritual needs of the monarch's household; indeed, in the early Middle Ages, when few laymen could write, a great many of the officials themselves were priests—so long did this go on in England that St. Thomas More was the first layman there to serve as lord chancellor. Most monarchs, regardless of how pious they were, attended daily Mass and regular confession. The singers and musicians of the court chapel were the best the sovereign could find. In time, these chapels often formed a separate jurisdiction from the country's dioceses, sometimes united with the military ordinariate for service chaplains. But royal weddings were usually performed in the parish church of the ruler's principal residence.

The liturgical year played an important role at court. The three major feasts, of course—Christmas, Easter, and Pentecost—were lavishly marked, while New Year's Day generally featured Mass and a levee with the diplomatic corps and other notables; so too with the feasts of the ancestral saints, national patrons, and patrons of the local knightly orders. Veneration of the Virgin Mary—especially under her best-known title from among local shrines—also played a big role. But there were three particularly general royal feasts in the year: the Epiphany, Maundy Thursday, and Corpus Christi. Presenting gold, frankincense, and myrrh; washing the feet of a number of poor men; and marching humbly as a servant of our Eucharistic Lord were actions that such monarchs usually reveled in.

Popular belief invested the regal figures with miraculous powers—often conflated in the popular mind with various ancestral saints. So the kings of France and England were believed to be able to heal scrofula, "the King's Evil;" the king of Castile to exorcise demons; and in Catholic times it was believed that the king of Denmark could heal epilepsy. The Holy Roman emperor was held to have some influence over the weather, and even today in Central Europe people speak of a fine warm day as *Kaiserswetter*. If the monarchs believed themselves mystically tied to their people and lands by the coronation, most of the people believed their rulers to be sacred figures.

Apart from this demi-priestly role, the Catholic monarch had two others, which were also invested with a sacred air because of the first one. The first was as chief protector of his realm. The king was fount of honor, chief of knighthood in his country. When, at the coronation, the bishop presented him with a sword, he offered a prayer:

> Take the sword lifted from the altar by our hands—unworthy, yet consecrated by the authority of the holy Apostles—which is granted to you in virtue of your kingship and ordained by God in virtue of our bless + ing for the defense of the holy Church of God. And remember that which the Psalmist prophesied, saying: "Gird your thigh with your sword, mighty one"; so that you might wield it with the same force of justice, destroy with power the mass of iniquity, and fight for

> and protect the holy Church of God and her faithful people; and that you might faithfully cut off and rout both false men and enemies of the Christian name; that you might mercifully help and defend widows and orphans; restore that which is desolate and, having restored it, preserve it; avenge injustice; and confirm that which is well disposed. In so doing, as an outstanding devotee of justice, made glorious by the triumph of virtue, may you be worthy to reign without end with the Savior of the world.

Thus the new ruler had committed to him the safety of both Church and people in his realm and was to defend them equally. And he had to be ready to give his life, if necessary, for his people and his realm.

But as that foregoing prayer also makes clear, he was to protect the weak and ensure justice, and indeed, the monarch's third basic role was as fount of justice, the chief judge of the realm. As business grew, he necessarily did less and less of the actual working and appointed ever more judges to "do justice in his name." So it was that any site where a judge presided was, and is, a court. In monarchies today, courts generally have the royal arms up, and all are charged with keeping "the King's Peace." We retain this concept in American law to this day, with our breaches and justices of the peace.

Such, basically, was Catholic monarchy from its inception clear down to the time that Blessed Emperor Charles inherited the throne. As we shall see, he did his best to live up to its expectations.

Chapter 3

A TALE OF TWO HOUSES

Two households, both alike in dignity,
In fair Verona, where we lay our scene,
From ancient grudge break to new mutiny,
Where civil blood makes civil hands unclean.
From forth the fatal loins of these two foes
A pair of star-cross'd lovers take their life.[1]

—William Shakespeare

Emperor Charles married Zita of Bourbon Parma, but while they were very much in love and both sides approved of the match, the age-long rivalry between the Habsburgs and the Bourbons—and before them the Valois, the Bourbons' predecessors on the French throne, and like them a branch of the House of Capet—in large part created the world we live in. There had, however, been similar marriages before: in 1615, Louis XIII of France married Anne of Austria, daughter of the Habsburg Philip III of Spain. But instead of lasting peace between the two houses, the union produced Louis XIV, who not only fought a number of wars with Austria in Germany and manage to acquire a

[1] Shakespeare, *Romeo and Juliet*, prologue, lines 2–6.

fair amount of real estate as a result but he was also able to put one of his grandsons on the throne of Spain and cost the Habsburgs that country's empire. The second union, of the dauphin Louis and the archduchess Maria Antonia in 1770, was the culmination of the "Diplomatic Revolution" fourteen years earlier. This eminently logical desertion by these two Catholic nations of their respective Protestant allies was tested in the Seven Years War, and survived. But when they came to the throne four years after their wedding, King Louis XVI and Queen Marie Antoinette had no idea of the horrors awaiting them. Nor, for that matter, did Charles and Zita.

The origins of both the houses of Habsburg and Capet are remote in the past; indeed, they date to the decline of Charlemagne's empire and the failure of the Carolingians. The first definite ancestor we have for the Capets/Valois/Bourbons is Robert the Strong (c. 830–866). The forebear of the Habsburgs was one Guntram the Rich (920–973), who in turn was part of a clan in Alsace called the Etichonids, the earliest member of whom we have any record of lived back in the 600s. The feebleness of Charlemagne's successors brought the son of Robert, Odo, to the throne of France in 888. Meanwhile, the Etichonids were happily ruling southern Alsace, until Guntram's son, Lanzelin (d. 973), conquered Aargau in modern Switzerland. His son, Radbot, in turn built a castle in Aargau, which he named "Habichtsberg." He and all his descendants would be named Habsburg afterwards. One source of friction between the kings of France and the later Holy Roman emperors was that they both claimed to have a right to be considered successors of Charlemagne; in the list of both kings and emperors, he appears as Charles I.

For the next few centuries, the Capets were busy, essentially creating France. Along the way, they produced such kings as Robert the Pious and St. Louis IX. In the meantime, the Habsburgs, as subjects of successive emperors, nevertheless expanded their holdings within the empire, picking up new real estate in Alsace, Switzerland, and Swabia. Thus it was, as we saw earlier, that Rudolf von Habsburg would be elected Holy Roman emperor in 1273, three years after St. Louis died. He ruled until 1291, and during that time acquired the little duchies of Austria and Styria. The first night Rudolf entered Austria, he arrived at a small castle called Eckartsau. It would one day, far in the future, play an eerily ironic role in the family's fortunes. Despite his success at acquisitions, however, he was unable to secure the imperial throne for the Habsburgs after his death. Adolf of Nassau succeeded him, but on the latter's death, Rudolf's son was elected. He, too, however, failed to secure the succession: six Luxembourgs and Wittelsbachs would succeed in turn (including Charles IV, who would establish the constitution under which the Holy Roman Empire functioned until its end). But in 1438, Albert II was elected to the imperial throne, and the Habsburgs would occupy it (with one short exception) until it ended.

Meanwhile, in France, the main line of the House of Capet died out and was succeeded by a younger branch, the House of Valois. As the Habsburgs were consolidating their power base through marriage, the Valois were fighting the Hundred Years War with England. Under Charles VII—and with the aid of St. Joan of Arc—the English were finally defeated. Other than the heavenly aid given to and brought by the Maid of Orleans, a key factor in the French victory over the English was the switching of sides by the Duke of Burgundy. Descendant of yet another branch of the Capets, the duke not only controlled the Duchy of Burgundy in France but the neighboring county in the Holy Roman Empire (called *Franche-Comte*, "Free County"), as well as what are now the Netherlands, Belgium, and Luxembourg. Successive dukes dreamt of establishing a state independent of either France or the empire that would run from Switzerland to the sea. So taken was Duke Philip the Good with the idea that in imitation of the sovereign houses of Europe, he founded a knightly order—the Order of the Golden Fleece. This, of course, did not sit well with the French, and successive kings and dukes quarreled, until Duke Charles the Bold was killed by the victorious French in the battle of Nancy. The king of France wanted to have Charles's daughter, Mary of Burgundy, marry his son. Instead, she married Archduke Maximilian, son of the Holy Roman emperor.

Succeeding his father in 1493, Emperor Maximilian I—despite the loss under his watch of most of the Swiss territories—ruled not only the remaining Habsburg lands in Swabia, Alsace, and Switzerland but also today's Austria, Czechia, and Slovenia, as well as the huge Burgundian territories, which would one day pass to his son, Philip of Burgundy. Young Philip, in turn, married the daughter of Ferdinand and Isabella of Christopher Columbus fame. They produced a son, Charles, who in 1516 inherited the throne of Spain and was already ruling his grandmother's

Burgundian possession, where he had been born. When his grandfather, Emperor Maximilian I, died in 1519, another imperial election was required.

This imperial election was interesting because for the first time in a while there were not only serious opponents to the Habsburg heir but—in deference to the empire's not merely covering Germany and northern Italy but in some vague way, all of Christendom—they were both of them from "outside": Francis II of France and Henry VIII of England. For Francis in particular, Charles's election was fearsome: Habsburg-ruled areas faced France on every frontier. He began a French tradition that would characterize that nation's policy for over two centuries: Francis not only would oppose Charles V's empire on every frontier but also would support anyone else who did the same. To a large degree, this effort has left its mark on our own world to this very day.

Charles V's empire thus included the Habsburg lands in central Europe, the Low Countries, southern Italy and Lombardy, Spain, the Canary Islands, and the Greater Antilles. Mexico, Central America, and Peru were added to his domains during his reign, and he chartered the first universities in the Americas, at Mexico City and Lima. The addition of the Holy Roman Empire did not increase his power greatly, but it certainly augmented his prestige. His was truly an empire upon which the sun never set—the first such in history. Steeped in medieval philosophy and theology, he dreamed of creating a Universal Christian Commonwealth, on roughly the same basis as had Theodosius the Great.

But the year in which Charles came to office, Martin Luther began his revolt against the Church, which eventually became a political as well as a religious struggle. The French were always keen on chopping the emperor down to size, and after the Turks conquered most of Hungary in 1526, it fell to Charles V to try to keep them at bay. From time to time, various popes joined the ranks of his enemies. Nevertheless, he won as great a deal as he lost when, worn out after thirty-eight years of non-stop campaigning, he decided that no man should have to endure what he had. So, to his younger brother Maximilian II, he left Austria and the imperial title; to his son Philip II went Spain, the Italian territories, and the New World. In 1558, he died in monastic retirement at Yuste.

The year 1526 saw another acquisition by the House of Habsburg that would be quite decisive in their history. The Czech royal Přemyslid dynasty had joined with the House of Habsburg several times throughout history. Judith of Habsburg married King Wenceslas II and gave birth to Elizabeth, the last princess of the Přemyslid dynasty (1292–1330) and mother of Holy Roman Emperor Charles IV of Luxembourg (1316–1378). Later, Elizabeth of Luxembourg (1409–1442), the granddaughter of Charles IV, married Albrecht II of Habsburg (1397–1439). Their granddaughter Anna Jagellonica (1503–1547) married Ferdinand I of Habsburg (1503–1564), who was elected king of Bohemia in 1526. From 1526 to 1918, the Kingdom of Bohemia was ruled by Habsburg and Habsburg-Lorraine monarchs, the last of whom was Blessed Charles I.

To the Spanish Habsburgs went the duty of expanding Christendom in the New World and fighting the Protestant Dutch and English on the high seas. The Austrians dealt with the Protestant Germans and the Turks. Both occasionally allied against common threats, as against the Turkish Navy, which led to the great victory at Lepanto in 1571. Meanwhile, the French fought a vicious religious civil war—in the course of which the Valois became extinct and were replaced with another Capet branch, the Bourbons. Although the Catholics were victorious in that conflict, the Bourbons continued the Valois rivalry with both branches of the House of Habsburg. Not only did Henry IV, Louis XIII, Louis XIV, and Louis XV support the Turks (in return, however, for their making life somewhat bearable in the Holy Land for the local Christians), they launched a series of wars with the Habsburgs.

The Thirty Years War started out in 1618 as a dispute between the Catholic emperor Ferdinand II and his Protestant nobility. Successive Danish, Swedish, and French interventions kept the pot boiling, humans dying, and Germany being devastated for the next three decades, until all sides agreed to the Peace of Westphalia out of sheer exhaustion. Its vagueness guaranteed future conflict. There then followed, for some eighty years, the first set of World Wars mankind would know—one result of which was that each was known by a different name among Americans. So ensued the War of the Grand Alliance (King William's War) 1688–1697, the War of Spanish Succession (Queen Anne's War) 1701–1714, and the War of Austrian Succession (King George's War) 1741–1748. All of these wars featured France and Prussia fighting Great Britain and Austria, with the lesser European states choosing sides. When they had finished, several things had happened: the French had lost Nova Scotia to Britain, paving the way for the future loss of Quebec; the extinct Spanish branch of the Habsburgs was replaced by Louis XIV's grandson, thus establishing the Spanish Bourbons, who are with us today; the Spanish Netherlands (now Belgium and Luxembourg) and Lombardy went to Austria; and the line of the Austrian Habsburgs, although extinct in the male line, retained the throne in the person of Maria Theresia. Her husband, Francis of Lorraine, was elected Holy Roman emperor; ever since, the family name has been Habsburg-Lorraine. Two Spanish Bourbon princes (one of whom was later king of Spain as Carlos III and founded California and Los Angeles) founded two younger lines: Bourbon of Two Sicilies and Bourbon Parma. It was from this last that the future Empress Zita would descend.

But Maria Theresia was bitter over her experience with Britain as an ally, and France was growing similarly cold with Prussia. At last, in 1756, the two major Catholic countries in Europe allied. This pact was sealed in 1771 when Louis the Dauphin, heir to the French throne, married Maria Theresia's daughter, the archduchess Maria Antonia. In the immediate, however, the alliance was tested that very year when the first of these eighteenth-century world wars to be started in the New World was ignited; the cause was the murder by allied Indians of French soldiers in the custody of a young British colonial officer, a Captain George Washington. Lasting until 1763, this conflict cost France her colonial empire in North America, but it also ended Frederick the Great's dreams of expanding Prussia further.

The next world war pitted France, Spain, the Netherlands, and the rebellious British colonists against their mother country and their loyalist neighbors. Austria joined the League of Armed Neutrality (made up of most of the other European powers), which at length successfully threatened the British. While it allowed the French and Spanish to pay off old scores, the war bankrupted France. This in turn led to the French Revolution that—after murdering Louis XVI and Marie Antoinette—managed to cover the continent in blood and bring Napoleon to power. Although making himself "Emperor of the French" in 1804, he sought legitimacy for his new monarchy. Two years later, Maria Theresia's grandson Francis II abdicated the throne of the Holy Roman Empire to keep Napoleon from taking it, but in 1810, to avoid the final ruin of Austria after yet another defeat, he gave his daughter Marie Louis in marriage to the conqueror. Two years after that, the Russian campaign began the unravelling of the Napoleonic Empire, and by 1815 (despite the Waterloo interruption), Napoleon was banished to St. Helena and the Congress of Vienna had—as it thought—put the revolutionary genie back in the bottle.

But in fact, it had not. The period after the overthrow of Charles X of France in 1830 saw the Bourbon clan in France and Spain and the Braganza dynasty of Portugal split along ideological lines. In all three cases, the older lines (called respectively the "Legitimist," "Carlist," and "Miguelist" claimants) held out for a traditional monarchy centered on altar (the place of the Catholic as moral guide of society), throne (a monarch whose authority was rooted in tradition, and held sufficient power to "protect his people from their politicians"), local liberties, and class solidarity rather than conflict. Their liberal cousins and opponents simply wanted to remake the given country into a version of Britain's figurehead monarchy. This led to civil wars and defeat for the traditional sides. Nevertheless, all three deposed families moved to Austria, where the Habsburgs were seen as friendly to such causes.

But the Habsburg realms themselves were not to be spared the horrors of revolution. A wave of it spilled across Europe in 1848; in Austria, it led to unrest in Hungary (only put down with Russian aid and that of the subject Croats, Romanians, Slovaks, Serbs, and some Magyars who rallied to the dynasty), Bohemia, Austrian Italy (routed by Field Marshal Radetzky), and Vienna itself. Unrest in the capital led to the flight of Metternich and the abdication of Emperor Ferdinand II; he in turn was replaced by his eighteen-year-old nephew, Franz Josef.

The long reign of Franz Josef—from 1848 to 1916—not only saw Europe entirely transformed, it saw the young emperor (as with Queens Victoria and Elizabeth II) metamorphose from gallant young sovereign to a legendary figure seemingly etched in granite. It was, in any case, the events in Franz Josef's reign that set the stage for the hard and painful road his successor would have to tread. Franz Josef started out with the assurance of having overcome his peoples' share of bloodshed in 1848. But in 1853, he made a decision that would haunt the rest of his reign: when Russia asked for his aid in the Crimean War (the tsar reminding him of their aid to Austria in 1848), he refused it. The tsars would not forget. The following year, he married his mother's niece, the young Bavarian princess Elizabeth—the "Sissi" of cinema and story. Passionately in love with his wife, Franz Josef—as he would with his children—always put duty first. Among other things, this often meant setting aside his great interest in and love for the arts (a side of him almost forgotten today). The neurotic and beautiful empress, despite her own love for Franz Josef, found it increasingly difficult to deal with life at court, as would their son, Rudolf (born 1858).

Yet if he was harsh with himself and his family, the emperor was very easy-going on servants. Rising always at 3:30 a.m. for his bath, the emperor did not object to the usual drunkenness of his valet. But on one occasion, the hapless servant was so inebriated that he was forced to grasp Franz Josef's shoulders to keep himself upright. Annoyed as he was, rather than firing the man (for court employees were rarely fired), the emperor simply had him transferred to the kitchen—"where he would be observed." As was customary, this transfer brought with it a rise in salary.

Amusing as many of the anecdotes surrounding Franz Josef were, in 1859 his betrayal (as they saw it) of the Russians bore its first fruit. The little Italian kingdom of Sardinia, having joined the Crimean War at the side of Britain and France precisely to purchase their connivance at Sardinian aggression, called in its marker, as far as France was concerned. They convinced Napoleon III, then emperor of the French, to make war on Austria; in return for doing so, Napoleon was promised Savoy and Nice. Both emperors went into the Franco-Austrian war convinced of their military abilities; each was horrified by the carnage he saw on the battlefield. The Austrians were defeated, but barely, and Napoleon III duly received Lombardy and passed it on to Sardinia, receiving Nice and Savoy as promised. The Sardinians quickly invaded Modena, Parma, Tuscany, and the Papal State of Romagna. The rulers of these states fled to Austria: one of these was Robert, the young Duke of Parma. In exile, his second wife was Princess Maria Antonia of Portugal, who was the youngest daughter of Dom Miguel I, rightful king of Portugal. Their daughter would one day be Empress Zita. The following year, the Bourbons of the Two Sicilies were likewise deposed—this time by Garibaldi; they too sought refuge in Austria. At the same time, the Papal States were invaded; Umbria and the Marches fell quickly to the invaders (although French troops kept them out of the area around Rome). What was left of the papal army was besieged at Ancona, and it was only with great difficulty that Franz Josef's ministers prevented him from entering the war to relieve the doomed garrison.

The next debacle to confront Franz Josef was in Germany, where Prussia wished to play the same role as Sardinia had in Italy. So long as Frederick William IV—the "Romantic Upon the Throne"—ruled the country, Austria's hegemony in the Germanic Confederation (invented at the Congress of Vienna as a sort of replacement for the Holy Roman Empire) was unchallenged. But when Frederick William's younger brother, William I, came to the throne—and appointed as his chancellor the ambitious Otto von Bismarck—tensions emerged. Prussia and Franz Josef's younger brother,

Maximilian, would constitute the emperor's greatest concerns for the next few years.

In the immediate, however, events to the north were more pressing. Two duchies in the north of Germany, Holstein and Schleswig, were both ruled by the king of Denmark. But their administration was separate from the Danish realm and each other; in addition, Holstein was part of the Germanic Confederation. The king of Denmark decided to unite them with each other and his other realms, thus effectively withdrawing Holstein from Germany. Austria and Prussia were agreed that this was not something they wanted, and so they declared war on the Danes on February 1, 1864. Although greatly outnumbered and outgunned, Denmark valiantly struggled on, surrendering only on October 30 of that same year. The victorious allies divided the regained duchies, with Schleswig being occupied by Prussia and Holstein by Austria. As intended by the canny Bismarck, this was a recipe for later turmoil.

While the war raged, however, Franz Josef's younger brother, Maximilian, began to pursue dreams of his own. Having served as Viceroy of Lombardy-Venetia, as well as successfully reorganizing and modernizing the Austrian Navy—and, with the birth of Rudolf, no longer being direct heir to the throne—the energetic archduke was restless. So too was his wife, the former Belgian princess Charlotte. From 1859 on, Maximilian had been approached by various groups of Conservative Mexicans keen on reversing their defeat by the anti-clerical Liberals in the latest Mexican Civil War. Mexico had, after all, become independent from Spain as an empire; despite the execution of Agustin I Iturbide (who had accepted the crown only after it was rejected by various European princes), it was still regarded as such by many on the Mexican Right. Initially, the young archduke refused the various requests, but when France under Napoleon III invaded Mexico and seized the capital—lending his voice to that of the Mexicans—Maximilian changed his mind. He accepted the offer in October of 1863, renounced his Austrian rights (Franz Josef disapproved of and warned against the whole enterprise), and left Austria by ship the following April, while the Danish war was still raging.

The Mexican adventure is renowned to this day. Contrary to much that has been published, Maximilian was popular with many of his new subjects, and his new army was soon joined not only by them but by volunteers from his and his wife's native lands, as well as Turkey and Egypt. It became apparent that he and Carlota would not be able to have children; his initial reaction was to invite his and Franz Josef's youngest brother, Ludwig Viktor, to come to Mexico as his heir. Maximilian negotiated a marriage for his brother with Isabella, princess of Brazil, daughter and heiress of that country's emperor, Pedro II. This brother was not the marrying kind, however, and refused. Maximilian and Carlota adopted the grandson of Iturbide as their heir. From him descend the Gotzén-Iturbide family, whom many Mexican monarchists consider heirs to the throne. But that throne became increasingly shaky when the American Civil War ended and the newly re-United States were once again able to intervene south of the border. (Such intervention had been responsible for many Liberal victories in the years since independence.) Napoleon III, not wanting to get involved with the United States in a war, withdrew in 1866, while the Americans rushed arms and supplies to Maximilian's enemies. Things looked bleak indeed for Mexico's second emperor.

Nor was 1866 a very good year for his older brother. Tension had built up over the administration of the duchies conquered from the Danes, and Austria and Prussia began gathering allies. Alas for Austria, as in 1859, Russia opted to remain neutral—another fruit of Franz Josef's Crimean War decision. Most of the small northern German states sided with Prussia, as did Italy. But Hanover, Hesse Kassel, Hesse Darmstadt, Nassau, the Free City of Frankfurt (capital of the Confederation), Saxony, Bavaria, Wurttemberg, and Baden allied with Austria. War broke out in June; superior technology and training told, and in six weeks, the Prussians were victorious. The first five states were annexed to Prussia, and their dispossessed monarchs retreated to Austria. Although the Austrians had badly defeated the Italians, Prussia insisted as part of the peace that their allies be given Venetia. For the first time since 1438, the Habsburgs had no influence over Germany and Italy.

Almost a year exactly after the disastrous Austro-Prussian War began, another tragedy hit the House of Habsburg. As the onrush of American aid to the rebels began to be felt, Maximilian's position continued to erode. Napoleon III had urged him to leave the country, but he refused, instead allowing his empress to go on a mission seeking aid. Carlota fruitlessly visited Rome and Vienna; suffering a complete mental breakdown, she lived the rest of her life in seclusion in a Belgian castle, only dying in 1927. Maximilian and his two senior generals were captured; given the chance to save their lives if they renounced their allegiance to him, the two Mexicans refused and were executed with him. The final words of the last emperor of Mexico (so far) were, "I forgive everyone, and I ask everyone to forgive me. May my blood, which is about to be shed, be for the good of the country. *Viva Mexico, viva la independencia*!" It was a sentiment that would be repeated later, by another Habsburg. Maximilian's body was brought back to Austria by the same ship that he and Carlota had taken to Mexico. He would be entombed with his fathers in Vienna's *Kaisergruft*.

Apart from his brother Maximilian's death (the second great tragedy Franz Josef would have to endure after the death of his little daughter), the nationalities issue came to the fore once more after the terrible defeats in 1866. The squabbles of Czechs and ethnic Germans in Bohemia, Poles and Ruthenians in Galicia, and Magyars, Slovaks, Romanians, and Serbs in Hungary were almost endemic, and balancing them while ensuring that life went on and the country as a whole continued to prosper was a difficult and delicate proposition. But Franz Josef's loss of prestige after his defeats meant that a more permanent solution had to be found than the unitary neo-absolutism Franz Josef had come to power with in 1848. The solution hammered out by Franz Josef and various statesmen was called the *Ausgleich*; this arrangement separated Austria and Hungary, with the latter becoming once more a separate kingdom, of which Franz Josef would be crowned king that very year. The remainder of the country, which circled around Hungary like a crescent, would also be a constitutional monarchy, over which he would remain emperor. Although the two halves would have separate governments, there would be a few joint ministries dealing with foreign affairs, defense, and the like. Each half also had a two-chamber parliament. But where the minorities in Austria had a great deal of autonomy, those in Hungary did not, and since they had been loyal to the dynasty in 1848, this was keenly resented by them. This became even worse as the nineteenth century wore on and the Hungarian ruling party attempted to "Magyarise" these minority peoples.

Things were complicated a few years later when, in 1871, the German Empire came into being after the French were defeated in the Franco-Prussian war. Many among the Germans in the dual monarchy began to look to Berlin for leadership rather than Vienna. This Pan-German Movement also had an anti-Catholic edge—the *Los-von-Rom* or "Away-from-Rome" movement. At the same time, however, Bismarck began to send out signals of reconciliation to Austria-Hungary; an alliance to keep France weak and isolated was what the wily old Iron Chancellor had in mind. Although Crown Prince Rudolf disapproved, Franz Josef (who took little notice of his son's views) ploughed straight ahead. In 1873, the sovereigns of Germany, Austria-Hungary, and Russia signed the Three Emperor's League, which would guarantee peace for over a decade.

In the meantime, Franz Josef's extended family—and the supply of heirs to the throne—had been steadily growing. Of course, he had his son Rudolf. Maximilian had died childless, and the youngest brother, Ludwig Victor, was not interested in marriage. But there was one more brother:

Karl Ludwig. He had originally married a Saxon princess in 1856, but she died childless two years later. In 1862, however, the archduke married Princess Maria Annunciata, daughter of the king of the Two Sicilies whom Garibaldi had deposed. The couple would have three sons: Franz Ferdinand (b. 1863), Otto Franz (b. 1865), and Franz Karl (b. 1868). In 1875, when the deposed Duke of Modena died, he left his fortune to the eleven-year-old Franz Ferdinand on the proviso that he took the name Austria-Este. Taking his military duties (and his pleasure in the hunt) very seriously, Franz Ferdinand would be in no hurry to get married.

But where Franz Ferdinand and his father were both dutiful and devout, Otto Franz was of a different type altogether—for all that his father favored him. As he grew into manhood, his amorous and bacchic adventures became the stuff of gossip throughout Vienna. In a less charming man, a wave of moral disapproval might have been the result. Instead, his failings were winked at by the public—at least those who knew of them. But his uncle the emperor was rather less amused and strongly resolved that the "Gorgeous Archduke" should marry a woman who would be a strengthening influence on him. His choice fell on Princess Maria Josepha of Saxony, Austria's wartime ally against Prussia. Daughter of King George (whose devotion to the Sacred Heart of Jesus was renowned), she had inherited both her father's piety and single-minded loyalty. She would need them. It would not be a happy marriage, as anyone who knew the couple might have known. But the wedding nevertheless took place on October 2, 1886. In the beginning, at any rate, Otto did his expected part. On August 17, 1887, Archduke Karl Franz

Joseph Ludwig Hubert Georg Otto Maria—the subject of this book—was born.

CHAPTER 4

PIETAS AUSTRIACA

Vienna runs a close second with Madrid in its celebration of the Corpus Christi processions. Every shop and place of business is closed. The Emperor of Austria in person takes his place in a procession, falling into the ranks behind the clergy, followed by the court, the ministers, the municipal authorities, and the trade guilds. There are waving plumes, caparisoned horses, with all the noble Hungarian body-guard glittering in their mediaeval trappings. There are benedictions and genuflections at the successive stations; and as the crosses and the sacred symbols are held on high, the people drop devoutly on their knees in the mud or the dust.[1]

—WILLIAM S. WALSH

As recounted earlier, every Catholic monarchy developed its own devotional style, and this was certainly true of the House of Austria. The Habsburgs shared much in common with their brethren, but they also had some religious features unique to themselves. Taken together, their various devotions and venerations were dubbed *Pietas Austriaca*,

1 William S. Walsh, *Curiosities of Popular Customs* (F. B. Lippincott Company, 1897), 288.

"Austrian Piety." Arising from a combination of standard monarchical practices, the family's medieval roots, the local traditions they found in their various countries, and the Habsburg role as defender and renewer of Catholicism during the Counter-Reformation, this method of devotion was adhered to publicly by every member of the family. For some—as perhaps Charles's great-uncle Ludwig Viktor and his own father—these things might have been mere formalities, as in a great deal of public religiosity today in the Anglosphere. But most were fairly sincere, and in the case of Charles, he did his utmost to live by it, and made it his own. It is fair to say that without some understanding of the *Pietas Austriaca*, it is impossible to grasp Charles's character. It should also be remembered that his empress, although not born to a then-currently ruling clan, nevertheless was brought up with the memory of the roughly equivalent *Religion Royale* of the Bourbons.

At the basis of such devotion was a rite touched on before: the coronation. Every Christian nation that had the rite put great store in it, as it combined the sacramental of anointing and oath to defend the Church with a similar oath to defend the laws, rights, and territories of the given realm, and investiture with the country's crown jewels. The regalia were themselves often suffused with deep national symbolism, redolent of the nation's history and traditions.

The medieval Holy Roman emperors were eligible for four of these rites: elected at Frankfurt, they initially had the Crown of Charlemagne bestowed on them at Aachen, Charlemagne's capital of Aix-la-Chapelle. Then down to Italy, to be crowned king of that country with the Iron Crown of Lombardy (so called from the band of iron within made from a nail of Christ's passion) at either Milan or Pavia. Following this came the coronation for the Kingdom of Burgundy at Arles (last received by Charles IV in 1355). Finally, the emperor would actually be crowned as such by the pope at St. Peter's in Rome. But Charles V was the last Habsburg to be crowned either king of Italy or Holy Roman emperor—both by the Pope at Bologna in 1530. He was also the last to be crowned king at Aachen; due to the hostility and proximity of France to that city, the ceremony from then on took place at Frankfurt until Francis II was crowned in 1792. Fearful that Napoleon would try to take the Holy Roman throne for himself, Francis had made himself emperor of Austria as Francis I and abdicated his older title, hoping thereby to dissolve the age-old entity and so keep it out of the hands of his usurping future son-in-law.

But while there would be no coronation as emperors of Austria for the Habsburgs who succeeded him, they reigned in 1815 over three countries that did still boast the rite: Hungary, with its Holy Crown of St. Stephen; Bohemia (including Moravia and Austrian Silesia—modern Czechia), and the Crown of St. Wenceslaus; and the Lombardo-Venetian Kingdom, which still preserved the above-noted Iron Crown. Franz Josef's uncle Ferdinand, who succeeded to the throne in 1835, quite happily received all three crowns. But for Franz Josef, the Iron Crown was out of the question thanks to the successive losses of both parts Lombardo-Venetia. Likewise, although he had wanted to be crowned at Prague, the politics of Czech nationalism rendered it impossible. The Hungarian coronation in 1867 came at the price of the earlier mentioned *Ausgleich* and the creation of Austria-Hungary. When Charles's time would come, he would look on reception of the Holy Crown of St. Stephen as tying him forever to Hungary, as marriage would to his wife. Moreover, he planned—once peace came—to be crowned king of Bohemia as well. It is impossible to exaggerate the importance of this rite and its meaning to both Charles and Zita, whose French Bourbon, Valois, and Capet ancestors had undergone a similar ceremony at Reims.

In the view of the Habsburgs, coronation gave them a responsibility before God not only for their people's bodies but for their souls—a responsibility that would only lessen under the Enlightenment-loving Joseph II, but rush to the fore once more under Francis II. This meant patronizing the orders and monasteries they had inherited with Austria, such as the Benedictine Melk, the Cistercian Heiligenkreuz, and the Augustinian Klosterneuburg. After the onset of the Protestant revolt, it also meant bringing in new orders to deal with various needs: Piarists, Hospitallers, and above all the Jesuits, just to mention a few. The last named were given control of elite schools and often gave confessors to the reigning emperor. So too with such orders as the Dominicans, Franciscan, Carmelites, and Servites. Imperial funds went into building convents and parish churches across the Habsburg lands, as well as hospitals and the like. For the same reason, as the Habsburgs acquired new lands from the Turks and the Poles, they sponsored the Byzantine Rite Ukrainian, Ruthenian, Romanian, and Croatian-Serbian Catholic Churches. But unfortunately, protecting the Faith and saving souls sometimes required sterner measures, hence the horrors of the Thirty Years War (prolonged for thirty of those years by external intervention) and subsequent forbidding of public Protestant services. Moreover, there was the fear (justified in the case of the War of Austrian Succession by the actions of many Silesian Protestants in cooperating with the Prussian invaders) that such folk would conspire with the Habsburgs' enemies. This attitude may seem harsh to us moderns, but we too ban and punish those whose ideas we consider a threat to society, as witness the European criminalization of Holocaust denial and American treatment of so-called "hate-speech." "Heretic" may be almost an epithet of pride today; in days gone by, it carried the same regard as "racist" or "bigot" do now. So do every society's rulers attempt to safeguard their subjects from what they consider evil.

An important part of Habsburg spirituality was maintenance of what can only be called inherited obligations toward Rome, the Holy Land, and various foreign missions. Apart from the defense of the Papal States—which Austria became unable to do after the 1859 defeat—the emperor had to maintain several educational and religious institutions in Rome: Santa Maria dell'Anima (which to this day boasts that it "together with the Principality of Liechtenstein is the last existing remnant of the Holy Roman Empire"), the Campo Santo Teutonico, the Pontifical Croatian College of St. Jerome, the Pontifical German and Hungarian College, and the Pontifical Bohemian College. In common with the kings of France and Spain, and in succession to the Holy Roman emperors, the Austrian emperors claimed the right of *Jus Exclusivae* at papal conclaves. That is to say, they did not claim the right to name the pope but to disqualify, if they thought him opposed to their interests, a single cardinal at a conclave. Although exercised several times in the seventeenth, eighteenth, and early nineteenth centuries by the three powers, it had not been used since 1831, although in 1846 the cardinal sent with the imperial veto arrived too late to enter the conclave; that was just as well, because the man he would have vetoed became Blessed Pius IX.

In common with the kings of Spain, Sardinia, and the Two Sicilies (and the Dukes de La Trémoille, now represented by a branch of the Princes de Ligne), the emperors of Austria had for typically arcane genealogical reasons a claim to the title of "King of Jerusalem." The French alliance with the Turks had given that country almost a monopoly on protection of the Catholics of the Holy Land, which, to be fair, they had used very well. But Franz Josef took his obligations toward the Holy Land very seriously. In 1854, he founded an Austrian Hospice in Jerusalem (his brother Maximilian scouted out the property) and stayed there in 1869, at which time he was made a knight of the Holy Sepulchre. His eventual heir, Franz Ferdinand, also joined the order in Palestine.

One other area in which Austria attempted to unseat French religio-political supremacy was in the area of foreign missions. Not merely in the Holy Land but throughout the Ottoman and Chinese Empire, and many other places, the French had made themselves sole defenders of native Catholics. But under Franz Josef, Austrian protection of and aid to the Church in places and situations closed to the French blossomed. In northern Germany and Scandinavia, where the Church had begun to peek out from the ruins of the Reformation (thanks in no small part to Romanticism), the

Austrians funded new churches. They did the same in Albania and Macedonia—parts of the Ottoman Empire beyond French protection. In the 1840s and '50s, the emperor contributed heavily to the work in what is now South Sudan of men like Fr. Ignatius Knoblecher and the Comboni missionaries. As a result, Pope Leo XIII put the newly revived Coptic Catholic Patriarchate in Egypt under Austrian protection. But one of the biggest missionary recipients of imperial largesse was the Leopoldine Association, which until 1914 donated millions of dollars to the struggling Church in a faraway country—the United States of America. Founded in 1829, it also dispatched such missionaries as Venerable Frederic Baraga to our shores.

The concrete expressions of Habsburg piety were and are to be seen all over their former possessions; as might be expected, the very center of this spiritual empire is in its temporal heart the Burgkapelle of the Vienna Hofburg. To this day, the chapel hosts the annual Mass and chapter of the Order of the Golden Fleece, presided over today by Emperor Charles's grandson. The nearby Augustinerkirche was both parish church—and so wedding chapel—for the family as well as last repository for their hearts. In keeping with old custom, their bodies would in turn be entombed at the Kaisergruft of the Kapuzinerkirche, while their viscerae were sent to a crypt at St. Stephen's Cathedral—itself a mighty sign of imperial patronage. To this day, the Viennese square "Am Hof" boasts a beautiful bronze column commemorating the Virgin's intercession in warding off Swedish invasion in 1645.

Indeed, Marian devotion was and is a strong keynote of the Pietas Austriaca. There are many shrines of Our Lady all over the former empire. But perhaps the center of them all is the great shrine of Mariazell, the home of an image of the Virgin called *Magna Mater Austriae*, the "Great Mother of Austria." She is and was, however, venerated not only by the members of the Habsburg dynasty and the Austrians but by Hungarians, Czechs, Slovaks, Slovenians, Croatians, Poles, and Bosnians. At the beginning of the Thirty Years War, Ferdinand II led an army to victory carrying the banner of Our Lady of Victories; he was constrained the following day to execute a group of Czech rebels and then set out to Mariazell to pray for their souls. He had already vowed to Our Lady of Loreto in 1598 that he would free any lands he might inherit from heresy; in the wake of his victory, he spread devotion to her under this title. But just as the Habsburgs placed their struggles with sin and heresy under the Virgin's mantle, so too with the ongoing wars with the Turks. In 1684, to commemorate the relief of the siege of Vienna by the Turks the previous year, Pope Innocent XI placed the feast of the Holy Name of Mary on the universal calendar. Twelve years later, an icon of the Virgin in the Byzantine Catholic town of Pocs began weeping; when Prince Eugene of Savoy crushingly defeated the Turks at Zante a few months afterwards, it was attributed to her intervention, and the icon was brought to St. Stephen's Cathedral, where it remains. Prince Eugene also attributed another such success to the Virgin in 1716, whereupon the pope put the feast of Our Lady of the Rosary on the calendar to commemorate it. The presence of *Mariensäulen*, "Mary Columns"—pillars surmounted by a statue of Our Lady—in virtually every larger town the Habsburgs ruled is a continuing testimony to their love of the Virgin.

So too with their veneration of Christ himself. Gathered over centuries, the dynasty's collection of relics in the treasure chamber of the Hofburg included a number associated with Our Lord, including several pieces of the true cross (devotion to which was a large part of the Pietas Austriaca). Of course, as rulers of Austria and protectors of Heiligenkreuz Abbey, they would also from time to time venerate the large chunk of the cross which is enshrined there, a gift from a Babenberg duke who had been on crusade. Indeed, *crusade* was a word that resonated with the Habsburgs, as they spent centuries fighting for the cross of Christ against heretics and Muslims. In the course of the Czech protestant rebellion that precipitated the Thirty Years War, a group of rebellious nobles had Emperor Ferdinand II a virtual prisoner in the Hofburg. They demanded that he sign a decree giving them religious liberty, or else! One of them dared to grab him by the shoulders and said, "Give in and sign!" But at that point, the crucifix he kept always with him spoke and said, "*Ferdinande, non Te deseram.*" (Ferdinand, I shall not desert thee!) Just at that point imperial cavalry came riding up and Ferdinand's tormentors fled. In any case, the cross symbolized to the Habsburgs the spirit of sacrifice for God and their people that was expected of each of them if they wished to reach heaven. The same was true of innumerable other pieces in their relics collection, to include the holy lance, believed to be that which had pierced the side of Christ, and the agate bowl that some believed to be the Holy Grail, the vessel in which Jesus had first transubstantiated wine into his Blood at the Last Supper, and which was used to catch some of that which flowed from his side the following day.

So too with Habsburg devotion to the Blessed Sacrament. On the one hand, this devotion could be very public, as with the Corpus Christi processions the emperors marched in—"God's Court Ball," as the locals called it. Soldier's dress uniforms and noble costumes, knights and religious of various orders, civil officials, and behind it all under the canopy, the Host in the monstrance, to whom Church and state alike gave due homage on this feast day. But it could also be very private indeed, and successive emperors made a point of spending time before the Blessed Sacrament in prayer whenever personal or public affairs demanded it. Masses accompanied any formal occasion at court.

One of the most important of these was the foot-washing on Maundy Thursday, a rite the emperor had in common with the kings of France, Spain, Portugal, Two Sicilies, England, Sardinia, and Bavaria. It was one of the most glittering events at court, and deserves an eye-witness account:

> Shortly after ten o'clock the floor began to fill with score upon score of officers in full uniform, from the different regiments of the kingdom, making a brilliant and imposing scene. In the assemblage were many of the most distinguished members of the Austro-Hungarian court, including ministers of state, archdukes, generals of infantry and cavalry, and vice-admirals of the war-fleet. Chatting with officers in gold-embroidered blue and scarlet uniforms were knights of Malta with

white cross on sleeve and breast, Hungarians with high yellow boots and a leopard's skin thrown over the left shoulder, and in marked contrast to these the Polish aristocrats in flowing robes of black mourning for their lost kingdom. In the royal box above were the ladies of the court. At half-past ten the clergy entered the room, followed by the twelve oldest poor men of Vienna (for whom the service is performed), dressed in old German costume,—black, with white cape collars and knee-breeches.

Many of the aged men were quite feeble, and were assisted to their chairs by their relatives, who stood behind them during the service. Earlier in the morning the Emperor, Francis Joseph I, accompanied by his suite, attended high mass in the royal chapel, and upon his return entered the hall, followed by his cousin, nephews, and a largo cortege. The Emperor wore the uniform of a general of infantry and took his place at once at the head of the table, making the number thirteen, while in the rear stood thirteen of his body-guard. Then appeared from an anteroom twelve of the nobility, each carrying a tray containing the first course of a feast to be served to the Kaiser's guests.

The dishes were all placed upon the table by the Emperor himself, but no sooner had he done this than, with the assistance of his brother and the archdukes, he replaced them upon trays held by the thirteen guards, who removed them. It seemed a little hard on the old men to see the tempting viands so quickly taken away, but we learned later that each one received at his home the food and dishes as well, which were made for this occasion, as it had been found that the dinner was much more enjoyed in this way than before such a grand assemblage. The repast was beautifully prepared and handsomely garnished, served in four courses, each presented and removed in the manner described, after which the tables were taken away.

Footmen then removed the shoes and stockings from the old men and spread over their knees a long white linen roll, after which the chaplain began the Gospel for the day. At the words *et coepit lavare pedes discipulorum* the Emperor knelt and began the ceremony of the foot-washing, one prelate holding a basin while another poured the water. The Emperor continued kneeling until he had performed this service of humility for each of the twelve, after which he took from a salver silken bags, each containing thirty pieces of silver, and hung one about the neck of each of the old men. This ended the service; but we lingered long enough to see these honored guests assisted to the royal carriages to be sent home in the care of members of the Kaiser's body-guard, carrying the sizable wooden chest of provisions and a large flask of wine. When the Empress is at home she performs a similar service for the twelve oldest poor women of Vienna, but in case she is not, as happened this year, they are not present at the ceremonial, but receive at their homes an equal share of the royal bounty. It is not uncommon later to find these royal gifts in an antiquarian's shop,—the original recipients frequently desiring the florins they

> will bring more than the distinction of possessing the gifts themselves.
>
> The men and women who can count more than one hundred years are annually included in this royal invitation, but the majority of them receive this honor but once. This year the oldest was ninety-six and the youngest eighty-eight years of age.[2]

Nor was there a lack of devotion to the saints. Although a Babenberg, St. Leopold III served as a good patron for the Habsburgs in Austria. In addition, the family was devoted to Saints Stephen of Hungary and Wenceslaus of Bohemia, as well as St. Michael the Archangel. To these, in the seventeenth century, were added a devotion to St. Joseph. In 1675, Emperor Leopold I (who would later withstand the siege of Vienna), made St. Joseph co-patron with the great archangel of the Holy Roman Empire. Two years later, he declared him patron of the Habsburg dynasty as well, and honored him further in 1678 by naming his newborn son Joseph.

These devotions were all fairly well established, both in Catholicism and among the Habsburgs. But a relatively new one arose in seventeenth-century France: that of the Sacred Heart. It had always had a sort of royal aspect in that St. Margaret Mary Alacoque revealed that Jesus had ordered her to tell Louis XIV of France to put the Sacred Heart on his military banners, and to consecrate his country thereto.

---

2 Correspondence of the *Springfield Republican*, April, 1895, quoted in Walsh, *Curiosities of Popular Customs*, pp. 675–76.

Louis did not, but many other monarchs became interested: the exiled James II and Mary of Modena from England; Augustus II and Augustus III, electors of Saxony, kings of Poland, and grand dukes of Lithuania; their rival for the Polish and Lithuanian thrones, Stanisław Leszczyński; Felipe V of Spain; Maria I of Portugal; Maximilian III, elector of Bavaria; and the daughter of Stanislaw, the Queen of France's Louis XV, Marie Leszczynska. Unable to influence her husband, she did bring her son, Louis the dauphin, and his heir, likewise named Louis, to the love of the Sacred Heart, something that remained when the boy succeeded his grandfather as Louis XVI in 1774. During his later imprisonment, he vowed to consecrate France to the Sacred heart if he regained his power; alas, he did not, dying on the guillotine.

As a result of the French Revolution that murdered him and his Habsburg wife, however, the Sacred Heart became the badge of many of the Catholics who fought it. This was particularly true in the Vendee and Tyrol; in both regions, the Sacred Heart remains the official symbol today. Devotion to the Sacred Heart grew particularly among Catholics interested in political and social questions of the day. The French Legitimists, Spanish Carlists, and Papal Zouaves were instrumental in spreading it. But among the Sacred Heart's biggest royal clients in the late nineteenth century was King George of Saxony. This devotion he would pass on to his daughter, Maria Josefa. Given her marriage to the dissolute Archduke Otto, she would need it.

Book Two

IMPERIAL LIVES IN TANDEM

Chapter 5

BIRTH AND EDUCATION OF A PRINCE

Lord, if it please you, hear our prayer, and by your inexhaustible power protect your chosen one, Charles, now marked with the sign of our Savior's holy cross. Let him treasure this first sharing of your sovereign glory, and by keeping your commandments deserve to attain the glory of heaven to which those born anew are destined; through Christ our Lord.

—Rite of Baptism, Roman *Rituale*

As earlier noted, the birth of young Archduke Charles on August 17, 1887 did not cause much of a stir outside his immediate family. He was born fourth in line to the throne, but as mentioned, this was likely to change, especially if Cousin Rudolf, the crown prince, had sons. Even if he did not, the as-yet unmarried uncle Franz Ferdinand was quite likely to. What Charles's advent did do, for a short while, was to rekindle his errant father's interest in Charles's twenty-year-old mother, Archduchess Maria Josefa, at least for a while. Two years older than his bride, Archduke Otto's bachelor's adventures—often with Crown

Prince Rudolf—had resumed shortly after his marriage. But fatherhood calmed him down, at least for a while. The archducal family lived at Persenbeug Castle on the Danube, and Charles was baptized two days later in the castle chapel. As with so many of the Habsburg properties, Persenbeug had passed in and out of family hands, but it has remained in the ownership of one or another branch of the family since 1800—so it is that the chapel where the newborn archduke was baptized and the Kaisersaal where the ensuing celebrations took place are unchanged.

The little family had another home, the Villa Wartholz in Reichenau-an-der-Rax. Where Schloss Persenbeug was a medieval castle renovated to nineteenth-century standards, Villa Wartholtz had only been built in 1872, in the latest historicist style. Charles's grandfather and Otto's father, Archduke Karl Ludwig, had bought it especially for the hunting. But the area, once the railroad came through, became a resort for the aristocracy and wealthy bourgeoisie. Both houses had lovely gardens and ponds that the young Charles would enjoy playing in, albeit almost drowning in one at Persenbeug. But the family would often be posted in different places, owing to varying military assignments for Charles's father. After Charles's birth, they lived in Brno from 1887 to 1890; his father was transferred to Enns in 1890–1891, but as there was no suitable housing for them, Charles and his mother stayed at Villa Wartholz. When Archduke Otto changed to infantry, the family moved to Prague Castle (1891–1893) and finally to Sopron (1893–1896). There Otto was posted to Hussar Regiment No. 9, while his family stayed in the palace of Count Ladislav Pejačević on Petofi Square.

But Charles was only two years old when another of the tragedies that plagued the Habsburgs in the twilight of their reign occurred: the death of Crown Prince Rudolf and his mistress, Baroness Maria Vetsera, at his hunting lodge of Mayerling. This was a very strange occurrence, much like the Kennedy assassination in its mixture of strange circumstances and conflicting theories. Certainly it appeared to be suicide; Franz Josef had to get a medical opinion that the late prince had not been in his right mind, and Rudolf's wife had received what certainly looked like a suicide note. As against this, Charles's future wife, Zita, maintained that the deaths of Rudolf's mistress and himself were murders carried out at the behest of foreign political figures. Hoping to use the antagonism between father and son to their advantage, they found Rudolf unwilling to betray Franz Josef, and so silenced him. Franz Josef, in this reading of the event, preferred to avoid war by going along with the suicide theory. To complicate things further, it is a strongly held belief by many of the monks at Heiligenkreuz—whose predecessors were apparently told so by the servant who brought the bodies to the abbey where they were both initially held—that Rudolf's fingers were broken, apparently snapped while holding a table against the bedroom door. Were that true, of course, it would rule out both his killing himself and his mistress. Intact, however, would be the mysteries of who and why. Whatever the case, that particular story could only be proven or otherwise by reexamination of the remains. In all likelihood, as with the Kennedy affair, the disappearance of Judge Crater, and any number of other such strange tales, we are highly unlikely to come to complete resolution this side of the grave. What is certain is that Franz Josef had Mayerling pulled down and replaced with a Carmelite monastery, whose sisters to this day pray for the repose of the souls of the tragic pair.

Another certainty is that with Rudolf gone, the line of succession altered again. Charles's grandfather was now next in line, then Uncle Franz Ferdinand, then Otto, and lastly Charles. At this point, his education became a burning consideration. An attractive infant and tot, as he grew older, the little archduke began to show a tremendous concern for others. Once, climbing some stairs with his nanny, and noticing that she was beginning to huff and puff, he stopped and said, "Why don't we rest a little?" He was always looking for gifts to give to servants and was enchanted with the rudiments of his religious education. But there was nothing of the annoying prig about him, hence the near-drowning at Persenbeug. Charles loved playing soldiers, and even as a child he picked up English from his Irish nanny, Miss Bridie Casey. "He was happy about life and keen that others should be, also."[1]

The stay in Sopron marked him in several different ways. Although only spending three years there, from the time he was six until age nine, it was at Sopron that Father Artur Tormássy joined the family as Charles's Hungarian-language tutor. He would give him daily lessons for the next nine years, until the archduke left high school, and corresponded regularly with him in Magyar after that. The ease this gave

---

1 James and Joanna Bogle, *A Heart for Europe* (Gracewing, 1993), p. 5.

the young heir in such a difficult language stood him in good stead for the rest of his life.

But there was another significant individual in Sopron at the time: an Ursuline nun, Mother Vincentia Fauland of the Child Jesus. A native of Graz in Styria, she was the administratrix of the Ursuline school in Sopron. But there was another side to her: from the age of sixteen, Aloysia (as she was born) was favored with the stigmata. The Ursulines had only accepted her after long and careful observation, and her mother superior kept a diary of her unusual subject's visions. Mother Vincentia also had the gift of prophecy; this being known to a number of people, it was noted when she said of young Charles, "Yes, one has to pray a lot for him, because he will become Emperor and he will have to suffer a lot. He will be a special point of attack for hell."[2] In response, a group of her acquaintances and followers began praying for the young archduke. They and their successors would continue to do so until he died, after which time they began to pray for his beatification. This was in fact the origin of the *Kaiser Karl Gebetsliga für den Völkerfrieden*, the "Emperor Charles League of Prayer for Peace among Peoples." Having successfully seen his beatification through, the league now superintends his *cultus* and works for Charles's canonization. We shall see more of them in a later section. But this was the first indication that he himself might one day be emperor, and it was one of which very few were aware.

2 Heinz von Lichem, *Karl I: ein Kaiser sucht den Frieden* (Tyrolia, 1996), p. 72.

When Charles was seven, his education began in earnest. In addition to Father Tormássy, the young archduke was given a heavy daily academic load: modern languages, history, geography, the classics, and religion were the bulk of it all, with one Count George Wallis as overall tutor. This was a relatively happy time for Charles's parents, as evidenced by the arrival of a younger brother, Maximilian Eugen, in 1895. Charles was delighted with the new arrival but had absolutely no idea of where he came from, supposing in the end that one of the servants must have brought him as a gift. But wherever the child had indeed come from, Charles doted on him, and as soon as he was able to, Maximilian returned the favor.

The following year, however, things began to change. Charles's grandfather, the heir to the throne, had made a pilgrimage to Egypt and the Holy Land, which were particular areas of interest to the Habsburgs. In Cairo, he met his eldest son, Franz Ferdinand, who was struggling with tuberculosis. He then went on to the Holy Land as his brother had, visited Jerusalem and Bethlehem, and then the River Jordan. In the heights of religious enthusiasm, he drank the water. The typhoid fever he contracted stayed with him, and although seeming in good health when he returned to Vienna, he took a swift turn for the worse, dying on May 19 at age sixty-two. This meant that once more the line of succession shifted; the unmarried Franz Ferdinand was now heir, while Otto was second in line, and Charles third.

This brought about a change in all their lives. Attention focused on Franz Ferdinand, the eldest of the three brothers. As earlier mentioned, he was unmarried at the time, and both devout and devoted to hunting. The new heir had also loved traveling and had literally been around the world before his father died. Franz Ferdinand had been posted to Sopron a few years before his brother, and then to the western Hungarian city of Gyor, where was garrisoned the cavalry regiment the emperor had given him command of. The new heir's time in Hungary had not been wasted; he had several Hungarian tutors, one of whom, Father Joszef Lanyi, would become a lifelong friend. Walking in the streets with no ceremony, he got to know the Magyars, and he cultivated friendships with leading members of the Hungarian Catholic Party. However, he began very much to resent the then current Liberal Party leadership of the Hungarian Kingdom. Not only did their Magyarisation policies build resentment among the various nationalities who had rallied to the dynasty in 1848, Franz Ferdinand feared their pro-German attitudes and suspected them of disloyalty to the dynasty. Franz Ferdinand's tuberculosis flared up at the time of his father's death so that he was unable to attend the funeral.

Franz Josef resolved that since the brothers were now closer to the throne, they should have suitable dwellings in town. To Franz Ferdinand he assigned the Palace of the Upper Belvedere—built by Prince Eugen of Savoy and today an art museum. To Otto and his family went the palace at Augarten; located near the Imperial Porcelain Factory, it is now the residence and school of the Vienna Boys Choir. Those who knew him at this age have constantly commented about how Charles's generous and truthful nature continued to mature during these years. He was not given to lying, and he was very prayerful at Mass. Having already received the Brown

Scapular in 1896 (given by a Dominican priest, with the admonition, "Wear it immaculate and pure until you can return it in death to the Heavenly Mother!"), he received his first Communion at the chapel of Villa Wartholtz.

Yet another horrible tragedy struck the Habsburg clan in 1898. The empress Elizabeth, Franz Josef's much loved (and loving) consort, as beautiful as she was troubled, was murdered by an anarchist on a ferry boat in Lake Geneva. Today the center of an international cult—much inspired by film—she was and is a much-misunderstood figure. Married to Franz Josef at an early age, the Wittelsbach princess had difficulty with her domineering mother-in-law, who was also her aunt. Increasingly, she found court life hard to bear and began to travel; this became something of a mania after her son Rudolf died. Despite it all, her death was yet another heartbreak for her husband.

The following year, there occurred an extraordinary event in the life of the Church and of Charles himself. Under the influence of a mystic, Blessed Maria Droste zu Vischering, Pope Leo XIII resolved to consecrate the whole world to the Sacred Hear of Jesus. The pope set June 11, 1899 as the date upon which he would do the deed, and he invited all the bishops of the world to do the same in their own cathedrals. So it was that on that day, at St. Stephen's Cathedral in Vienna in the presence of the emperor and the court, the archbishop consecrated the people and the country to the Sacred Heart. Charles had come down with whooping cough, however, and could not travel to the capital, but he insisted on performing the consecration at the chapel at Villa Wartholtz. This was not too surprising, because he had already cultivated a devotion to the Sacred Heart. He used to read the monthly *Messenger of the Sacred Heart* cover-to-cover and would try to find new subscribers for it. He was also a great fan of the *Daily Prayer Book of the Sacred Heart of Jesus*, which he would often be seen using for the rest of his life. The First Friday Devotion had also become a cornerstone of his prayer life and would remain so.

Later that year, at age twelve, Charles began his formal education at the Schottenstift (Irish Monastery) in Vienna. Founded by Irish monks in 1155, it had had quite an eventful history. In 1807, in accordance with an imperial decree, the monks opened a high school, which soon became quite prestigious. This was where Archduke Charles was sent to complete his secondary education. Here, amongst boys of various backgrounds, he had to prove himself. Thanks to his easy manner and lack of formality, he was soon very popular, his nickname being "Arch-Charles" in reference to his rank. He studied, in addition to the liberal arts he had already begun, such hard sciences as chemistry and physics.

During his second year at the Schottengymnasium, 1900, two major events occurred. One was that after years of happy game-chasing bachelorhood, Franz Ferdinand had fallen in love. The object of his affections was a devout and fun-loving Bohemian noblewoman, Sophie, Countess Chotek. Noble but not royal, alas—not marriageable. Franz Josef was furious, and the court chaplain was against it. But Franz Ferdinand had conquered a deadly disease, travelled the world, and formed his own ideas regarding the future of the empire. He was not to be balked: finally, the willful archduke prevailed and was given permission to marry, but morganatically. This meant that while Franz Ferdinand would still one day be emperor, his wife could never be empress. Nor would their children inherit the throne. Otto might or might not become Kaiser if he outlived his brother, but Charles surely would; moreover, it would befall him to produce children for the dynasty. The second great event was that his father—long since returned to his philandering ways—had caught syphilis. Untreatable then, it was deadly, and accompanied by horrendous physical and mental decay. This diagnosis ensured that, in all likelihood, it would indeed be Charles who succeeded, sooner rather than later.

With this in mind, it was decided that he should not take exams with his peers when he finished his course of instruction at the Schottengymnasium—it was considered unseemly to have these students in essence compete against the heir to the throne. The emperor decided to send him for a year or two on European tours to familiarize himself with their ways of doing things and improve his languages. In this manner, he also visited a number of foreign courts. Always returning to Villa Wartholz, Count Wallis and his other tutors continued his education.

Apart from cultivating a charming manner, the young archduke's devotional life also continued to grow. During this period, when the Los-von-Rom (Away from Rome) movement was growing among Pan-Germanist minded Catholics, Charles refused to hear the pope insulted in his presence. On October 18, 1903, he went to the consecration of the Canisiuskirche in Vienna's ninth district, which was built under the special patronage of his mother, Maria Josefa; Franz Josef was also there.

Spring of 1904 saw Charles go to a fashionable resort, Brixen (now Bressanone) in South Tyrol. There he met Count Arthur Polzer-Hoditz—whom we shall meet again—for the second time. The first occasion had been when Charles was still a boy. But now, the sixteen-year-old was both well-informed and articulate: "For all his *joie de vivre* he liked serious conversation. I was often amazed at the clear and straightforward judgements he expressed on men and things. His judgements were always charitable, never malicious."[3] This was a good sign, because as far as the emperor was concerned, Charles's boyhood was over; the next year, he entered the Imperial and Royal Army.

3 Arthur Polzer-Hoditz, *The Emperor Charles* (Putnam, 1930).

Chapter 6

TO BE A SOLDIER

Receive this sword, in the name of the Fa+ther, the + Son and the Holy + Spirit, and may thou use it for thy defense, and that of the Holy Church of God, and to the confounding of the enemies of the Cross of Christ, and of the Christian faith: and as far as human frailty shall permit, may thou harm no one with it unjustly. And may He deign to grant this to thee, Who with the Father and the Holy Spirit etc.

—The Blessing of a New Knight,
from the Roman *Pontificale*

The next few years were filled with study and travel. Charles's parents rarely saw each other as his father's disease made its dreary road to death. The young heir himself was often at Villa Wartholtz but would also accompany his mother to Miramar Castle near Trieste, from whence his Great Uncle Maximilian had pursued glory in Mexico. He would, however, also visit his father frequently.

His military obligations began in earnest when Charles reached eighteen years of age. He was posted in September of 1905 to the barracks of the Seventh "Duke of Lorraine" Dragoons (demolished on January 27, 2012) in Bilina,

Bohemia. Commissioned a lieutenant, he was very quickly an important part of the life of the regiment. The Seventh had been founded in 1663 and participated in all the wars of the dynasty ever after—down to and including World War I. Although it would be dissolved in 1918, 1990 saw its recreation as a "Traditional Regiment," with Archduke Johann Salvator becoming honorary colonel five years later. In 2004, the NCO academy in Enns took on the regiment's traditions.

Of the army he was joining, Charles himself would say many years later—almost toward its end—on October 24, 1918, "All the people of the monarchy have found a common home in the army. For that reason, it has been enabled to accomplish so much." Its future commander-in-chief would have his view of his peoples formed in great part by watching them cooperate more or less in harmony in the army. "The Imperial army was supranational. Among its ranks, members of twenty different nations, in return for knowledge of 86 German words of command, were vouchsafed equal treatment."[1] Although its ranks were primarily Catholic, there were large numbers of Protestants, Orthodox, Jews, and Muslims to be found therein. Nevertheless, "Religious tolerance, even in the days of the Josephinian Enlightenment, did not imply a totally secularist agenda. The dynasty's own piety was always expressed in the army's ethos and customs. The Habsburg army's rallying cry was 'With God and Kaiser for the Fatherland.' When the gifted

[1] Richard Bassett, *For God and Kaiser: The Imperial Austrian Army, 1619-1918* (Yale University Press, 2015), p. 3.

Croat general Jellacic was made governor (Ban) of Croatia, his instalment speech was rich in devotional phrases invoking the Virgin Mary."[2] If God came first, however, Kaiser was not far behind: "From the moment on 5 June 1619 that it saved the prayerful Archduke Ferdinand from the clutches of the Protestant Bohemian nobility, it sealed an unbroken bond between sovereign and soldier."[3] This bond would endure through the conflict that ended the Empire: "By 1914 [the army] had not fired a shot in anger in a generation. Unlike its Serbian and Russian opponents, the Austro-Hungarian army went into the First World War entirely unprepared to fight a modern war. It fought without interruption for more than four years, defying Entente expectations that it would quickly fall to bits through internal tensions and nationalist rivalries."[4] The close bond with the dynasty that held the forces together under the unbelievably horrific conditions, say, of the Italian front in the glacier-ridden Alps, was manifest in the military education given all archdukes; that of the heir to the throne was particularly intense.

It was while he was at Bilina that Charles was made a member of the Order of the Golden Fleece—of which, as future emperor of Austria, he would one day be grand master. Founded in 1430 by Duke Philip the Good of Burgundy, it had come to the House of Habsburg with the rest of the Burgundian inheritance. Its members drawn from the higher echelons of the Austrian nobility, it was and remains today one of the most elite European orders of knighthood.

---

2 Ibid., p. 4.

3 Ibid.

4 Ibid.

Its statutes were written in fifteenth-century French, and it was typical of the young Archduke Charles that he insisted on reading the difficult language with the help of his tutor—he did not want to commit to anything he did not understand or could not fulfill. One cannot overestimate the influence of the code of Chivalry on Charles's life. It was integrally united with his view of the military, and so of politics. These comments of his son, Archduke Otto, on chivalry and knighthood might well express Charles's own views:

> The first task of chivalry was the service of faith, and most beautiful expression of this servitude were the knightly orders, who were called to defend the Christian West, to protect the holy places and at the same time to accomplish the works of Christian charity with their soldierly function. Knights who did not belong to a religious order were no less bound by religion. Certainly, it was a faithful age in general—but that was not crucial. On the contrary, it could be said with equal justification that the faithful knights had shaped their epoch.
>
> The faith, the anchorage in the transcendent, led to the selflessness of the service. Exemplary of this was the Burgundian knighthood [the Order of the Golden Fleece], which, as the backbone of a multi-ethnic state, had to seek a balance between the nations, between Germans and Frenchmen. The knights as civil servants of the state embodied the exact opposite of the bureaucracy, the rule of the desk or the office, and the

Burgundian ideal continued to live in the administrative apparatus of the old Austria into our century.

An important role was played by the concept of personal honor. One respected God and therefore also his image on earth, man. The ideal of faith in daily life set the higher standards that can be expected of a man of honor. Certainly, his way will be no easier. But that is not the purpose of life on this earth as soon as one realizes that it is only a fleeting prelude to our existence.

It is also related, according to Thomas Aquinas, to the chivalrous virtue of high-mindedness, that is, to think great things about oneself, and, trusting in God, to do great things. From the high-minded man the word of the Psalmist applies: "Nothing is the villain in his eyes."

After all, one of the most important criteria of chivalry is personal courage, which is not to be afraid, but to overcome it and to act in spite of all anxiety, as conscience dictates. Courage must therefore not be understood exclusively in the sense of soldierly virtue, but also as a fearless appearance for what one believes in. Moral courage often demands much more from us than the physical one. It also presents a constant challenge. To become a hero in the sense of the warrior can be the act of a moment; moral heroism, however, means commitment, binding for the whole life.[5]

---

5 Otto von Habsburg, "Chivalry Today in the Technological Age," Memento, Author: Erich Feigl, ed. Chancellery of the Grand Priority of Austria of the Ordre Militaire et Hospitalier de Saint-

To understand Charles as a soldier and a statesman, then, it is important to keep these two factors in his formation: the transnational mutual loyalty of the Habsburgs and their army and his commitment to the ideals of chivalry.

Training at Bilina was not all military, however. His civilian tutors continued to push as much into his head as they could. The intensity of this civil education may well be wondered at. In most countries in the world today, national leadership is considered a trade to be acquired through on-the-job training for elected officials. But as young Charles moved ever closer to the crown, the then-perceived necessity for a ruler to know as much about his own country and the rest of the world as possible became ever more pressing to his great-uncle, uncle, mother, and tutors. But it was not merely technical knowledge but ethical and religious that had to be acquired. In any case, Charles's time at Bilina was sufficiently pleasant for him to return when emperor and judge a shooting competition. The prize he awarded is preserved in the Regional Museum at Teplice.

In the meantime, Charles's father's condition slowly worsened. He was being nursed at the residence in Augarten. While visiting Vienna, Charles had a mishap skating and had to recuperate there as well. This would be the last time father and son spent any real time together. In October of 1906, Otto's health took a sudden turn for the worse. Maria Josepha hurried up from Miramar to see him, but she returned as his condition improved. Nevertheless, on the feast of All Saints, Archduke Otto died at age forty-one—and

---

Lazare de Jerusalem, pp. 13-16.

Charles was one more step closer to the throne. Despite the coolness between his parents, Charles had loved his father dearly and was devastated by the loss—as was seen plainly during the obsequies on November 6.

Charles arrived in Prague, the capital of Bohemia, in 1906, as a nineteen-year-old archduke. He began his university studies at the Charles-Ferdinand University. His curriculum included legal studies, history, and economics—that is, select disciplines important for the heir to the throne. He studied as a private pupil with prominent Czech and German professors of this oldest Central European university (founded by Emperor Charles IV in 1348). His academic results were very good, as evidenced by reports of the period, and as the future king, Charles learned much about the historical issues of the Kingdom of Bohemia, which was an irreplaceable part of the monarchy. It was decided to install him and his tutors—Counts Wallis and Polzer-Hoditz—in Prague Castle to engage in further studies alongside what he received at the University in history, economics, and law (especially the Hungarian Constitution). The surroundings in which the archduke was living could not help but impress upon him the importance of his eventual inheritance. In his apartment was the window out of which two Catholic Councillors had been thrown on May 23, 1618, which led to the confrontation with Archduke Ferdinand the following month. The Castle itself had been the stronghold of such emperors as Charles IV, who reorganized the Holy Roman Empire, and Rudolph II, who made Prague a center of literature and alchemy. St. Vitus Cathedral held the shrines of its name saint, as well as St. Wenceslaus (the

"Good King Wenceslaus" of the Christmas carol), and St. John Nepomuk, who died rather than reveal the confession of a queen to her tyrannical husband.

Prague itself, ancient capital of Bohemia, was one of the three major cities in the empire, after Budapest and Vienna. Like the province itself, it was divided between Czechs and ethnic Germans—and their competing nationalisms—the Czech variety of which had a lingering sympathy for Jan Hus, the famed heretic of the fifteenth century, whose devotees had fought a bloody civil war before at last being suppressed. This sojourn in Prague, therefore, also gave the archduke some firsthand knowledge of the current challenges facing the empire. Charles felt quite rightfully at home in Bohemia. Altogether, he lived there for six years, a relatively long period that is often only briefly mentioned in his biographies in relation to his military service. The truth is that, until recently, not much was known about his stay in Bohemia, which deeply shaped his personality.

On his birthday in 1907, Charles came of age and took his place in the ranks of the senior archdukes. After some further study, he went back to his regiment—this time at Brandys nad Labem. The evaluation made of him at this period is fascinating for the description of his qualities:

> "KA, Military Qualifications: Archduke Charles Franz Joseph: In 1908 the lieutenant was fit for war, with German, French, Italian, English, Hungarian language skills and . . . Bohemian for service use sufficiently, as a stable character, with lively temperament, excellent intellectual gifts, with extraordinarily rapid conception

> . . . described. He has a good understanding of tactical situations, is a very passionate and very dashing rider with very good horse skills. As a dresser of man and horse independently very good usable, corresponds in field service and as a patrol commander excellently; He is well-versed in shooting, and even as a very good shooter he instructs in it very well; leads a platoon and a squadron singly and in association very well. . . .
>
> Exemplary zealous, benevolent and filled with a strong sense of duty, he knows how to preserve male discipline and military spirit. Exercises the best influence on camaraderie in the Officers Corps. A particularly intelligent, usable, excellent officer. Has decidedly attachment and love for the [Cavalry] Arm, shows excellent diligence and ambition, is an initiating, dashingly riding cavalry officer, which excellently meets in every respect.

Commenting on Charles's military interests, Zita Ballinger Fletcher opined:

> Charles' decision to pursue a military career was noteworthy. As a royal family member, Charles was not obligated to pursue a profession. Royal family members often held titles and positions for show but were not committed to working or being dedicated professionals. Karl was a rare exception.

Spurning the luxuries enjoyed by so many of his relatives, Karl lived a simple soldier's lifestyle. He dedicated himself to his career and enjoyed marching, drill and cavalry exercises.

For much of his life, he lived in military housing—even as a married man, with his wife Zita and their many children.[6]

The following year was Emperor Franz Josef's diamond jubilee. Unlike the golden anniversary a decade earlier, which had been rather subdued through being overshadowed by Empress Elizabeth's murder, this one was quite simply an imperial and royal blowout. In a thousand towns across the Dual Monarchy, old places and buildings were renamed and new ones christened in honor of the man who, in six decades, had made the transition from teenager to living monument. The successive familial tragedies that had befallen him had fixed the old emperor ever more deeply in the hearts of his people. When, two years after the diamond jubilee, ex-president Theodore Roosevelt visited Vienna and met with the old monarch, the former chief executive asked him what he thought his role was. Franz Josef ruefully answered, "Protecting my people from their politicians."

While that may sound like a mere clever line, it was not. The truth is that from the time of the Ausgleich in 1867, the old emperor had had to play an incredible balancing act: his Hungarian kingdom's dominant politicians tended to be Protestant and independence-minded, as well as pro-German; their attempts to Magyarise the non-Magyar but varied majority in Hungary (Slovaks, Croats, Romanians, Serbs, Rusyns and Germans, to name a few) caused constant difficulties in the immediate and would explode in 1918. The Austrian half featured full participation politically for

6 Zita Ballinger Fletcher, "Blessed Karl: A True Soldier," June 29, 2019, http://www.emperorcharles.org/blog/2019/6/29/blessed-karl-a-true-soldier.

Germans, Czechs, Italians, Slovenes, Croats, Poles, and Ruthenians, and so the Austrian Parliament became ever more deadlocked. Franz Josef had increasingly to use emergency powers to keep the government functioning. Shuffling cabinets, playing one nationalism off against another, and all the while avoiding so far as possible great gestures or enormous changes so as to allow the majority of his subjects sufficient peace with which to live their lives. It was a policy that had paid off: the economy was growing, net incomes were rising, and the newfangled inventions of the nineteenth century—from the railroad to the telephone—were slowly spreading through Central Europe. It was a delicate balance, and the emperor—remembering only too well the horrors of 1848, even if few others in public life did—was dead set against anything that might upset the applecart.

His immediate heir, however, was of a decidedly different cast of mind. Despite the constant slights his wife received because of her status, his marriage had proved an extremely happy one, but it also gave Franz Ferdinand an understanding of the aspirations of the Czechs, and so of the other peoples of the monarchy. Although Franz Ferdinand had the reputation of disliking Hungarians, one of his closest friends, Fr. Joszef Lanyi, remained with the family from 1900–1906—and baptized Franz Ferdinand's children as a calculated snub to the court bishop who had opposed his marriage. Although sharing his uncle the emperor's deep Catholic faith, belief in the dynasty, and in the empire itself, he believed that radical restructuring of both the internal constitution of the monarchy and its foreign policy were necessary if Austria-Hungary was to survive in the long-term.

Franz Ferdinand gathered around him a group of very able advisers, of whom the chief was ethnic-Romanian Aurel Popovici. They came up with a plan for a United States of Greater Austria. This comprised a division of the existing country into fifteen more or less ethnically coherent states, with a sprinkling of autonomous German settlements scattered about. This would, of course, enrage nationalist Magyars; a more moderate approach saw the future emperor being crowned king not only of Bohemia but of Croatia (then in a personal union with Hungary similar to Hungary's own with Austria), which in turn would be united with Austrian Dalmatia, to form a third or fourth partner in the monarchy. However unpopular these ideas made the heir with the dominant set in Hungary, it gave him quite the following among the Slavs. Franz Ferdinand also favored scrapping the alliance with Germany and returning to the Russian alliance—possibly gaining France as an ally, were that possible. These glaring differences with Franz Josef's policies led to increasing distance between Franz Ferdinand and his imperial uncle.

Where did Charles stand in all of this? On the one hand, he shared Franz Josef's desire for continuity and for the continued role of altar and throne in the life of the empire's peoples. But he agreed with Franz Ferdinand's desire for change. Having played a major role in organizing the family jubilee celebrations at Schonbrunn, there he confessed to Count Polzer-Hoditz his fears: "This was the first time that the usually so happy and optimistically inclined Archduke expressed dark views about the future. . . . He spoke of the tradition of his House, which consisted in adherence to the federalistic principle. We have, he said, departed too greatly from that principle, which we would have bitter cause to regret."[7] Having travelled as a boy extensively through the empire, Charles had seen the sheer multiplicity of its peoples. As far as foreign affairs went, his travels in Alsace-Lorraine (the latter of which he bore in his family name) convinced him that the two provinces' proper place was with France. This would bear fruit, of a sort, in the future.

In the immediate, Franz Josef's politicians thought of a jubilee gift for their nominal master that he would not be able to resist. Thirty years before the great event, at the Congress of Berlin which ended the Russo-Turkish War, the Turkish provinces of Bosnia and Herzegovina were allotted to Austria-Hungary to occupy and govern, but only in trust for the Ottoman Empire, who would retain a phantom sovereignty. The population was made up of Catholic Croats, Muslim Bosniaks, and Orthodox Serbs, who under Ottoman rule had been kept mutually hostile. The Austrians introduced modernization of all types and spent a fortune in doing so. A party grew up among the Croats urging annexation to Austria in hopes of being united to Croatia. The Muslims were content so long as they had some sort of connection to the sultan. Many of the Serbs would have liked annexation to Serbia. Surely, annexation of Bosnia would only formalize what had already been the case for three decades? Who could object to that?

---

7 James and Joanna Bogle, *A Heart for Europe: The Lives of Emperor Charles and Empress Zita of Austria-Hungary* (Gracewing Publishing, 2000), p. 25.

Quite a few, as it turned out. An international crisis was precipitated, but Germany stood by Austria, and Russia's reforming prime minister, Pyotr Stolypin, was dead set against war. Turkey was bought off, and the Serbians and Montenegrins grudgingly accepted the *fait accompli.* It was a difficult victory because Bosnia's very place in Austria-Hungary required negotiation with the Hungarians; it became a sort of co-dominium between the two halves of the monarchy. But this meant no union with Croatia, and so disaffection spread even among the local Croats. The most popular member of the Austrian establishment in the province was—ironically, in view of future events—Franz Ferdinand.

In the summer of 1908, Archduke Charles was called up for regular military service at the garrison in Brandýs nad Labem, as lieutenant in Dragoon Regiment Seven, the Duke of Lorraine. During this time, he stayed at the chateau in Brandýs, whose owner and Charles's distant uncle, Archduke Ludwig Salvator of the Tuscan Habsburg line, was away touring the Mediterranean. The Renaissance chateau, located twenty-five kilometers from the center of Prague, had belonged to the Habsburgs as a royal summer residence since 1547. The history of the chateau was unique in that all the Habsburg monarchs had stayed there for a time. As the commander of the Fifth Squadron, Archduke Charles crossed the Elbe River to Stará Boleslav every day on a bicycle or on horseback. The cavalry barracks and riding hall stood in close vicinity to the churches of St. Wenceslas and the Ascension of the Virgin Mary. Stará Boleslav is the oldest pilgrimage site in Bohemia, where St. Wenceslas, the patron saint of Bohemia, was murdered and buried in 935.

The Palladium, a bronze relief of the Virgin Mary and Baby Jesus, said to protect the Czech lands and accompanied by many legends and dramatic events, is also venerated there. With the knowledge of Charles's entire life today, we can consider the coincidences or follow the ways of God: in his spiritual life, Charles was deeply affected by the pilgrimage tradition of Stará Boleslav. His predecessors, the Habsburg monarchs, also had much in common with this Czech St. Wenceslas and Marian tradition. In one of the photographs that has survived from 1908, Archduke Charles is seen entering the Basilica of St. Wenceslas to celebrate the feast of Corpus Christi.

Eyewitness accounts, town chronicles, and even film footage and photographs preserve the memory of Charles's stay in this typical Czech town. They testify to his good and open nature. He was very well-liked there and in the surrounding villages in the Brandýs region. He took part in social life and, above all, spoke very good Czech. He mixed with local citizens and helped selflessly when needed, both with money and intercessions. During his stay in the town, the district office was reinstated, a brigade riding school was established, and a new city hall was opened in Stara Boleslav in 1911. A grammar school (*realgymnasium*), established in Brandýs nad Labem in 1913, carried the archduke's name. So it is no wonder he was so popular there and affectionately referred to by the people as "our archduke."

Meanwhile, the Archduke Charles was becoming better known in the capital. Vienna society, ever looking forward to scandal, could not believe that there was nothing of his father in the young man's make up. Starting in December of

1908, rumors began to be spread about that the young man was sowing his wild oats in the company of various actresses. Soon, even Franz Josef and Franz Ferdinand began hearing this talk. While the emperor did not believe it—having known both his errant nephew and the latter's son—an investigation was begun. Eventually, the rumors were traced to a musical comedy star. This lady borrowed an expensive piece of jewelry from a friend and told all and sundry that it was a gift from the archduke. That rumor was successfully squelched—but how many more might arise.

Particularly because Franz Ferdinand's children would not be able to inherit the throne, it became increasingly obvious that Charles must marry. But whom? Much as he enjoyed his stays with Franz Ferdinand, Sophie, and their children—who as a family were quite happy—there could be no question of a morganatic marriage. But an arranged marriage—with those of his own parents and Crown Prince Rudolph on his and everyone else in the family's minds—would not do either. Fortunately, an answer soon appeared. After Charles's grandmother died, his grandfather, Archduke Karl Ludwig, had married Infanta Maria Theresa, the daughter of Miguel I, the exiled king of Portugal. From this union came Franz Ferdinand and Otto's half-sister, Archduchess Maria Annunziata. Maria Theresa had a sister, Maria Antonia, who was the second wife of Robert, Duke of Bourbon-Parma. As we saw, he too had been deposed in 1860 by the Sardinian invasion. As might be imagined, the various children of this extended family had played together when young, and one of the Bourbon-Parmas was the Princess Zita. In 1909, Charles and Zita encountered one another again at their mutual Aunt Annunziata's home at the Imperial Kurhaus in Franzenbad (Františkovy Lázně).

Chapter 7

A PRINCESS ENTERS

O God, who by Thine own mighty power, didst make all things out of nothing: who, having set in order the beginnings of the world, didst appoint Woman to be an inseparable helpmeet to Man, made like unto God, so that Thou didst give to woman's body its beginnings in man's flesh, thereby teaching that what it pleased Thee to form from one substance, might never be lawfully separated: O God, who, by so excellent a mystery hast consecrated the union of man and wife, as to foreshadow in this nuptial bond the union of Christ with His Church: O God, by whom Woman is joined to Man, and the partnership, ordained from the beginning, is endowed with such blessing that it alone was not withdrawn either by the punishment of original sin, nor by the sentence of the flood: graciously look upon this Thy handmaid, who, about to be joined in wedlock, seeks Thy defense and protection.

—Rite of Matrimony, Roman *Rituale*

As we saw earlier, the Bourbon dynasty from whence Princess Zita came had a history paralleling in drama and length that of the Habsburgs. Her particular branch, the Bourbon-Parmas, were very close to the Count de Chambord, grandson of the deposed and exiled Charles X of France. Known to his supporters as Henri V, King of France, he had come closest to regaining his throne in 1873, when, in the wake of being defeated by the Germans and the overthrow of Napoleon III, he was invited back but refused to accept the republican tricolor flag and decided against the offer. He returned to Schloss Frohsdorf, near the Bourbon Parma house of Schloss Schwarzau. Thanks to the decades' long presence of his family there, the neighborhood of Frohsdorf had many residents of French descent. Henry dying childless, he left his chateau of Chambord to his cousin, Robert of Bourbon-Parma (Zita's father), and Frohsdorf to his Spanish cousin, Carlos VII. Don Carlos had already inherited the ongoing struggle between his grandfather, the rightful King Carlos V of Spain, and the younger branch of the family. This was eerily reminiscent of the struggle in Portugal that had ousted her grandfather, Miguel I. In all three lands, the older line of the ruling house had struggled not merely to regain the throne but to return to the Church her goal of guiding society, establish a monarchy with sufficient power to answer challenges successfully, and turn back the tide of centralization. All of this was in young Zita's background.

But so too was a lot of jollity. Her father had been married twice—first in 1869 to Princess Maria-Pia of the House of Bourbon-Two Sicilies. The happy couple were married in the Sistine Chapel by Blessed Pius IX. She bore the duke twelve children, of whom nine survived infancy. Maria Pia died in 1882, and Robert married a second time to Princess Maria Antonia of Braganza, whom, as we have seen, was the daughter of the rightful king of Portugal. She would bear

Robert eleven children, of whom Zita, born in 1892, was the fifth. Although the duke had lost his country, he was still extremely wealthy, with properties scattered across Europe. Among these were the Chateau of Chambord, as we have seen, Schloss Wartegg in Switzerland, Schloss Schwarzau in Austria, and the Villa at Pianore on the Italian Riviera. This was where Zita was born.

Certainly, Zita's childhood was quite different from Charles's. Her parents were happy with each other, and the large brood kept life at Schwarzau and Pianore very "kid-friendly," as we would say. When he was a boy, Charles would come over to Schwarzau to enjoy the company of Zita's older brothers, Sixtus and Xavier. "We were children in the same family circle," Zita later recalled. There were games, riding, shooting—and every six months, the whole Bourbon-Parma clan, servants and all, would move back to Pianore, or vice versa. It was also a very devout household. In 1900, she began taking catechism lessons and made her first Communion when she was ten years old.

The following year, she began school at the Salesian Sisters convent in Zangberg, Bavaria. Young Zita studied languages, math, history, art, and music, learning to play the piano and organ there. But in 1907, Zita and her sister were called home to Pianore; their father was gravely ill, and indeed, the duke died on November 16. Zita's maternal grandmother, the dowager queen of Portugal, had become a nun in 1897 at the Benedictine monastery of Sainte Cecile de Solesmes—cofounded as the sister foundation to his own abbey of men by Dom Prosper Gueranger. But in 1901, she and her sisters had been driven out by the anticlerical government of

France and found a new home at Ryde on the Isle of Wight. There she fell in love with Gregorian chant and the liturgy of the Church; two of her sisters would become nuns there. But while she considered the religious life strongly herself, God had other plans for her. In 1909, she graduated and returned to Schwarzau.

Dark-haired and beautiful, her happy experiences at home and in school combined to give Zita a vivacious manner, which did not lessen her piety one iota. Based upon her family traditions and her own studies, she had strong political views. Moreover, she combined all of those qualities with a very strong will and sense of right and wrong. Above all, Zita looked at marriage in a very specific light.

Zita, many years later, described her meeting with Archduke Charles:

> We were glad to meet again and became close friends. On my side feeling developed gradually over the next two years. He seemed to have made up his mind much more quickly, however, and became even more keen when, in the autumn of 1910, a rumor spread about that I had got engaged to a distant Spanish relative, Don Jaime, the Duke of Madrid. [Penultimate Carlist claimant to the Spanish throne; when he died childless in 1931, he was succeeded by his elderly uncle, who also died childless in 1936.]
>
> On hearing this, the Archduke came down post-haste from his regiment at Brandeis and sought out his grandmother, the Archduchess Maria Theresa (who was also my great-aunt) and the natural "confidante"

> in such matters. He asked her whether the rumor was true and when told it was not, replied: "Well, I had better hurry or else she really will get engaged to some one else."[1]

Not long after this incident, the emperor called Charles to Vienna for a heart-to-heart talk. There had been rumors linking Charles romantically to various noblewomen. But still smarting from the affair of Franz Ferdinand over a decade before, Franz Josef told his great nephew that he must make a choice from one Europe's other imperial or royal houses. Little did the exasperated old monarch know that his requirements for his heir were to be fulfilled with a love match! Of course, his own had been one such, and a disaster, but the strong-willed Zita was no Sissi.

In May of 1911, the Archduchess Maria Theresa invited both Charles and Zita with two of her sisters for a week-end at her hunting lodge in Sankt Jakob in Walde, in Styria. There, nine years before, young Charles had shot his first gamecock under the guidance of the imperial huntsman Erhard Orthofer. Now he was on a far sweeter hunt. "It was here, during a week of beautiful May weather away from military duties and official work that Charles was able to get to know Zita. They spent long hours talking together and it was here that he proposed marriage to her. They were away from the nods and smiles and interest shown by others at balls and dances, and could be themselves."[2] Alas, in 1922

---

1 Gordon Brook-Shepherd, *The Last Habsburg* (Weidenfeld & Nicolson Ltd., 1968), p. 18.

2 Joanna and James Bogle, *A Heart for Europe: The Lives of Emperor*

this romantic haven burned down, save its clocktower. On the site is a Gasthaus run by the Orthofer clan, whose dearest possession is the imperial table at which the couple sat; Zita herself would return here at age ninety-one.

When the news went through their extended family, there was joy mingled with relief. Zita was not only lovely, clever, and in every personal way popular, she was eminently qualified genealogically. The emperor was particularly pleased with everything about her—not least her merry personality. The official announcement was made of the engagement at Pianore on June 13, 1911, the feast of St. Anthony. The wedding was set for Schwarzau on October 21. But before the autumnal nuptials, there loomed two official duties. The one was simple enough; Zita must make a pilgrimage to Rome and get the blessing of Pope St. Pius X on the forthcoming wedding, but Charles must represent his great uncle at the coronation of the newly acceded king of Great Britain and Ireland, George V.

His readiness to do so solved a protocol issue. Austria-Hungary had been unrepresented at the coronation of Edward VII in 1902. Franz Josef had been too old to travel that far and Franz Ferdinand's marriage presented all sorts of problems with etiquette. Sophie would not have been able to dine with her husband, sit with him, or even ride in the same carriage. But this time, as heir presumptive to Franz Ferdinand, Charles could represent the country and the dynasty at what was certainly the largest gathering of royals

---

Charles and Empress Zita of Austria-Hungary (Gracewing Publishing, 2000), p. 29.

in Europe since Queen Victoria's funeral. The forty-one who were to be present represented every country in Europe (save France, Portugal, and Switzerland), the Ottoman Empire, Ethiopia, China, Japan, Siam, and Morocco. Charles set off for London.

Meanwhile, Zita went to Rome at Charles's request to seek the papal blessing upon their marriage. As a child, she had been there for the silver jubilee of Pope Leo XIII in 1902. But this occasion was different. To honor the princess's engagement to the archduke, the pope would offer Mass for Zita and her family in his private chapel and grant them a private audience afterwards. Pius settled with them in his library and started out by saying, "I am very happy with this marriage and I expect much from it for the future. . . . Charles is a gift from Heaven for what Austria has done for the Church." So far, so good. But a bit later, things became a little peculiar when the pope referred to Charles as the heir apparent. Tactfully, Zita pointed out that Charles was in fact only second in line to the throne, after Franz Ferdinand, but the pope said that nevertheless he would soon be emperor. Taken aback, Zita replied that Franz Ferdinand would surely not abdicate. But St. Pius X, looking a bit perturbed, said "If it is an abdication . . . I do not know."[3] His words would haunt those present in the years to come.

In the meantime, Charles had arrived in a London filled with foreign guests. As something of a junior royal, the archduke found himself lodged in Belgravia in the same house that another guest—Queen Victoria's grandson, Prince

---

3 Ibid., p. 32.

Arthur, Duke of Connaught (future governor-general of South Africa)—would die in in 1938. The *Lady* magazine, reporting not only on the coronation itself but the plethora of balls, banquets, and other goings on gave minute descriptions of each of the foreign royals. Of Charles, it gushed, "And the Archduke Charles Francis Josef of Austria representing his uncle the Emperor, a handsome young prince who, by the way, was formally betrothed the day before he came to England to the Princess Zita of Bourbon-Parma, a daughter of the late Duke of Parma and sister of the present. The bride-elect is only 19 and very pretty, and she is the 12th child in a family of 20 brothers and sisters!"[4] It was here, of course, that Charles made the acquaintance of George V, a meeting that would have a key effect later on.

Once back home and reunited with his fiancée, Charles found the ensuing months prior to the wedding quite busy. He and Zita enjoyed each other's company, and the week before their wedding, they went to Wiener Neustadt for the Austrian Flying Week in honor of the dual monarchy's nascent air force. But at the same time, they had serious discussions regarding their similar views on religion and politics. The night before the wedding, Charles told his bride, "Now we must help each other get to Heaven." For them both, marriage was a sacrament, a sacred and holy thing, as was the crown whose burden the two of them would have to shoulder together one day.

The wedding itself took place at the chapel in Castle Schwarzau. It is today virtually unchanged, but because the

---

4 Ibid., p. 34.

castle is now a woman's prison, it is hard to see nowadays. It was quite different on October 21, 1911, when a huge number of Habsburgs and Bourbons gathered to celebrate what looked to have the makings of an extremely happy marriage. Film clips show a happy extended clan, and even Franz Josef is smiling and jolly. He had every reason to be. The day before, Zita was treated by the local villagers in costumes, songs, flowers, fireworks, and a torchlight procession. One of the guests was an individual fated to play an important role in their lives: an Hungarian naval officer named Nicholas Horthy.

Charles was dressed in the uniform of the Seventh dragoons with his Golden Fleece order around his neck, while Zita's satin dress was festooned with Bourbon lilies and she wore a tiara given by Franz Josef. Charles entered the chapel between his mother and the emperor. The celebrant was an old friend of the bride's family, Msgr. Gaetano Bisleti, who was also an envoy from St. Pius X. (He would be made a cardinal just over a month later; in 1922, as cardinal protodeacon, he would announce the election of Pope Pius XI and later crown him with the tiara.) The ceremony was in French, in deference to the bride's origins, but the sermon was in Italian. Charles had the words engraved in the rings that the couple exchanged: *Sub tuum praesidium confugimus, sancta Dei genitrix* (Under your protection and umbrella, we flee, Holy Mother of God). When the banquet was finished and a fitting toast given by the emperor, the couple departed by car on their honeymoon to Villa Wartholz. The villagers lined the road, and air cadets from Wiener Neustadt dropped flowers on the newlyweds from the sky. The archducal pair made a short pilgrimage to Mariazell to dedicate their marriage and their lives to the Magna Mater Austriae. From there, they stopped at the "Gasthaus Elephant" in Brixen in what is now South Tyrol, and thence on to Dalmatia, where such resorts as Franz Ferdinand's island of Lokrum beckoned.

The honeymoon concluded, it was time to return to normality, which, in their case, meant the life of a young officer of dragoons and his wife at Brandys. Thirty thousand people headed by the governor of Bohemia, Prince Franz von Thun und Hohenstein came to welcome them, and the arrival of Charles and Zita was the event of the year. There is a famous story about their first winter together. Motoring out from the castle where they lived in town, their car broke down, and they stopped at a nearby house while it was being fixed. The lady of the house gave them refreshments and chatted with the pair, not knowing who they were. But realizing they were heading back to the garrison at Brandýs, she asked if they could bring her son, a soldier in the regiment, his laundry and a packet of money. The archduchess took the clothes, the archduke the money, without either of them revealing their identities. Both were duly delivered to the lad, who knew exactly who his benefactors were. He told his mother, and she in turn related it to all and sundry. It was typical of the tales that would emerge about the friendly and unassuming young couple. The "high couple" led a quiet and happy life in Brandýs until the spring of 1912, when the Seventh Dragoon Regiment was transferred to the Kolomiya garrison in Galicia. Charles and Zita said goodbye to their beloved town and travelled for six weeks in great discomfort to the Austrian-Russian border (in the territory of present-day Ukraine).

It was at Kolomiya that their firstborn, who would be named Otto after Charles's beloved but doomed father, was conceived. "In 2007 the city greeted their son . . . the outstanding European Otto von Habsburg. In his opening speech this 95-year old imperial descendant joked: 'Last time I was in Kolomyia 95 years ago.'"[5] Although the villas "Emilia" and "Wilhelmina"—whose owner Charles and Zita often visited—survive, their home was destroyed in Soviet times, and the space is occupied by a closed machine factory. The pair travelled extensively in the area; one such jaunt was to the village of Mykulychyn, where their friend Prince Johann III of Liechtenstein had a hunting lodge which Charles's father had enjoyed hunting from. April 22–23, 1912, the pair went grouse hunting; the following June, the archduke returned to hunt deer, driving in the first automobile seen in those parts. One local villager was so astounded that the archduke asked him if he'd care to take a ride; he did, and the result was an exciting tour for the farmer and another story that made the rounds!

In the summer, Charles was thrown from his horse and received a bad concussion. Granted sick leave, he and Zita returned to Villa Wartholz. September 12–15 saw Vienna host a Eucharistic congress in which the newlyweds took part. Recovered by their first anniversary, Charles was able to greet the arrival of Otto on November 20, 1912. Five days later, the baptism occurred at the Villa's chapel, with

---

5 Kolomyia City, *Kolomyia Colorful City.*

the emperor as godfather. Franz Josef had two further gifts for the young family. Already, on All Saints Day, Charles had been promoted to major; he was transferred to the Thirty-Fourth Infantry based in Vienna. Moreover, Franz Josef gave the archduke and his little family the castle of Hetzendorff, near Schoenbrunn, to live in. Here, too, his evaluation by his superiors is fascinating. "KA, Military Qualifications: Archduke Charles Franz Joseph. Here, too, the commander certified: '. . . he is safe and skillful in spite of his brief service with the infantry in conducting a battalion; summarizes and judges tactical situations quickly and correctly; is of remarkable decisiveness; disposes calmly, surely and definitely; has repeatedly commanded the regiment and very well met it; . . . a particularly excellent military officer, excellent staff officer, will undoubtedly acquire within a very short time the excellent suitability for regimental commander; is recommended for a favor."

Now that they lived in the capital, Zita took up the roll of imperial hostess, which Franz Ferdinand's wife could not. It would have been very easy to have annoyed either Franz Ferdinand or the emperor, or else add their own Hetzendorff as the center of a third coterie. But the young couple steered clear of any such infighting and remained on friendly terms with both. There were reasons for this.

Franz Josef was a spartan man, who by now had dedicated his whole life to his empire's well-being. As noticed, he worked very hard to keep the dual monarchy on an even keel, regardless of personal sacrifice. This was an attitude Charles and Zita admired and learned from. In return, the old emperor was enchanted by his great niece-in-law and overjoyed at Charles's ability to find happiness with tradition.

Franz Ferdinand, on the other hand, appreciated Charles and Zita's domesticity, which was beginning to resemble his and Sophie's. Writing to his mother about his home life, Franz Ferdinand had said, "You don't know, dearest Mama, how happy I am. . . . I cannot thank God enough for my good fortune. . . . She is everything to me, my wife, my adviser, my doctor, my friend—in one word my whole happiness. . . . And our children! They are at once my wonder and my pride. I could sit the whole day admiring them, I love them so much. And in the evening at home, when I smoke my cigar and read my newspapers, and Sophie knits, the children play about, and everything is so delightful and cozy!"[6]

This domesticity did not prevent Franz Ferdinand—who loved travel—from taking his beloved wife on private overseas trips, where there was no question of protocol. This also allowed him, as future emperor, to begin to set the stage for the change of alliances he wished for. In November of 1913, Franz Ferdinand and Sophie went to Great Britain, where they stayed with King George V and Queen Mary at Windsor. They then moved on to Sherwood Forest to enjoy the hospitality of the Duke of Portland at Welbeck Abbey. (To this day, St. Mary's Catholic church near Worksop treasures the memory of their Mass attendance there.) The other guests included the Austro-Hungarian ambassador, the

6 Friedrich Wassensteiner, *Franz Ferdinand – Der verhinderte Herrsher* (Verlag Kremayr & Scheriau GmbH & Co. KG, 2014).

Duke and Duchess of Devonshire, Lord Curzon, the Marquis of Titchfield, Lord and Lady Salisbury, and ex-Prime Minister Arthur Balfour. One can only wonder what this acquaintance with the leading lights of Britain's Conservative Party might have led to one day had Franz Ferdinand succeeded his uncle.

Beyond that, Franz Ferdinand knew that Charles agreed with him on the necessity of federalizing the empire so that the Hungarians' subject nationalities would thereby become reconciled to living with the Magyars and each other. He resented Franz Josef's exclusion of him from government business and planned not to follow in that particular mode. According to Count Polzer-Hoditz:

> The Archduke Franz Ferdinand complained . . . that he had so little influence on the Government, and often did not hear of important decrees, even such as might have a future prejudicial effect, until after they had been published. He used regularly to add 'When I am Emperor, I shall have Charles with me in the Hofburg and let him work with me.' The heir to the throne, he went on, must be informed on all points; moreover, he had the right to advise on measures which might have a decisive effect in the future. Only in this way could a change of rulers be affected without violent upheavals.[7]

It is remarkable that Franz Ferdinand showed no rancor to Charles for the fact that he would inherit the throne rather

---

7 Arthur Polzer-Hoditz, *The Emperor Karl* (Putnam, 1930).

than his uncle's children. But so it was. In these few happy years at Hetzendorf, Charles and Zita indulged their simple tastes and their similar senses of humor, content that their high destiny lay some years away and that they would be groomed for it by Charles's uncle. In the meantime, January of 1913 saw Charles taking intensive general staff studies; having mastered tactics over many years, he was now being initiated into the secrets of strategy and supply.

In the meantime, Franz Ferdinand was becoming increasingly convinced that there were plots afoot to kill him. As the empress Zita would later recall:

> At the beginning of May, 1914, we were in Vienna and Uncle Franz Ferdinand rang up one evening asking us to come over to the Belvedere for supper. It was just a small family meal with the heir-apparent, his wife and children, and ourselves as the only guests.
>
> Everything passed off normally—indeed, quite gaily—until after supper, when the Duchess of Hohenberg went to take the children up to bed. After his wife left the room. The Archduke Franz Ferdinand suddenly turned to my husband and said:
>
> "I have something to say but I must say it quickly as I don't want your aunt to hear anything of this when she comes down. *I know that I shall soon be murdered.* In this desk are papers which concern you. When it happens, take them. They are for you."
>
> My husband protested: "Surely, you must be joking." But his uncle replied: "No, I'm serious. After

> all, everything is ready. The crypt in Artstetten is now finished."
>
> Before anything more could be said, the Duchess reappeared and we all did our best to pass the rest of the evening as though nothing out of the ordinary had happened.

In retrospect, this statement seems chilling not merely because we know Franz Ferdinand was correct but also because of the millions who would die as a result. But who did he suspect wanted him out of the way? There were a number of plausible candidates: Pan-Germans who feared his ascension to the throne might end their dreams of incorporating German-speaking Austria into Kaiser Wilhelm's realm; Hungarian Liberals, who feared his accession would mean the loss of their Slavic subjects; or various varieties of Slav nationalists, who feared that his popularity, once wearing the crown, would end their dreams of separate nationhood. All of these could tolerate the status quo, so long as Franz Josef lived, but none of them thought that would last more than ten years. The prospect, however, of a vigorous middle-aged man upon the throne with a strong young heir—and both popular—would banish their goals to the remote future if at all.

But how could the heir to the throne be so certain in what he wanted? His actions on June 13, when he hosted German Kaiser Wilhelm II at Konopiste, speak both to Franz Ferdinand's independence and to the understanding he had of *realpolitik*. On his Uncle's behalf (probably at the urging of the foreign minister and the chief of staff), Franz Ferdinand asked for and received the kaiser's assurances of support if Austria-Hungary ever had to go to war with Serbia. But he explained to the kaiser his opposition to such a step, pointing out that Austria had cultivated Bulgaria as an ally but was having trouble keeping Romania out of the Russian alliance. In the archduke's opinion, reconciling Romania and Bulgaria and keeping them both as allies was the best option to keep Serbia isolated and Russia out—but this would be difficult as long as the Hungarian government oppressed the Romanians in Hungary. Knowing the influence the kaiser had with the Hungarian Liberal government, he asked and received an assurance that Wilhelm would recommend to Tisza amelioration of their conditions. The events in Sarajevo would later change all that.

That he had to go to Bosnia he had known since 1913, when the emperor assigned him the job of attending military maneuvers in June of the following year, after which he was to tour Sarajevo. Because military commanders were absolved of status requirements, he would be able—for the first time in their marriage—to take Sophie to an official function and have her recognized as his wife. Some sources maintain that he had been warned by the Russian government not to go. What is certain is that as he was the most popular of the Habsburgs among the South Slavs, the Serbian nationalists among them feared his accession to power, and not just them.

Enter an important figure named Dragutin Dimitrijević. A colonel in the Serbian army and chief of Serb Military intelligence, his code name was "Apis." In 1903, he had been responsible for the overthrow and murder of the

Serbian king, Alexander Obrenović, and his queen, Draga Mašin. The pro-Austrian royal couple eliminated, the officers invited the exiled Peter I Karađorđević to return, and coincidentally, the new king was far more pro-Russian than his predecessor.

At any rate, having eliminated a pro-Austrian king, Apis thought eliminating the Austrian emperor should be easy enough, and so tried to assassinate Franz Josef in 1911. Failing at that, he set his sights on Franz Ferdinand. Using government money, he formed the Black Hand, a supposed Bosnian nationalist group. They set up the ambush for Franz Ferdinand, scheduled for his visit—June 28, 1914.

There were signs and portents aplenty. Historian Karl Schrittwieser notes, "Franz Ferdinand visited Náměšť nad Oslavou on 19 June 1914. A day later, he arrived here with his wife and three children here at the castle [Chlumnetz, now Chlum]. The family was able to spend two days together here. On the morning of June 23, before leaving for the station, Franz Ferdinand presented his longtime confidant, Franz Janacek, with a gold watch, asking him not to leave the Duchess and the children if anything happened to him." Some sources claim that he said, "I know that the bullet has already been poured for me, but duty demands that I go to Bosnia." There were more issues facing the doomed couple when they arrived at the station. The saloon car on his special train overheated and had to be left behind when they set out on the twenty-fourth. The electricity failed on the train, and all the cars had to be lit with candles, leading Franz Ferdinand to remark that reminded him of cemeteries.

Nevertheless, the archduke and his wife pressed on with their various activities until the night of June 27.

But Franz Ferdinand was apparently not the only one in a prophetic mood at that time. In Arad, Hungary (now Oradea, Romania), Bishop Joszef Lanyi had gone to bed (whom we have met as Franz Ferdinand's tutor and baptizer of his children). He then had a most remarkable dream:

> At a quarter past three on the morning of the 28th June 1914, I awoke from a terrible dream. I dreamed that I had gone to my desk early in the morning to look through the post that had come in. On top of all the other letters there lay one with a black border, a black seal and the arms of the Archduke. I immediately recognized the latter's writing and saw at the head of the notepaper in blue coloring a picture like those on picture postcards which showed me a street and a narrow side-street. Their Highnesses sat in a car, opposite them sat a general, and an officer next to the chauffeur. On both sides of the street there was a large crowd. Two young lads sprang forward and shot at their Highnesses. The text of the letter was as follows: "Dear Dr Lanyi, Your Excellency, I wish to inform you that my wife and I were the victims of a political assassination. We recommend ourselves to your prayers. Cordial greetings from your Archduke Franz, Sarajevo, 28th June, 3.15 a.m." Trembling and in tears I sprang out of bed and I looked at the clock, which showed 3:15. I immediately hurried to my desk and wrote down what I had read and seen in my dream.

> In doing so I even retained the form of certain letters just as the Archduke had written them. My servant entered my study at a quarter to six that morning and saw me sitting there pale and saying my rosary. He asked whether I was ill. I said: "Call my mother and the guest at once. I will say Mass immediately for their Highnesses, for I have had a terrible dream." My mother and the guest came at a quarter to seven. I told my mother the dream in the presence of the guest and of my servant. Then I went into the house chapel. The day passed in fear and apprehension. At half-past three a telegram brought us the news of the murder.[8]

A most peculiar tale, indeed, and it is interesting to note also that it occurred seven hours before the death. Yet as Abbot Wiesinger observed, it was very well attested, as witnessed by other researchers: "Indeed, it is only through personal ties with the case that I have been able to preserve these facts. My great-uncle, the late Bishop Count Nicholas Szechenyi, served as bishop of the same diocese administered by Dr. Lanyi. I have also been able to interview an intimate associate of Dr. Lanyi's brother, the Jesuit priest Eduard Lanyi. Eduard was one of the two witnesses who signed Dr. Lanyi's notes and sketch."[9]

As all the world knows, that horrible murder took place on June 28, 1914. Although they did not know it at the

---

8 Alois Wiesinger, *Occult Phenomena in the Light of Theology* (The Newman Press, 1957), p. 106.

9 Stephan A. Hoeller, "The Bishop's Dream of Murder," *FATE Magazine,* April 1962; vol. 15, no. 4.

time, millions across the globe died with Franz Ferdinand and Sophie. One way or the other, it had transpired as several had predicted—Mother Vincenzia Fauland; the future saint, Pope Pius X; Franz Ferdinand himself; and lastly, Bishop Lanyi: Charles was now heir apparent to the aged Franz Josef. He would have only a little over a month to enjoy that status in peacetime.

Chapter 8

HEIR TO A WAR

O GOD, Who dost stamp out wars and vanquish the assailants of them that hope in Thee, help us when we cry to Thee, that the ferocity of our enemies may be brought low, and we may praise Thee with unceasing thanksgiving.

—Collect, "Mass in Time of War,"
Missale Romanum

Telegrams from Sarajevo went out to Franz Josef at the Kaiservilla in Bad Ischl (Who when informed of the missive's contents declared, "Again . . . again . . . again . . . This is terrible! Every sorrow has befallen me on this earth."), to the Hohenberg children at Chlum (who were initially told their parents were just hurt), and to Charles and Zita at Villa Wartholz. They were horrified for many reasons: they had loved Franz Ferdinand and Sophie, and they were very worried about the Hohenberg children. But they were also only too aware that they were now in the immediate center of things and nothing could ever be the same. Charles called the emperor and arranged to meet him at the train station—a huge mob accompanied them back to Schoenbrunn. Having held his composure up to this point, Franz

Josef broke down into tears and said, "I am spared nothing." All those who have had a relative die with whom there was distance will understand the old man's feelings. Meanwhile, rioting broke out in Sarajevo, as Croats attacked the Serbs they thought were connected to the archduke's murder.

The bodies were brought back to Vienna by ship and train, arriving on July 2. There had been a great deal of concern that Sophie would be slighted in death as she had been in life. The first hurdle Franz Ferdinand had cleared himself, sparing both his uncle and his nephew the question of burying a commoner in the Kaisergruft—they would both be interred in the crypt he had built at Artstetten. Some connected to the court thought that the obsequies that were being planned (the couple would lie in state in the Hofburg before going to Artstetten) might give Sophie short shrift due to her morganatic status and asked Charles to approach the emperor. His response to his heir was, "What more do they want? She is getting exactly the same ceremony as my wife had." Indeed, "The bevy of criticism and insidious interpretations still being perpetrated in the historical literature of today about intentionally degraded ceremonial aspects will simply not stand up to examination of the sources and background materials of Habsburg tradition."[1] It is not to be doubted that Franz Josef—although believing himself to have been correct in his actions—felt a great deal of remorse toward his murdered heir and niece-in-law.

Initial reactions across Europe were sympathetic. The London *Times* opined:

---

1 Martina Winkelhofer, *The Everyday Life of the Emperor: Francis Joseph and his Imperial Court* (Haymon, 2012), p. 223.

> After all the awful blows that have fallen upon him as a sovereign and as a man, it was fondly hoped by all who have watched the vicissitudes of his troubled life that the head of the House of Habsburg, the oldest of European Sovereigns, might be suffered to close his days in peace. . . . Brother, son, and wife were torn from him, one after the other, by violent and sudden deaths. Now the pistol of a Slav assassin has taken the nephew who was to succeed him and the mother of that nephew's children. There are men and women in all states of life to whom fate seems ruthless, showering upon them one ruthless blow after another. But few amongst these children of misfortune can have had to suffer a succession of calamities so grievous as the stricken old man who sits upon the proudest throne on the continent.[2]

The *Tablet*, a Catholic weekly in England then and now, was great in its praise for the murdered heir: "By this senseless crime is lost to the world a Prince upon whom Catholic Europe had learned to build her highest hopes . . . a devoted Catholic and an eager soldier, a serious and earnest student of statecraft, as well as of the higher arts of war. . . . Whatsoever he set himself to do he seemed to do successfully, and his strong personality soon made itself felt as a power, first in the Empire and then in Europe."[3]

---

2 Joanna and James Bogle, *A Heart for Europe: The Lives of Emperor Charles and Empress Zita of Austria-Hungary* (Gracewing Publishing, 2000), p. 48.

3 Ibid.

It may well be that the Austrian government missed an important opportunity to mobilize that sympathy.

> After all, Franz Ferdinand had been murdered in the fulfillment of his duties as heir to the throne and official representative of the House of Austria. As General Inspector of the entire military weight of Austria, he was entitled to an honorable military funeral. It was highly irregular to prohibit the presence of foreign heads of state at the funeral; worse, it was a grave political error. If the political aspects of the tragedy had been placed in the foreground, i.e. the assassination by an anarchist of a future head of state, a funeral replete with other European heads of state would have sent a powerful signal to the rest of the world. In the agitated, nearly hysterical pre-war atmosphere which prevailed throughout Europe at that time—the last card—the harmonious appearance of all European leaders together—was not played. It was simply neglected.[4]

Whether or not that is true, one of the ironies of the July crisis was that Franz Ferdinand's death gave both the foreign minister, Leopold von Berchtold, and the army chief of staff, Conrad von Holtzendorf, practically unlimited power. The murdered archduke had detested both men and campaigned for their removal; unsuccessful in that quest, he had managed to prevent them from dragging Austria-Hungary into war with Serbs in September of 1913 when the Serbs invaded

---

4 Winkelhofer, *The Everyday Life of the Emperor*, p. 224.

Albania. Little though the emperor might regard his then-heir's views on administration, he did listen to him in regard to foreign policy. With the archduke out of the way, that balance was gone. Both Berchtold and Conrad von Holtzendorf insisted that war was the only answer. The emperor's response was, "Those who want war have absolutely no idea what war is."[5] He still insisted that there should be no declaration of war unless Serbia refused to cooperate with an investigation.

Nikola Pasic, the Serbian Prime Minister, did not have an easy path ahead of him. On the one hand, although he was not involved with the overthrow and murder of the king of Serbia in 1903, he had benefitted by it. How much he knew about Apis's involvement with the murder is hotly debated by historians. Certainly, he was sufficiently afraid of Apis to have him executed on trumped up charges in 1917 when the Serbian government had been driven from the country. Certainly he had much to fear from what an independent Austrian investigation might uncover. Moreover, he was facing elections the following November, and appearing weak in front of the Austrians was the last thing he wanted to do.

Germany gave Austria-Hungary a blank cheque in terms of guaranteeing them against Serbia's great ally, Russia. Kaiser Wilhelm and his country were in an assertive mood. The Prussian idea of empire was very different from Austria's—and very much nationally minded. Moreover, although the kaiser was keen on being seen as his country's "Supreme

---

5 Katrin Unterreiner, *Emperor Franz Josef, 1830-1916: Myth and Truth* (Brandstätter Verlag, 2015), p. 100.

Warlord," the fact was that his ability to direct affairs independently of his chancellor had eroded. Bethmann-Hollweg was keen on Austria going to war with Serbia. Among other things, while Germany had few nationality problems (save with the Poles in the East and the Alsatians and Lorrainers in the West), it had huge social problems. As with Britain, France, and to a lesser extent, Austria-Hungary and Russia, Germany's impoverished industrial proletariat had been eating up Socialist propaganda and were becoming an increasing threat to stability. Surely a war would unite all Germans in one great effort! Of course, in terms of colonial and military affairs and industrial might, Germany had become the great competitor of the British Empire and, naturally, was as keen to hold on to Alsace-Lorraine as France was to get it back.

Apart from Franz Ferdinand, the other great pusher for peace in Central and Eastern Europe had been Pyotr Stolypin, reforming prime minister of Russia from 1905 to 1911. Apart from the many internal reforms he had pushed through, he had banned Rasputin from Russia and pursued a pacific foreign policy. Indeed, Stolypin made it clear that Russia would not be in a position to fight a modern war without three decades of internal development first. There are many today who believe that had he stayed both prime minister and alive (he was assassinated by a Leftist Revolutionary a few months after his resignation), Russia would have been spared the war, the revolution, and the civil war—three great calamities that alongside the Second World War are seared into the Russian soul.

But there was a war party among officialdom in Russia as well. Although Russia in some ways was the mirror image of Austria-Hungary—its double-eagled golden imperial standard was a reminder of the Romanoff dynasty's claim to the Byzantine heritage, as the Habsburgs' was of the Holy Roman, and the tsar claimed by virtue of his position to be the chief layman of Orthodoxy, as Franz Josef did of Catholicism—there were many differences. While Russia's industrial base was smaller, it was rapidly growing, and already had a proletariat. Russian agriculture—despite the Stolypin reforms—was far less efficient than Austria-Hungary's, as was its infrastructure. Russia, too, had a nationality problem, although its major minorities—Poles, Finns, Estonians, Latvians, Lithuanians, Belarusians, Ukrainians, Georgians, Armenians, Turkestanis, and on and on—were either few or positioned more or less to the frontiers of the country. Still smarting from their defeat in 1905 by the Japanese and the resulting unsuccessful revolution, the Russian war party saw in a war for Serbia and against Austria-Hungary and Germany a quick escape from their various internal problems. Sazonov, the foreign minister, was by no means a member of the bellicose faction, but he would feel determined to defend Serbia, saddened as he was by the archduke's murder.

France had an anti-clerical government and suffered from the same Socialism issues that dogged Germany. Allied to Russia in the Triple Entente, the most warlike French were spoiling for a chance to get Alsace-Lorraine back. Many in the government had an ideological hatred of Austria-Hungary, as the kind of Catholic monarchy their predecessors had overthrown in 1789, 1830, 1848, and 1870. This antipathy was certainly not shared by all in the French government, but as we shall see, it would be sufficient.

The British Empire had no initial interest in going to war. But the fact remained that German industrial output was rapidly overtaking British—and the threat of a German navy able to rival the Royal Navy on the high seas was a long-term nightmare. Nor had Whitehall forgotten German support for the Transvaal and Orange Free State during the Boer War. Britain, too, suffered from industrial unrest. At the moment, however, her big problem was the Home Rule issue in Ireland. In the first weeks of July, British officials were entirely focused on that rather than the trouble in the Balkans.

Last of the European great powers (other than Spain, which had been scrupulously neutral since her drubbing by the United States in 1898) was Italy, formally allied to Germany and Austria-Hungary in the Triple Alliance. Formally, because while the three countries were obligated to come to one another's aid in the event of any of them being attacked, they were not so obligated if one of them should declare war against a fourth power. Irredentists wanted to, as they saw it, complete the Risorgimento by taking the Italian-speaking parts of Tyrol and Istria from the Austrians, as well as the Croatian Dalmatian coast (the notion being that it had once belonged to an independent Venice). Of course, Austria had been, with France, the guarantor of the independent Italian States before 1860; even with the annexation of Rome from the pope in 1870, however, a great deal of rancor remained, both on the part of those who had supported Italian unity and those who opposed it—and millions of Italians had emigrated after that unity was achieved.

There were in every country of Europe sizable numbers of people who more or less supported the idea of war against one or more of their neighbors: some for the sake of nationalism, some to alleviate internal strains in society, and some just because they felt Europe had been at peace too long and needed shaking up. They looked at the brilliant full-dress uniforms of their own soldiers and dreamed of Napoleonic glories. From highest chiefs of staff to lowest street thugs, not a one had any idea of the horrors of modern warfare. They might have had they looked more closely at the bloody civil war in the United States a half century before. From this conflict had emerged ironclads, submarines, trench warfare, targeting civilian populations to weaken the war effort, and the demand for unconditional surrender. Add fifty years' worth of advances in military technology into that cauldron and you would have a perfect witches' brew of slaughter.

Historians have argued and will continue to argue over who bore what responsibility for the outbreak of war. Certainly, not even the war parties in each country had any idea of what they would be unleashing. The idea for the Austrian foreign minister and the chief of staff was a quick war before Russia or anyone else could react. Their investigation had shown the role played by the Serbian army officers Apis and Vojislav Tankosić and the civil servant Milan Ciganović in ordering the murder of Franz Ferdinand. After waiting for the July harvest to be brought in, the Austrian government issued an ultimatum to Serbia on July 23. The Austrian embassy staff in Belgrade were told to evacuate if no response was received within forty-eight hours.

This ultimatum was received while the prime minister was out stumping for votes in the countryside with other major cabinet figures. It was couched in very reasonable terms—so much so that Berchtold feared it might be accepted. Amongst other things, it insisted—in the light of the alleged involvement of Serbian government officials in the Sarajevo affair—on Austrian officers being allowed to conduct their own investigations on Serbian soil. With Pasic out of the capital, Crown Prince Alexander, the regent, went to the Russian legation to ask for assistance. The tsar counselled him to accept the ultimatum. But the prime minister and the regent convened the Serbian cabinet, and it was decided to accept all but one of the requirements: that being the allowing of Austrian investigators to operate independently within Serbia. Despite the efforts of Britain to mediate and Kaiser Wilhelm and Tsar Nicholas to avoid war, the latter two found themselves overruled by their governments. Austria-Hungary declared war on Serbia, Russia declared war on Austria-Hungary, Germany declared war on Russia, France declared war on Germany, and Germany, keeping with long-ago prepared plans, invaded Luxembourg and Belgium, thus triggering a declaration of war by Great Britain (one of the guarantors by treaty of Belgium's neutrality). The guns of August opened fire. On August 3, British foreign secretary Sir Edward Grey looked out his window in Whitehall and saw the street lamps being extinguished. He declared, "The lamps are going out all over Europe, we shall not see them lit again in our life-time." It may well be argued that they have not been since.

What was Charles's place in all of this? Despite being heir to the throne, he was not consulted in any way and had to await developments with the rest of the dual monarchy's subjects. As he told his wife, "I am an officer with all my body and soul. But I do not understand how anyone who sees his dearest relations leaving for the front can love war." It was a decent question, sparked by the rapturous crowds seeing soldiers off at every major train station in the country—a scene repeated all over the continent. Moreover, for the Bourbon-Parmas, this war would be something of a civil-war. For Zita's brothers, Xavier and Sixtus, were resolved to fight for France, their ancestral homeland; their younger brothers, Felix and Rene, joined the Austrian Army. The duo were allowed to leave via Switzerland, as were a number of other allied political and military figures who had been caught vacationing by the outbreak of war. A number of royals were faced with the same problem in Germany and Great Britain. When the Bourbon-Parma brothers arrived in France, they were told that as Bourbons, it was illegal to serve in the French army. Fortunately, Belgium's gallant ruler, Albert I, the "King-Knight," as his subjects called him, enrolled them in his battered ranks at the far north end of the western front.

For Charles, in the immediate, apart from the melancholy parting with his two brothers-in-law—bosom friends since they were all children together—it meant separation from his family. Zita, Otto, and little Adelheid would move to Schoenbrunn to be close to Franz Josef, while Hetzendorf was shut up for the duration. Shortly before leaving, Charles was walking with Zita near Schoenbrunn. After chatting about other things, he turned to her and said:

> I leave with a heavy heart because when this war is over, whatever happens in it, this Austria-Hungary that I know and love will no longer exist. Either there will be two purely German Empires in the heart of Europe with a big Slav group beside them. Or, more likely, the Slav group will be pulled to Russia and we in turn will be swallowed up by Prussia.
>
> It's like La Fontaine's fable of the *pot de fer* and the *pot de terre* who go walking out together. The Germans are the pot of iron and if we go too far and too fast walking hand in hand with them we will bang together as in the story and it will be the Austrian pot of clay that will be shattered.[6]

The archduke joined the army headquarters at Przemyśl (the third largest fortress in Europe, at the time), now on the Polish border with Ukraine. But he was soon given a new job; based in Vienna, he would be the emperor's liaison with all his regiments, visiting each in turn and reporting to his great uncle on conditions. In this work, he acquired a nickname that would stay with him throughout the war: *Karl der Plötzlich* (Charles the Sudden), for his quick and often unexpected visits to frontline units. When in Vienna, he worked closely with Franz Josef, who ensured that he was

6 Gordon Brook-Shepherd, *The Last Habsburg* (Weidenfeld & Nicolson Ltd., 1968), p. 153.

thoroughly briefed in everything. He could not, however, convince the emperor to do what he considered key to victory: sacking the nominal commander-in-chief, Archduke Friedrich (whom he considered "a doll" beside his energetic chief of staff)—and that chief-of-staff himself, Conrad von Hotzendorf. Basically, Charles disliked Hotzendorf for the same reasons Franz Ferdinand had: moral, because of the chief's married mistress, with whom he spent too much time in any case; professional, due to the chief's habit of only sporadically informing Fredrich, Charles, or the emperor himself of his plans; and, as Franz Ferdinand had thought but events proved, tactical: the chief's offensive strategy had needlessly cost the lives of 189,000 soldiers and officers by the end of 1914. Charles believed the emperor himself should take direct control of the forces, but the elderly monarch felt it to be beyond him.

One of the many issues facing Austria-Hungary was that the country was very much the junior partner in the alliance with Germany; moreover, there had never been any pre-war consultation on joint actions. Each were responsible for the sectors that faced them—Serbia and Russia for Austria, Russia and France for Germany—and it had been France that claimed Germany's attention in the first months of the war. Apart from fairly easily repelling a Russian incursion into East Prussia, Austria was expected to carry her war with the Russians on her own, for the time being. Weeks after Charles was recalled to Vienna and his roving commission, Przemyśl found itself besieged by Russian troops surging into Galicia. Lemberg (L'viv) fell, and apart from the surrounded fortress, the Austrians had been pushed back to the Carpathians. But in November, the Germans relieved the pressure on Austria by invading Poland and capturing the industrial city of Lodz from the Russians.

On January 22, 1915, Charles was sent as the emperor's emissary to Kaiser Wilhelm II, who was ensconced at German Army headquarters in Charleville, France. Not allowed to make any agreements of his own, Charles discussed with the kaiser various ways peace might be achieved, but nothing concrete was achieved other than establishing a cordial personal relationship between the two.

Going back and forth between Vienna and the front as much as he could, Charles still managed to make time for his family. Zita bore him two more sons: Robert, on February 8, 1915, and Felix, May 31, 1916. This personal good fortune was matched on the battlefield. Although Przemyśl fell to the Russians in March, two months later a fresh Austrian offensive drove the Russians back almost entirely out of Galicia.

While the see-saw was going back and forth in Galicia, however, a new threat opened up to the southwest. Italy had remained neutral; this was accepted by Germany and Austria-Hungary since they had not been attacked, and the treaty had been purely defensive. Moreover, where the king's murdered father, Umberto I (called "the good," by his people) had been pro-Austrian, Victor Emmanuel III—doubtless mindful of his namesake under whom Sardinia had conquered the rest of Italy—was keen on annexing Trentino and Trieste. Both sides were engaged in negotiations with Italy's foreign minister to bring the country into the war. But in the course of secret negotiations in the first part of 1915, the British and French promised the Italians the territory they wanted in Austria in return for Italy's joining them as combatants. The treaty of London having been signed on April 26, war was declared on May 23. But the Italian political leadership soon discovered two glaring facts: the Austrian populace felt as betrayed by Italy as their leadership did and the Italians themselves were woefully unprepared for war. That having been said, it is a tribute to both armies that they were able to function in a horribly hostile environment—the "White Hell" of the Alps. After the initial clash, the two armies settled down to fortified lines and lobbed shells at each other through the Alps in hopes of causing avalanches above the enemy positions.

In June of 1915, Charles was able to fulfill an obligation of sorts for his murdered uncle. Franz Ferdinand had shared his nephew's devotion to the Sacred Heart and had given 50,000 kroner for the purchase of a building in Hall, Tyrol. The structure had been a College of Noble Canonesses, founded in 1569 by the Servant of God Archduchess Magdalena of Austria, a daughter of Emperor Ferdinand I. It was suppressed by Joseph II in 1783 and turned into an armory. Franz Ferdinand had led the campaign to buy and refurbish it as a monastery for the Daughters of the Sacred Heart and a basilica and place of pilgrimage for the patronal devotion of Tyrol. In March of 1913, Franz Ferdinand had begun the Nine First Fridays, partly in preparation for the consecration of the basilica, which was scheduled for July 30, 1914. But just a month earlier, on June 28, he had been murdered in Sarajevo; the examining doctor had found a Sacred Heart Medal on his chest. Given the outbreak of the war, it was impossible for Charles to take his uncle's place at the ceremony. But a year later, he went to Hall on pilgrimage; a photograph of June 23, 1915 shows him kneeling before the Blessed Sacrament in the basilica. A few days later, he returned to Hall again, on the first anniversary of Franz Ferdinand's death. In the basilica today, as at the Heldentor in Vienna, a plaque commemorates the first and last victims of the World War, Franz Ferdinand and his nephew.

As heir and especially as emperor, Charles tried to cultivate a special relationship with each of his countries. That between Charles and Tyrol was shaped by their shared devotion to the Sacred Heart of Jesus. He called Tyrol his "dear, little Sacred Heart country," and when once the authorities' representatives of Innsbruck welcomed him in their city, he reminded them in his answering address of the confidence that the Tyroleans should have in the Sacred Heart of Jesus. The Pan-Germanists were made unhappy by these words, but they gave all the more joy to the Tyrolean people. Charles made it known that after the conclusion of peace, he wanted to assert his influence so that the seminaries of the monarchy would be run on the model of the Innsbruck Canisianum, because the archduke took special pleasure in the Sacred Heart devotion of the "Canisians." Certainly, in the aftermath of Italy's intervention, Tyrol would need the blessings of the Sacred Heart.

Almost a year after Italy entered the war, and after a great deal of bickering between Hotzendorf and Franz Josef, Charles was sent to that front in command of the Twentieth "Edelweiss" Corps of the Eleventh Army. His command consisted of four regiments of Tyrolean Kaiserjäger, and four regular infantry regiments, one of each being Upper Austrian, Salzburger, Romanian, and Czech. Spending a great deal of time among them, the archduke was popular among his men—going so far as to rescue one during a flash flood. The stage was set for a massive offensive in which he would be a junior commander, although Charles had grave misgivings about its likely success, he put himself into it. As the attack began, Charles issued an order to his officers: "Any commander who has too great a loss for no good reason will be ruthlessly held accountable by me. The vigor and offensive spirit of our splendid troops is so great and there is so much rage against the treacherous hereditary enemy, that the leadership must make sure that the troops do not suffer even heavy losses through unstoppable forward storms." At first it was a great success, with the Austrians smashing through the Italian lines. But the terrain slowed them down, and suddenly Charles found himself and his troops literally without a road forward. Then, on June 4, the Russians launched the Brusilov offensive, named after its able commander.

Once again, the Russians swarmed into Galicia. Half the troops on the Italian front were recalled, as was Charles. On July 1, 1916, he returned to Galicia to take command of "Army Group Archduke Karl," a provisional force made up of the First and Seventh Armies. Working with German reinforcements, the Austrians stopped the Russian assault and then pushed it back. Once again, Charles showed his personal bravery and concern for his men at the front.

But no sooner had the Brusilov offensive been dealt with, then a new threat emerged. Like Italy, Romania had been an ally of Austria before the outbreak of war, and like Italy,

Romania had stayed neutral. There were, of course, many ethnic Romanians living in Transylvania, Bukovina, and Banat, whose fathers had rallied to the dynasty in 1848 and fought the Hungarians. But the Ausgleich of 1867 had effectively put them under Budapest's Magyarising sway, opening them up to propaganda from the Romanian Kingdom. As with Italy, the British and the French tempted Romania to betray its former ally in return for a promise of postwar expansion; the result was the August 17 Treaty of Bucharest. Ten days later, 440,000 Romanians swept over the virtually unguarded border and pushed deep into Transylvania. However, being even less prepared for war than Italy, they outran their supply lines and settled down. In September, the Bulgarians invaded the Romanian coastlands, and a German-Austrian counterattack pushed the Romanians out of Transylvania. But by that time, Charles was busy elsewhere.

In October, Franz Josef called him back to Vienna, wanting to further his education in civil affairs. But first, he was to represent the old emperor at another meeting with Kaiser Wilhelm. This did not go well; Charles had advocated for peace, only to find the kaiser mesmerized with hope of final victory. Yet, at the same time, Wilhelm observed about himself, "If people in Germany think I am the Supreme Commander, they are grossly mistaken. The General Staff tells me nothing and never takes my advice. I drink tea, go for walks, and chop wood."[7]

---

7 Hajo Holborn, *A History of Modern Germany, 1840-1945* (Princeton University Press, 1982).

Returning to the Romanian front with Zita, Charles first went to the capital of Transylvania, Clausenburg (Cluj), on October 28. The archducal couple were put up at a palatial residence (now a hospital). During their week there, Charles met with notables, reviewed troops, saw St. Michael's church and the Tailor's Tower, and gathered information about the area, while Zita visited troops in the military hospitals. None of the Austrian soldiers were ethnic Romanians, it being military policy not to employ troops, if possible, where they might have to fight men of their own ethnicity. But there were a group of Romanian POWs whom Zita pleasantly surprised by addressing them flawlessly in their own language. On November 3, they reviewed troops at the railroad station and then took the train for Petrosani. From there, they went on to various other places on the Romanian front.

On November 11, 1916, Charles was at Schassburg (Sighișoara). A telegram arrived, summoning him to the capital—Franz Josef was deadly ill. On the sixteenth, it was announced that Charles would "have charge of the affairs of the realm conjointly with the Emperor." Franz Josef's condition worsened, however. The emperor continued a modified version of his normal routine, working on papers very diligently. On the morning of the twenty-first, Charles and Zita were received by him, and he worked on some recruiting papers. But exhausted as he was, he went to bed two hours early. Convinced that he was slipping, his staff sent for Charles and Zita, as well Franz Josef's two daughters. The four of them, plus various other high officials, were saying the Rosary when Franz Josef died in his sleep. Silently, the group filed out into an antechamber, and each present referred to Charles by the title he would bear for the rest of his short life: "Your Majesty."

Chapter 9

A KING IS CROWNED

Almighty and everlasting God, Creator of all things, Commander of angels, King of kings and Lord of lords, who caused your faithful servant Abraham to triumph over his enemies, gave many victories to Moses and Joshua, the leaders of your people, exalted your humble servant David to the eminence of kingship, enriched Solomon with the ineffable gifts of wisdom and peace. Hear our humble prayers and multiply your blessings upon your servant, whom in prayerful devotion we consecrate our king; that he, being strengthened with the faith of Abraham, endowed with the meekness of Moses, armed with the courage of Joshua, exalted with the humility of David and distinguished with the wisdom of Solomon, may please you in all things and always walk without offense in the way of justice. May he nourish and teach, defend and instruct your Church and people and as a powerful king administer a vigorous regimen against all visible and invisible powers and, with your aid, restore their souls to the concord of true faith and peace; that, supported by the ready obedience and glorified by the due love of these, his people, he may by your mercy ascend to the position of his forefathers and, defended by the helmet of your protection, covered with your invincible shield and completely clothed with heavenly armor, he may in total victoriously triumph and by his [power] intimidate the unfaithful and bring peace to those who fight for you, through our Lord, who by the vigor of his Cross has destroyed Hell, overcame the Devil, ascended into heaven, in whom subsists all power, kingship and victory, who is the glory of the humble and the life and salvation of his people, he who lives and reigns with you and the Holy Spirit forever and ever. Amen.

—Primate's Prayer,
Hungarian Coronation Rite

The solemn responsibilities that had descended upon the twenty-nine-year-old Charles were enormous. He must bury his great uncle, who, like Queens Victoria or Elizabeth II, had been around so long that not only had few of his subjects any idea of life without their elderly monarch but many ritual points for the requiem and entombment would have to be resuscitated; no reigning emperor having died since 1835. Away at war so much, he had not been able to build up the coterie of supportive followers that Franz Ferdinand had. Charles must try to assemble such on the fly, as he replaced civil and military officers he considered incompetent—and so gain control of the country's governing apparatus. That was essential if he was to deliver his peoples two boons: peace and internal reorganization. Both were key, in his view, if they and the empire were to survive. Against him was set a formidable array of opponents: most of his politicians, his country's enemies, and its allies.

It is also important to remember just what he had inherited. As emperor of Austria, he was of course the ruler of the non-Hungarian half of the monarchy. But as we saw in the first section, the "Empire of Austria" was only a sort of escape hatch created by Charles's grandfather to rescue the inheritance of the Holy Roman Empire. In that sense, he was "Successor of the Roman Emperors of that Roman Empire of the christened Constantine I, of the Catholic Byzantium of Justinian and, lastly, of Charlemagne, the progenitor of that empire that truly did last for 1,000 years from Christmas Day 800 AD until its dissolution under the attacks of the Bonapartist Republicans in 1806."[1] He was also Charles IV, Apostolic King of Hungary, in succession to all the long line of Hungarian kings since St. Stephen donned his crown in AD 1000, but thereby, he also became king of Croatia—the first of his predecessors in that line having been crowned in AD 925, and that kingdom having entered into personal union with Hungary in 1102. But he was not only the emperor of Austria and king of Hungary; Charles was also king of the Czech lands: Bohemia, Moravia, and Silesia (which became a republic on 28 October 1918, today's Czech Republic). In the thousand-year succession of Czech monarchs, he was the last king of Bohemia as Charles III. Alongside St. Wenceslas, he is also the second Czech ruler to enter the pantheon of Czech saints. Blessed Charles and St. Wenceslas of the Přemyslid dynasty, who is

---

1 James Bogle, "The Beatification of Europe's Heart: Emperor Charles of Austria," *The Remnant*, October 15, 2005, https://www.remnantnewspaper.com/Archives/archive-2005-1015-beatification_of_europe.htm.

still venerated as the founder of the traditions of Czech statehood, are linked in many ways—by both the similarities of their fate, as both ruled at difficult times and died at a young age, and bloodline.

Charles's first message to his subjects, although pro forma, bound him "to do everything to banish in the shortest possible time the horrors and sacrifices of war, to win back for my peoples the sorely-missed blessing of peace, insofar as this can be reconciled with the honor of our arms, the essential living requirements of my lands and their loyal allies and the defiance of our enemies." As with his poring over the statutes of the Order of the Golden Fleece, the essentially chivalrous nature of the new emperor-king allowed for no empty oaths or promises, no formal but meaningless gestures.

On November 30 came the time for the peoples of Austria-Hungary to bid Franz Josef farewell. His body had lain in state in the Burgkapelle of the Hofburg. From thence the funeral cortege wound its way through the soldier-lined streets of Vienna's first district, through silent crowds. Obviously, none of the sovereigns of the allied powers were present, but in the procession marched the king of Bulgaria, the German kings of Bavaria, Saxony, and Wurttemberg, more than forty other princes and princesses, and over fifty Habsburg archdukes and archduchesses. At St. Stephan's Cathedral, the cardinal archbishop of Vienna offered the Requiem Mass, assisted by four other cardinals, ten bishops, and forty-eight priests.

The obsequies completed, Franz Josef's coffin was placed back in the imperial hearse and wound its way back to the Capuchin church, underneath which were and are the imperial tombs. The old emperor's successor, in uniform and black mourning armband, led the procession of mourners accompanied by Zita—veiled and dressed in black—and little Otto, all in white with a black sash, walking between them. To many of the tearful onlookers, that little golden-haired boy looked like a ray of hope in all the darkness.

When the funeral cortege arrived at the Capuchin church, the door was closed. As ceremony prescribed, the court chamberlain knocked with his staff against the portal. The friar behind the door asked, "Who is there?" The chamberlain responded with the late emperor's name and all of his many stirring titles and decorations, only to receive a brusque: "We do not know him!" and the door slammed in his face. He knocked again, at which the door opened once more, and the friar asked the same question; this time, the chamberlain said, "Franz Josef of Habsburg, Emperor of Austria and Apostolic King of Hungary." This received no more of a sympathetic hearing than the first attempt, and the door slammed once more. Finally, on the third attempt and the chamberlain's identification of the deceased as "Franz Josef, a mortal, sinful man," the body was allowed inside. Franz Josef's remains were brought down into the Kaisergruft where they remain to this day amongst his ancestors and descendants.

This having been accomplished, Charles had now to deal with the present. He had inherited his great uncle's commander-in-chief, Archduke Friedrich (whom he had compared to a mere "doll" of Conrad von Hotzendorf's) and his two prime ministers, Ernest von Koerber for Austria and Istvan Tisza for Hungary. Charles was determined to take the reins of military and civil power away from those whom he believed had mismanaged it during Franz Josef's last years. On December 2, he dismissed Archduke Friedrich with the Maria Theresia Order and many thanks and took over the supreme command himself. It was equally apparent that von Koerber would also have to go. He and Charles had never gotten on. The Austrian Parliament had broken down in chaos early in 1914 over nationalist issues, and Franz Josef had dissolved it and ruled by decree, hoping to call for new elections when the autumn came to cool off hot heads. But that peaceful autumn never came. Now, von Koerber insisted that Charles recall the parliament. Given what had already passed, and the ambitious plans for reforming the Constitution that Charles had, the last thing he wanted was the added liability of babbling politicians, many of whom were now connected to openly treasonous exile groups. He dismissed von Koerber and replaced him with Heinrich Count von Clam-Martinic, an old collaborator of Franz Ferdinand's, who had been serving as a general in the army. Moreover, he was a German-Bohemian, but much respected by the Czechs as well.

Hungary presented some special challenges. Prime Minister Tisza was entrenched politically; moreover, he was a Magyar nationalist, whose loyalty to the dynasty was suspect by many, as it had been by Franz Ferdinand. The ethnic Hungarians over whom he presided were and are an unusual people. Proud of their history and their line of "apostolic" kings, what they held most highly in reverence was not the wearer of the holy crown of St. Stephen but the crown itself. The Magyars would not truly recognize as their king anyone who had not been crowned in due and ancient form. The rest of the empire was dependent upon Hungary's agricultural production. While Charles—as had Franz Josef—could rule the rest of his realms without being crowned, Hungary was different. But to be crowned with the holy crown of St. Stephen, he would have to swear to uphold the current constitution of Hungary, which Tisza believed would effectively kill any plans Charles might have for federalizing the monarchy or even just making Croatia an equal partner.

Nevertheless, while Charles consented to be crowned, this would be—as with his knighting—no mere formality. As Cardinal Csernoch, who performed the ceremony would later recall:

> He prepared himself conscientiously for this great ceremony. He examined every detail and pondered the inner meaning of it all. Like a priest before his ordination—that was how devout and prayerful the King was before his coronation. I often had the opportunity of speaking to him during the period of preparation beforehand, and I remember observing him at the rehearsal as well as at the coronation itself. It was moving to see how the difficult burden of the feelings of responsibility had imprinted itself on his young soul.
>
> It was neither the ornamentation nor the pomp that interested him, it was only the duty, that he was undertaking before God, before the nation, and before the Church. He wished to be worthy of this, for which he had been chosen.[2]

---

2 Joanna and James Bogle, *A Heart for Europe: The Lives of Emperor*

On December 27, 1916, the royal couple arrived (as we must call them in Hungary) at Budapest's West Railway Station and were met by innumerable dignitaries of various ranks. At 6:00 p.m., Cardinal Csernoch, who as primate of Hungary was to perform the ceremony, gave Charles the inaugural diploma and coronation oath to sign, which the new king would have to give to the Hungarian Parliament the following day. That having been accomplished, December 30 was officially designated coronation day. As Charles and Zita would be staying in the Royal Castle on Buda Hill, adjoining the Matthias Church where the coronation was to take place, the crown jewels remained one night in the rooms of the king, rather like a medieval squire keeping vigil over his arms and armor the night before his being knighted. The following afternoon, the crown and other regalia were transported to the Loretto Chapel of the Matthias Church.

For weeks prior, the proud Hungarian nobility were repairing or purchasing their splendid national costumes for the event. Carriages were repaired, and for a very short time, the war receded from Budapest's consciousness. The morning of the thirtieth began with both chambers of the Hungarian Parliament meeting in their grand building on the Danube, and a twenty-one-gun salute from Gellert Hill. At 8:45 a.m., the procession with Charles on horseback and Zita and Otto in an eight-horse carriage proceeded from the castle to the Matthias Church. They entered with drums, trumpets, and the ringing of the church's bells. Cardinal Csernoch received

---

Charles and Empress Zita of Austria-Hungary (Gracewing Publishing, 2000), p. 68.

them, and the royal party proceeded to the Loretto chapel where the crown jewels awaited.

Before the coronation actually got under way, Charles knelt before the cardinal at the top step of the high altar and swore to defend the Church. He then lay prostrate before the altar, just as priests do who are about to be ordained; during that time, the "Litany of the Saints" was chanted. Csernoch anointed him on the right hand and wrist, and between his shoulders in the small of his back, after which the ancient coronation mantle was placed around his shoulders. High Mass then began; the music was Franz Liszt's *Coronation Mass*, composed for Franz Josef's ceremony in 1867. When the *Graduale* had been chanted, the cardinal presented Charles with the sword of St. Stephen, praying in Latin:

> Accept this sword through the hands of bishops, who unworthy, yet consecrated by the authority of the holy apostles, impart it to you by divine ordinance for the defense of the faith of the holy Church and remember the words of the psalmist, who prophesied, saying, "Gird yourself with your sword upon your thigh," O most mighty one, that by it you may exercise equity, powerfully destroying the growth of iniquity and protect the holy Church of God and his faithful people. Pursue false Christians, no less than the unfaithful, help and defend widows and orphans, restore those things which have fallen into decay and maintain those things thus restored, avenge injustice and confirm good dispositions, that doing this, you may be

> glorious in the triumph of justice and may reign forever with the Savior of the world, whose image you bear, who with the Father and the Holy Spirit, lives and reigns, forever and ever. Amen.

Sword in hand, the new king cut the air in three directions to show his readiness to defend both Church and State.

Then the holy crown was placed upon Charles's head, with the prayer:

> Receive the crown of the King, which is placed on your head by our hands—unworthy hands, but yet the hands of Bishops. In the name of the Fa + ther, and of the S + on, and of the Holy + Spirit. May you understand it to signify the glory of holiness, honor and the work of bravery, and may you know that through it you are a participant in our ministry, so that, as we are understood to be pastors in interior matters and the guiders of souls, so you in external matters may assist us as a worshipper of God and a strenuous defender of the Church of Christ against all adversity; and that you may always serve as a useful governor and a profitable ruler of the realm that has been given to you by God and committed to your rule through the office of the blessings of us who act in the place of the Apostles and all the Saints; so that, adorned with the jewels of virtue among the glorious heroes, and crowned with the prize of eternal happiness, you may glory forever with our Redeemer and Savior Jesus Christ, whose name and authority we believe you bear.

Csernoch then placed the scepter in Charles's hand with the prayer:

> Accept the Rod of virtue and equity. Learn to respect the pious and to intimidate the proud; guide the straying; lend a hand to the fallen; repress the proud and raise the humble, that our Lord Jesus Christ may open to you the door, he who said of himself, "I am the Door, whoever enters by me, by me shall be saved," and let he who is the Key of David and the Scepter of the House of Israel, be your helper, he who opens and no one may shut, who shuts and no one may open; who brings the captive out of prison, where he sits in darkness and the shadow of death, that in all things you may imitate him, of whom the Prophet David said, "Your seat, O God, endures forever; a rod of righteousness is the rod of your kingdom. You love justice and hate iniquity, therefore, God, your God, has anointed you with the oil of gladness above your fellows."

Then the orb, representing Christ's rule over all the earth and the king's ruler over his peoples as Christ's deputy, was put in hand without any special prayer.

Finally, the cardinal led him to the throne and placed him on it, saying:

> Be steadfast and hold fast to that place of which you have become heir by succession from your forefathers, now delegated to you by the authority of Almighty God and transmitted to you by us and all the bishops

> and servants of God and when you see the clergy draw near to the holy altar, remember to give them appropriate honor that the Mediator between God and humanity may confirm you in this royal position as the mediator between clergy and laity and that you may be able to reign with Jesus Christ, our Lord, the King of kings and Lord of lords, who with the Father and the Holy Spirit lives and reigns forever and ever. Amen.

This completed, the palatine, Archduke Joseph, called out, "Long live the King!" To which the crowds inside and out roared back the response "*Eljen*" (Long live)!

Now it was Zita's turn. As Charles had done, she lay prostrate before the altar, was anointed, and then crowned with the queen's crown and touched on her right shoulder with St. Stephen's crown. She, too, received scepter and orb and was enthroned beside her husband. The "Te Deum" was sung, cannon fired, and all the city's church bells rung to announce to all Budapest that their king and queen were duly consecrated. The Solemn High Mass continued; when it was finished, Otto left the oratory from which he had observed the rite with King Ferdinand of Bulgaria and rejoined his mother. Together, they returned to the castle in the carriage they had come in.

Charles remained upon his throne, however, to perform a ceremony with roots deep in the medieval past. When pope and emperor were seen as the spiritual and temporal heads of one Christendom, there were several ceremonial roles they occupied jointly—either, for instance, could authorize notaries. Both could give the title "Count of the Lateran Palace." Both could create "Knights of the Golden Spur"—a knighthood that was an individual distinction rather than an order. The popes gave out their version until the time of Paul VI—so it is that the last member of the papal knighthood, Grand Duke Jean of Luxembourg, died in 2019. The Holy Roman emperors continued to give it out until the end of the Holy Roman Empire; at which time they transferred its awarding to their Hungarian coronations. Normally it would have been given out to well-placed noblemen.

But these were not normal times; there was a war on, a war in which the king himself had seen action at the front. As was typical with him, the knighthoods would be given to true knights, men who had proved their mettle in combat. This account comes from Count Miklos Banffy, who had stage-managed the coronation:

> When the church was almost empty, those appointed to be dubbed Knights of the Golden Spur filed in from a side-door: There must have been about fifty of them, all officers coming from service at the front. Most of them were in iron-grey uniforms, faded, mended, with worn leather belts and blackened straps. One could see at once how old their boots were. . . . In the forefront were men with wooden legs leaning on crutches, limping, knocking against each other, coughing and breathing heavily with the effort of moving . . . out into the glow before the altar there poured all the sad grey tragedy of war. . . . Some of them, those who had been most grievously wounded, sank down onto

> the seats provided for them. The others, whom fate had left physically intact, lined up at attention . . . their tunics stiff with medals and ribbons and orders, the outward symbols of their gallantry. No-one spoke . . . they just stood there, looking straight ahead with a stare that was both eloquent and at the same time passive. Their eyes were the eyes of men who, day after day, look death in the face.

In this, as in all else, Charles took ceremonial quite literally.

This task completed, he left the church and proceeded to the Trinity Column. There he met the cardinal, laid down crown, scepter, and orb, and before the cardinal, swore to protect the country, to confirm all rights and freedoms, and to give justice to each one. The palatine shouted, "Long live the king," thrice. The new king then returned to the church whilst cannon sounded and was girded with the sword of St. Stephen. He stepped back outside where a white horse was waiting. Charles then rode to St. George's square where a "Coronation Hill," constructed out of earth brought from every county in Hungary, had been raised. He rode up the hill, drew his sword, and pointed it in all four directions, symbolizing his willingness to defend his country from all comers.

Afterwards, the royal party returned to the castle where a highly ritualized banquet took place—only slightly less ceremonial and symbolic than the coronation itself, with the king and queen fully attired in crown regalia, as they had been when enthroned. All the highest dignitaries of Church and State were present and played very specific ceremonial roles. Toasts were offered—again in a prescribed manner—as was the end of the meal and even the washing of hands afterwards. The royal couple then went back to the West Train Station, and so home.

For many of the Hungarians, the coronation had simply been a rite reaffirming their national status. But it was much more to its recipients. Zita recalled:

> The thing that impressed both of us most about the whole ceremony was the moving liturgical side of it all—especially the oaths that the King took at the altar before his anointing to preserve justice for all and strive for peace. This sacred pledge given in the cathedral was exactly the political program he wanted to carry out from the throne. We both felt this so strongly that hardly any words were necessary between us.
>
> My husband did not express afterwards any feeling of nervousness that, by this coronation, he had made his attitude inflexible with regard to the Monarchy as a whole. He felt he had made the position clear to Tisza that he had consented to the ceremony for legal reasons, and that reform would still have to come later."

While many Hungarians saw this ceremony purely as an affirmation of Magyar nationhood, for the imperial and royal couple, it was much more. As king of Hungary, Charles felt himself also to be equally king of all the nationalities resident there—Magyars to be sure, but Slovaks, Romanians, Germans, and Croats as well—*to each of whom he had sworn to do justice.* By extension, he also felt that the coronation had also bound him in some way to his Austrian peoples. Back in Vienna, he would begin to discharge the obligations he had undertaken. It is impossible to overestimate how important an event this ceremony was in the lives of Charles and Zita. In many ways, it determined the course of the rest of their lives.

Chapter 10

THE PEACE EMPEROR

O God, from Whom are holy desires, right counsels, and just works, give to Thy servants that peace which the world cannot give; that our hearts being devoted to the keeping of Thy commandments, and the fear of enemies removed, our times, by Thy protection, may be peaceful. Through our Lord.

—Mass to Beg for Peace, *Missale Romanum*

Upon their return to the capital, Charles and Zita had much to do. In the wake of Archduke Friedrich's dismissal, headquarters of the Austrian high command was moved from the archduke's palace in Teschen (Cieszyn) to the modest "Kaiserhaus" in the spa town of Baden, southwest of Vienna. The family took up residence in the palace at nearby Laxenburg. Then, as now, a monastery of the Franciscan Sisters of Mercy of the Holy Cross was located close by the palace. In the sisters' journal for January 9, 1918, mention is made of the new imperial neighbor: "The imperial court took up residence in the 'Blauen Hof' in Laxenburg and Emperor Charles drives his car to Baden's war cabinet every day at 8 o'clock, and he always piously watches the window as he drives past the chapel [to] greet the Holy of Holies. Even today he does it that way." (This worship chapel was located in the northwest corner of the monastery wing on the first floor.) This fits in well with the traditional, well-known image: the emperor did not pass any church without saluting Jesus in the Blessed Sacrament and giving him honor. This is what he taught his children: that they should make the sign of the cross whenever they passed by a church in the car.

Moving the location of the High Command was relatively easy; forming a cabinet was not. As his private secretary, Charles appointed his old friend, Count Polzer-Hoditz. Heinrich Count von Clam-Martinic was already the choice for prime minister. But who to choose for foreign minister, who at once needed to be able to deftly search for peace while weakening the bonds that tied Austria to Germany? Out of an extremely limited pool, the emperor chose Ottokar Count von Czernin, who had at first glance seemed perfect: he radiated assurance and flair. Those qualities he had in plenty. He had, however, others. According to Polzer-Hoditz, he was "lazy, unstable in character, unpredictable in temperament, and arrogant to a fault."[1] These traits would emerge at the worst possible times later.

In the immediate, however, the winter of 1916–17 was very hard, and the brunt of it fell upon the poor, as always. With so many able-bodied men in the army, deliveries of basic things like coal suffered, especially in Vienna. Charles commandeered his own court carriages and used them to

---

1 Joanna and James Bogle, *A Heart for Europe: The Lives of Emperor Charles and Empress Zita of Austria-Hungary* (Gracewing Publishing, 2000), p. 72.

help keep the city's poor supplied. But misery and poverty were everywhere. So too was the emerging spirit of nationalism. Unfortunately, it was being helped unwittingly by members of the imperial government.

According to Polzer-Hoditz:

> At the beginning of the war Austrian patriotism, to the amazement of a great many people, was displayed by all nationalities and by all classes of the population. It should have been carefully guarded as a most precious possession. It was military justice which destroyed it. From the outset, the military authorities saw a traitor or an enemy in every Czech, every Serb, every Pole, and every Ruthenian. There began those senseless persecutions by means of which, aided by the supineness of the Government, the secession of the non-Germans in Austria was slowly but systematically effected. The Slavs whose sentiments were Austrian—and there were a large number of them—were forcibly driven into the camp of the traitors and the enemies. . . .
>
> . . . For the overwhelming majority of the peoples of the old Danube Monarchy, the Austrian and dynastic point of view was not an "affair of the stomach" to which level Count Czernin tried to reduce all patriotism, but an affair of the heart.[2]

This was an urgent problem for Charles, because already in 1915, various groups of exiles—Czech, South Slav, and so on—had declared themselves the provisional governments

---

2 Arthur Polzer-Hoditz, *The Emperor Karl* (Putnam, 1930).

of breakaway republics from Austrian rule. The Allies had not recognized them as such, yet. If they did so, it would make holding Austria-Hungary together infinitely more difficult—and encourage Britain, France, and the rest to push through to absolute victory rather than a negotiated peace. Worse yet, the more enfeebled these movements made Austria, the harder it would be to convince the Germans to end the war. Thus, the important thing to do was to cut the ground out from under the nationalists by renovating the imperial structure as both Franz Ferdinand and Charles himself had always wished to do. But having sworn to rule constitutionally at his Hungarian coronation, Charles did not feel he could simply impose such changes by fiat or that they were likely to work if he did. His plan was to recall the Austrian Parliament, lay reforms before them, have them adopted, and move on—having reduced the nationalist threat—to negotiate a peace. Unfortunately, it did not work out that way.

Polzer-Hoditz had come up with, at Charles' request, some concrete ideas for putting federalism into practice for the Austrian half of the monarchy. But neither Clam-Martinic nor any other cabinet member would endorse them. For Charles to assert his own ideas to Parliament when it convened over the heads, as it were, of his cabinet would be to violate the whole idea of constitutional monarchy—even if it might be the only way to save that monarchy. When Parliament finally reconvened in May of 1917, Charles's speech from the throne disappointed the nationalists without reassuring the old guard. As a result, the government of Clam-Martinic fell on June 23 when the nationalists torpedoed the budget, and Dr. Ernest von Seidler agreed to be caretaker prime minister.

Meanwhile, Charles had decided to ameliorate what he could do on his own, specifically in regard to his power of pardoning convicted criminals. As mentioned, many members of minorities had been tried and convicted of treason without due process, and these had contributed to their growing discontent, as well as a rise in popularity for the national councils in exile. Polzer-Holditz was assigned to sift through numerous cases of subjects—primarily Czechs—charged with disturbing the peace, insulting the imperial family, and the like. The result was an amnesty on July 2, 1917 which freed over two thousand prisoners. Initially, this act caused quite a commotion amongst the Czechs in the empire and abroad, especially those in exile who intended to rule the Czechs after the war. But there was not, at this juncture, any way Charles could follow up this gesture with significant change. Since there was little he could do in wartime to reform the empire, the search for peace became all the more important. That search would take every bit of skill and determination the emperor had, not least because his allies, his enemies, and most of his ministers were not in favor of peace except on their own terms.

At this point, we might stop and take a look at Charles's character and personality. As we have seen, he was personally brave and very devout, a loving husband and father. But what else might be said of him? According to his wife, he was both logical and practical, with a well-developed sense of right and wrong. What this meant was that once he resolved something had to be done, he would doggedly look for ways to accomplish it, unfazed by setbacks. He was not an "intellectual;" rather, his empress recalled, he would arrive at conclusions by instinct and common sense. In this he reminds one of Britain's Bonnie Prince Charlie: both were surrounded by older and more experienced politicians and generals who thought them wrong; yet in retrospect, had they been able to push their ideas through, in all likelihood, they would have won. Despite his elevated station, Charles's tastes were quite simple; he preferred folk music to symphonies and operas, and histories and travel books to fiction. He was much like his great uncle had been in terms of being fairly indifferent to cuisine and wines. But Charles was an avid hunter and horseman. He was particularly attentive to other people's views, attempting to understand them even if he disagreed. As a result, when he caught someone else's point, he would say "yes, yes," giving the impression—sometimes erroneously—that he shared it. Perhaps what would become his biggest Achilles' heel was his unending attempt to see the best in everyone. Of a noble disposition himself, he failed at times to see the deceitfulness in others.

If anything, the incredible pressures put on him by accession to the throne and the attempts to find peace and ameliorate his peoples' needs made him ever more pious; supernatural aid was needed to fund superhuman strength.

> Blessed Charles of Austria understood the veneration of the Sacred Heart and the worship of Jesus in the sacrament not in a separate juxtaposition, but in their unity and communion. In his devotion to the Lord, he clearly had in mind the whole of Jesus' reality, and

> this coexistence in the devotion to the Divine Heart and the Eucharist will be observed more often. The two dominant dimensions of his piety were related to the Eucharist and the Sacred Heart. In the sacrament of the altar he knew the suffering and loving Heart of Jesus to be present. . . . For the Eucharistic Emperor, as His Excellency Fischer-Colbry, Bishop of Kosice, called him, the Sacred Heart Litany and the Day of the Heart of Jesus were among his favorite prayers.[3]

He most definitely had a domestic agenda:

> At home, Emperor Charles established a Ministry of Social Welfare—the first of its sort in the world. Its mission was to deal with such social issues as youth welfare, war disabled, widows and orphans, social insurance, labor rights and job protection, job placement, unemployment relief, and emigration protection and housing. He commuted death sentences whenever he could, and constantly urged his Hungarian ministers to enact universal suffrage in Hungary (unfortunately, his ministers resisted his instructions and suffrage was not legislated during Charles' reign). Charles ordered rationing to be instituted at the palace, just as it was throughout the rest of Vienna. He organized soup kitchens, used the palace's horses and wagons to deliver coal to the Viennese, fought against usury and corruption, and gave away most of his

3 Ildefons Maria Fux, "Blessed Charles of Austria and his relationship to the Sacred Heart of Jesus," https://stjosef.at/artikel/sel_karl_v_oesterreich_herzjesu.htm.

private wealth by distributing alms beyond his means. He went among his people, suffered with them, and comforted them with his presence and words. His subjects called him "The People's Emperor," a title he cherished more than his noble and royal titles.

On the warfront, Emperor Karl halted strategic bombing of civilian populations and buildings, restricted the use of mustard gas, and was adamantly opposed to submarine warfare and the mining of harbors. He abolished the military punishment of binding wrists to ankles, prohibited duels, and forbade flogging. He decreed an amnesty for anyone sentenced by military or civilian courts on charges of high treason, insults to the Royal Family, disturbance of the public peace, rebellion or agitation. At risk to his own life, he visited the soldiers on the frontlines and in the hospitals, giving all of the moral support he could, and observing the fighting firsthand. As Supreme Commander, Karl would not send his men anywhere that he himself would be afraid to go. His trait of showing up unexpectedly at anytime, anywhere, caused his soldiers to affectionately nicknamed him: "Karl the Sudden."

His presence inspired courage and valor.

Morally, the Emperor was concerned for the spiritual welfare of his people. He had plans to build many churches throughout Vienna to make access to churches easily available to all Viennese. He also

> insisted that the name of God be cited in all laws and acts of his government, because laws should be motivated by the love of God and one's fellow man. He enacted laws to protect readers from obscene reading material, started a movement to provide soldiers with good books, and fostered the printing of Catholic reading materials by implementing the formation of a Catholic printing press. Although he incorporated many laws and movements to raise the morality of his people, he primarily led them by the example of his life.[4]

Charles had, of course, inherited the war in which he and his country were involved. It represented the culmination of a foreign policy of which he had not approved, although he was in no position to oppose it. Although personally friendly with Kaiser Wilhelm II, Charles was only too aware that his friend was not really in charge; moreover, he shared his late uncle Franz Ferdinand's distrust of Germany. Pan-Germanism and the creation of a German-led *Mitteleuropa* would, in Charles's eyes, be the doom of the multinational monarchy, with Austria-Hungary being progressively colonized by her neighbor. To both Charles and his uncle, a far better scenario would be an Austria-Hungary allied with France, possibly Great Britain, and perhaps even Russia. It is interesting to note that St. John Bosco (1815–1888), noted

---

4 Brother Nathan Cochran, "Why an Austrian Emperor Should be Canonized: An American Perspective," http://www.emperorcharles.org/why-canonize-an-emperor.

for his prophetic dreams, had one that is particularly apropos in 1873:

> Thus says the Lord to the emperor of Austria: "Be of good cheer and look after My faithful servants and yourself. My wrath is now spilling over all the nations because they want to make people forget My laws, glorifying those who defile them and oppressing My faithful adherents. Will you be the rod of My power? Will you carry out My inscrutable design and become a benefactor of the world? Rely on the Northern Powers, but not on Prussia. Enter into relations with Russia but form no alliance. Join forces with Catholic France; after France, you shall have Spain. All together, become one in will and action.

According to Don Bosco's biographer, Fr. Amadeus, "This letter was sent to the emperor of Austria in July 1873 through a [Countess Lutzow] who delivered it to him in person. He read it attentively and sent his hearty thanks to the sender, saying that he would avail himself of it." As it happened, when this letter was sent, the as-yet-unborn Zita's kinsman, the Count de Chambord was in negotiations with the then pro-Royalist French government to be restored to the throne as Henri V. In the end, he refused, fearful that he would be a mere figurehead, but who knows how things might have gone had Franz Josef offered France an alliance at that juncture? Alas, as with Louis XIV and the request for the consecration of France to the Sacred Heart as was requested by St. Marguerite-Marie Alacoque, it did not come to pass. Unfortunately, as Charles was to discover, the France of 1917 was not the still-Catholic France of 1873.

> Charles identified with his fellow soldiers and was constantly with his frontline troops during World War I. He toured many places along the frontlines and took time to personally speak with and decorate soldiers fighting for the Austrian Empire for the many diverse ethnic and regional backgrounds. This was unprecedented behavior for an Austrian Kaiser—throughout Austria's history, military leaders of aristocratic blood viewed themselves as too lofty to mingle with common soldiers. But Charles knew no classism.
>
> Some of the soldiers Charles spent time with on the frontlines included Hungarians, Austrians, Czechs and Poles. During one of these visits, one Polish soldier was so inspired by Karl's personal example that he later named his son Karol after him—this name-bearer was Karol Wojtyla, who became Pope John Paul II.
>
> Karl also took the time to write personal messages to men under his command during World War I. This, also, was rare—Germanic emperors historically usually gave harsh orders, rather than candid personal addresses to fighting troops. In his messages, Karl addressed soldiers under his command as comrades and fellow patriots rather than subordinates. He did not incite them to fight using hostile language or provocation against the enemy. Instead, Karl spoke of his intense awareness of his men's sufferings and those of

> their families at home, and constantly promised to do all in his power to work for peace.[5]

In any case, when the new emperor came to the throne, the war was going fairly well for the Central Powers, at least on the surface. In 1915, Serbia and Montenegro had collapsed, with the Serbian army and government in exile on the island of Corfu. As we saw, the following year, the Brusilov offensive was halted, and most of Romania occupied after her initial successes. A few days after Franz Josef died, the Somme offensive launched by the British back in July had finally ground to a halt. Russia and France were both in very bad shape. But for Charles, the situation seemed very ominous. The Central Powers were certainly also approaching the end of their tether. For Austria in particular, the desperation of the Allies could not bode well: it might lead them to recognize the nationalist exiles as governments. In that event, the road to their victory lay through the disintegration of the empire; yet German victory would effectively end Austrian independence. Above all, Charles feared the entry of the United States into the war on the side of the Allies. Immediately when he came to the throne, Charles asked his German ally to put forward peace proposals. So it was that on December 12, 1916, the famous "Peace Note of Germany and Her Allies" was issued.

The note, after going into detail about the horrors of the war, basically said that the Central Powers were ready to

---

5 Zita Ballinger Fletcher, "Blessed Karl: A True Soldier," June 29, 2019, http://www.emperorcharles.org/blog/2019/6/29/blessed-karl-a-true-soldier.

make peace, but also ready to go on indefinitely. It rehearsed their victories and ended by saying, "If, in spite of this offer of peace and reconciliation, the struggle should go on, the four allied powers are resolved to continue to a victorious end, but they solemnly disclaim responsibility for this before humanity and history." However, the document offered no points of negotiation, and was extremely vague. On December 18, Woodrow Wilson, president of the United States, issued a note praising the idea but complaining about its lack of specifics. Thus, the first fruits of Charles's effort went nowhere.

The emperor was getting desperate. The German navy had been arguing for the use of indiscriminate submarine warfare in order to choke off British trade and bring them to the bargaining table. Not only the German but most of the Austrian military and naval officials thought this a good plan. But Charles, with that peculiar intuition of his, knew that such a policy was not only inhumane, it would be disastrous. Constantly he would tell Kaiser Wilhelm that such an effort would bring America into the war; his German counterpart would reply, "It will work so quickly that England will be brought to her knees before America can do anything!"

At last, on January 20, Admiral Holtzendorf, chief of the German naval staff, came to Baden to argue the case of unconditional U-boat warfare to Charles and secure his agreement. At the meeting, not only the Germans but the Austrians argued against the emperor for it, with Holtzendorf personally guaranteeing that his submarines would end the war in four months. At last, after everyone else had left and Holtzendorf was left alone with Charles, he let the other shoe drop: "It is anyway too late for arguments. Our U-boats are already at sea with their new orders and a countermand can no longer reach them in time." The whole meeting had been a charade. When Charles met privately with Zita afterwards, he said, "This is the end. If America comes in we are finished for good. The Empire will be cut off from the outside world." From that point on, Charles, alone of the military or civil leaders of the Central Powers, could hear the clock ticking.

Unbeknownst to Charles at that moment, however, the French were becoming interested in approaching Austria-Hungary directly rather than through Germany. The catalyst for this development was Charles's brother-in-law and close friend, Prince Sixtus of Bourbon-Parma. In 1915, Sixtus, an officer in the Belgian army, as we saw, had written an article in a French magazine declaring that Austria was an important component in Europe and by no means anti-French. He concluded that the wrath dedicated to her in French periodicals would be better aimed at Germany. Thereafter, he was contacted by several high-ranking members of the French government—including, ultimately, the president, Raymond Poincare—about the possibility of getting in touch with Vienna to discuss peace. Sixtus, who was quite aware of the situation in Austria, said it was pointless until his brother-in-law was emperor. Very shortly after Franz Josef's death, Sixtus was approached by the same group, who asked him to contact Charles. At almost precisely the same time, Charles asked Zita to get in touch with her brother to see if peace talks could begin.

Albert I, the chivalrous "king-knight" of the Belgians, gave Sixtus and Xavier leave to travel to Switzerland, visit their mother, and open negotiations with the Austrians on behalf of the French. They arrived on January 29, 1917 and transmitted the terms the British and French were offering to their mother. The terms offered were fairly basic: Alsace-Lorraine to be returned to France; Belgium restored as an independent nation, with the Congo; Serbia likewise, with Albania added to her; and the cession of Constantinople to Russia. On February 13, Charles sent an envoy—another boyhood friend, Count Erdödy—to the brothers in Switzerland agreeing to three of the four points, but with an alternative for Serbia, which, after all, had been the cause of the whole thing. She and Albania would be united with Montenegro into a South Slav monarchy. Initially, Count Czernin appeared happy with the progress made, and in a note of the seventeenth, he urged that the process be concluded speedily. A little while later, however, he sent an unsigned note via Erdödy saying that a separate peace was impossible, because the alliance between Austria-Hungary, Germany, Bulgaria, and Turkey was unbreakable. It might also be noticed at this point that Alsace-Lorraine, being German (although as early as his teen years Charles had realized that its people were Frenchmen, albeit primarily German-speaking), and Constantinople, as Turkey's capital, were not his to negotiate with. Beyond that, much of his cabinet—and Czernin himself, from time to time—were certain Germany would win. Why even speak of peace when victory was assured? As Zita said, "The Emperor took pride in being a constitutional monarch and he was determined to stay one too—even in wartime. He was therefore obliged to bring Czernin in on this. In any case, Poincare would have asked: 'What does your Government and your Foreign Office think of all this?'"[6]

Nevertheless, in utmost secrecy, the two Bourbon-Parma brothers crossed the Austrian border on March 23, making their way to Laxenburg where the imperial family was staying. All had been prearranged; the reunion, after so many months and so many changes, was ecstatic. But after the more personal part of the visit was finished, Czernin joined the party and Zita left. Although questioning some aspects of the Alsace-Lorraine transfer in a somewhat cold and distant manner, he offered no objections. There had been no mention of Italy's claims, thus far. Afterwards, the brothers went back to Vienna and continued their conversations with Czernin at Erdödy's house. Sixtus and Xavier questioned the foreign minister's apparent reticence, Sixtus asking him point blank if he supported the proposals. He responded that he did but begged for prudence because of Germany's might. Sixtus replied that he guaranteed his prudence but demanded to know if he was really in support of his sovereign. "But of course! I am his Minister of Foreign Affairs," Czernin retorted. He would play a different tune later.

Meanwhile, at Laxenburg the next day, Charles took many hours composing a letter in French (with occasional telephone calls to Czernin in Vienna). Addressed to Sixtus, it was really to the leaders of the entente. Therein he committed himself to supporting the "just claims" of France to

---

[6] Gordon Brook-Shepherd, *The Last Habsburg* (Weidenfeld & Nicolson Ltd., 1968), p. 69.

Alsace-Lorraine, to Belgium's restoration with the Congo, and to the restoration of Serbia with a seacoast, with the proviso the Serbians break all connection with such organizations as the Black Hand. As the Russian Revolution had just broken out and the Tsar had abdicated on March 15, Charles tabled anything regarding Russian claims until a stable government should be in place there. Then Sixtus and Xavier left as secretly as they had come, excited to be bringing a letter that should have ended the war in fairly short order.

That still left Charles the need to try to get the Germans to accept the terms he had agreed to. On March 28, he sent a telegram to the German kaiser suggesting a meeting at their GHQ in Homburg vor der Höhe. The excuse he used was to introduce Zita to Wilhelm's wife Augusta—the two empresses had never met. But he did indicate he wanted to discuss substantial matters and that as he would bring his chancellor and foreign minister, Wilhelm should do likewise. His generals were already there.

Charles had already told Wilhelm that they had opened a channel to the allies back in February. On this occasion, Wilhelm asked who the intermediary was, and Charles refused to tell him, assuring him however that the discretion of said go-between was guaranteed. The German accepted this and then told Charles to go ahead. Now, prior to this time, much was made in Austrian official circles of the possibility of resurrecting the Kingdom of Poland—from the conquered Russian sector of the country—and giving Charles another crown. But he abandoned that idea and proposed compensating Germany for Alsace-Lorraine by uniting more closely to Germany and throwing in Polish-speaking Galicia from the existing Austrian territories. It was a much greater prize than the French provinces and shows the lengths to which Charles would go to end the war. But the while Wilhelm listened politely, the offer was neither accepted nor rejected. As Zita said, "If we had a friend in Germany it was the Emperor William. But he was completely under the thumb of his generals. This, I think, was largely because he was such a dreamer. He believed in his dreams and one of them, unfortunately, was that of final victory. And so he handed everything over to Hindenburg and Ludendorff."[7] About the only positive thing to come out of the Homburg conference was Zita shaming Hindenburg into halting the bombing of the Belgian royal family's headquarters.

Still and all, Charles was not yet prepared to go it alone. After all, the Germans had not rejected the terms. But the imperial couple had just returned to Vienna when the U-boat's chickens came home to roost. On April 6, 1917, the United States declared war on Germany, citing the attacks by U-boats on American shipping. But thus far, the United States had not declared war on Austria-Hungary; partly this was because the Austro-Hungarian navy had not been part of the fighting. As President Wilson said in his speech declaring war, "That government [Austria-Hungary] has not actually engaged in warfare against citizens of the United States on the seas, and I take the liberty, for the present at least, of postponing a discussion of our relations with the government in Vienna."

---

7 Ibid., p. 74.

Still, the writing was on the wall. Ten days after their return from Homburg, a letter was sent to Wilhelm from Vienna, signed by Czernin, stating plainly the exhaustion and starvation becoming widespread in Austria-Hungary and declaring, "We must make an end at any price by late summer or autumn of 1917." After going on to point out the effects of the Russian Revolution, the note declared, "If the monarchs of the Central Powers are not capable of concluding peace within the next few months, then their peoples will do it for them over their heads." Although Charles had written the bulk of the letter, he had Czernin sign it because he was not considered a "pessimist" in Berlin. Two days later, the response came back—it was simply a set of assurances of final victory—"time is working for us." If Charles was to save anything, he would have to do it without his allies.

Unfortunately for Charles, the French government of Aristide Briand, which had supported President Poincare's actions for peace, had fallen. His replacement, Alexandre Ribot, was far less interested then Briand had been, and America's entry into the war bolstered this indifference. Nevertheless, he met with British Prime Minister Lloyd George at Folkestone on April 11 to discuss the matter. At this juncture, the secret treaty with Italy and the territory promised the entente had made to gain Italian entrance into the war came up. They were made the worse because the Italian army had thus far failed in all its objectives and was in a stalemate with the Austrians—far from any realistic chance of occupying the promised territories. Since they had sworn an oath of secrecy regarding Sixtus's letter, they could no more discuss it with Italian Foreign Minister Sonnino than they could discuss their secret treaty with Italy with Sixtus. But given Sonnino's anti-clericalism and hatred for Austria-Hungary, it probably would not have changed too much. In the event, on April 19, the British and French sat down with the Italians at the Alpine town of Saint Jean-de-Maurienne. The result of their deliberations was that they declared that it would be inopportune to enter into negotiations with Austria-Hungary, as it might endanger the unity of the entente.

It is impossible not feel, over a century later, some horror at this turn of events. The Italians had been, to put it kindly, little help in the prosecution of the conflict, terrible as their losses had been. Oceans of blood had already been spilt up to that day in April of 1917, but oceans more would flow afterwards. Prince Sixtus wrote a mere five years later:

> From a general point of view it was evident that breaking the united peoples grouped around Austria from their common concord through and with her meant breaking a historical bulwark whose value and necessity had long been proven against whatever hegemony threatened Europe from east or west. . . . A separate peace with Austria would have realized the principal object of the war. . . . The general moral and economical exhaustion would not have reached the maximum level which it reached quickly after the war, all the more that Europe retained her customary life and order. Russian Bolshevism did not and could not enjoy the impunity which allowed it to organize its work of diabolical destruction. . . . The result must have been too magnificent and too clear in the eyes

> of the negotiators for them not to have put all their energy into achieving it. Every man of mind or heart should have seconded them. Three men who were, for the moment, three irresponsible sovereigns caused its wreck: M. Ribot, Signor Sonnino, and Count Czernin. Sonnino I can understand a little, but the others?[8]

The elected representatives of the people were not nearly so keen as the hereditary monarch to end the war, but then, he had seen combat, they had not.

But one who was—and for the same reasons as Charles had—was General Luigi Cadorna, Italian commander on the Austrian front. Knowing how exhausted his men were, and how unlikely victory could be under the conditions they faced, he had decided that the only way out was a separate peace. Ignoring his own prime minister but supported by the opposition and, so rumor has it, the king (who, like Charles, had spent the war close to the front, unlike "his" politicians), Cadorna sent a liaison officer to the German embassy in Switzerland. He told the military attaché that the army would make peace if Austria agreed to cede part of the Trentino. This opening went nowhere, however; the Germans did not pass it on to the Austrians immediately. When they did so, Charles did not respond, believing that the entente governments were still negotiating in good faith.

In any case, on April 20, Lloyd George met with Prince Sixtus in Paris and explained to him that Italy wanted Trentino, Dalmatia, and Trieste. Armed with this information, Sixtus

---

8 Prince Sixtus of Bourbon-Parma, "Afterthoughts," *Dublin Review*, 1922.

returned to Laxenburg once more, meeting with Charles on May 7. In response to the information his brother-in-law gave him, Charles agreed to cede part of Trentino—more than Cadorna had asked for. By this time, he had heard of the general's offer; perhaps, had he known the real intentions of the entente leadership, he might have negotiated directly with Cadorna and perhaps Victor Emmanuel III. With Italy out of the war, it would have strengthened Charles's hand tremendously in dealing with both his friends and his foes, and seeking an early peace. Alas, it did not happen.

Sixtus met with Poincare and Ribot in Paris on May 20; the president, as usual, was enthusiastic. But the prime minister, with whom lay the actual decision, was not. Three days later, he met Lloyd George in London, where nothing useful eventuated. In the meantime, Ribot broke his oath and showed Sonnino the Sixtus letters—without, of course, ever revealing to the Austrians the secret treaty with Italy. Sonnino was emboldened by what he considered a sign of Austrian weakness. In the end, after waiting in Westminster for some sort of word, Sixtus returned to his regiment at the front on June 25.

Lloyd George, on June 8, had already addressed the British Cabinet's Committee on War Policy. The question came up as to whether the Allies should try another offensive on the western front or reinforce Italy with British and French troops to try to defeat Austria. Lloyd George came down strongly for "a knock-out blow against Austria." Advocating such a course, when he knew that a negotiated peace was available without bloodshed, was simply monstrous. Indeed, if the question of guilt for starting the war shall be argued until doomsday, the question of who continued it is an easy one. In the end, although Lloyd George's generals overruled him about a direct assault on Austria, his refusal to accept the peace proposal ensured that four hundred thousand men died needlessly in the mud of Passchendaele.

Whilst that horror was progressing in August of 1917, the French general staff—independently of their politicians, and for the same reasons as Cadorna—dispatched a Major Abel Count Armand to negotiate with Nicholas Count Revertera von Salandra, the Austrian envoy to Switzerland (a close confidante of Charles who had masterminded the travels of the Bourbon-Parma brothers). In return for ceding Trieste and Trentino to Italy, Austria would receive Bavaria, Silesia, and all of Poland in its pre-1772 borders. None of this went anywhere; Czernin conducted the negotiations privately, but it is another interesting "what if."

So why did Charles not unilaterally pull out of the war? Several reasons. The Tisza government in Hungary was pro-German, and had Austria attempted to withdraw with entente guarantees, the Germans would not have hesitated to invade; indeed, some in the general staff favored it anyway, as a preventative measure.

In any case, the German generals—Ludendorff in particular—had come up with yet another mad scheme for a quick victory that would prove even worse than the U-boat plan. Since the overthrow of Nicholas II, the provisional government of Alexander Kerensky was attempting to soldier on. If Russia could be put out of the war, then all the German and Austrian troops engaged in the east could be thrown against the western front, and France could be overwhelmed before the United States could do anything about it. How best to cause Russia's collapse? To smuggle from his Swiss hideout back into Russia (on board a sealed train) an obscure Russian radical named Vladimir Lenin.

As with so many of these bright ideas of the German general staff, Charles immediately saw the problem. According to Zita:

> He tried to oppose the idea of smuggling Lenin into Russia in the German sealed train and tried to talk the German Government out of the scheme on three grounds. First, that this was an unfair and irresponsible thing to be done to the Russian people. Second that the more chaos was caused in Russia the more difficult it would be to find anyone to talk peace with. And third, that once Communism got established in Russia, it wouldn't stop there but would spread and both Germany and Austria-Hungary would be engulfed. Evil, he was convinced, could only breed evil. He put these arguments personally to the German Emperor and also through Government channels. And it was for these reasons that he refused point-blank to consent to the original German proposal, which was that Lenin's sealed train should cross via *Austrian* territory to the East.[9]

It is important to remember that all the while the war raged, diplomats conferred, and internal politics were dealt with, Charles and often enough Zita travelled their realms

---

9 Brooke-Shepherd, *The Last Habsburg*, p. 103.

extensively. Charles and Zita returned to Brandýs and Stará Boleslav every year on holiday and for imperial visits. On March 26, 1917, Emperor Charles honored Brandýs nad Labem and Stará Boleslav as the first city in the monarchy to be graced with an official visit. Local records, the press, and a documentary film capture the emperor's short stay in his favorite local places. In the spring of 1917, Charles and Zita travelled through Galicia to visit the whole front in this Crownland from the north to the south. Among other things, on May 5, they visited Cracow, where they were enthusiastically greeted. There, the future blessed met the future cardinal, one of the leading figures of the Polish Church of the twentieth century, the indomitable prince, Bishop Adam Stefan Sapieha.

In October 1917, Emperor Charles bought the chateau in Brandýs nad Labem from the estate of Ludwig Salvator, as his personal, family residence. The imperial couple (with Crown Prince Otto, as we know from his personal memoirs) visited Brandýs for the last time in August 1918. This last visit, when Charles apparently decided not to move his family to Brandýs, was said to be full of sadness.

Until the end of her long life, Empress Zita remembered her stay in Brandýs as the only time they had both been happy. Decades later, long after the blessed emperor had passed from living memory in the locale, his firstborn son, Archduke Otto, visited Brandýs nad Labem and Stará Boleslav to reaffirm old ties of friendship.

In late October 1917, two further blows were struck against Austria, although the first looked initially like a triumph. On October 24, the collapse that General Cadorna had feared came when Austrian and German troops broke through the Italian line at Caporetto. Resistance collapsed, and the Italians retreated beyond the line of the Piave River. The British and French ordered the Italians to fire Cadorna and rushed troops to the area. The new line held, but the Austrians were jubilant. Unfortunately, it was this victory that convinced Woodrow Wilson that he must somehow declare war on Austria-Hungary because American troops could not be deployed in Italy otherwise.

On November 7, the bad seed planted by the German high command in the soil of Russia flowered, and the Russian Provisional Government in Petrograd was overthrown by Lenin and the Bolsheviks. The stage was set for a horror that would plague the world for seven decades—and remains with us yet in some places. Charles had known what would come of it, and he would be proved right in every last horrible detail.

The winter of 1917–18 would be harder than the one before, and that had been brutal. But there was one last indignity before the old year limped out. The United States at last declared war on Austria-Hungary on December 7—which date, coincidentally, would some thirty-four years later see the United States themselves the target of an unprovoked assault. The major reason adduced for the declaration of war (Wilson not wanting to go on record as wanting to get involved in the Italian mess) was that on April 4, 1917, the American schooner SV *Marguerite* was boarded by sailors from an unflagged submarine and sunk in the Mediterranean. The witnesses testified that the submarine was probably Austrian because "Austrian was the language spoken by the officer of the submarine." Testimony that would not have held up in a court of law brought the United States into the war, and ultimately, due to Woodrow Wilson's insistence before and during Versailles, doomed the double monarchy, as it did those of Prussia and the other German states. According to Winston Churchill (no partisan of the Central Powers, to be sure), "Personally, having lived through all these European disturbances and studied carefully their causes, I am of the opinion that if the Allies at the peace table at Versailles had not imagined that the sweeping away of long-established dynasties was a form of progress, and if they had allowed a Hohenzollern, a Wittelsbach, and a Habsburg to return to their thrones, there would have been no Hitler."[10] If 1917 had been bad for the imperial couple and their peoples, 1918 would be far worse.

---

10 Martin Gilbert, *Road to Victory: Winston S. Churchill*, 1941-1945, p. 1314.

Chapter 11

BETRAYAL AND EXILE

Almighty everlasting God, in Whose hands are set the power and the government of every realm; look upon and help the Christian people, that the heathen nations who trust in the fierceness of, their own might, may be crushed by the power of Thine Arm.

—Collect, Mass against the Heathen

January of 1918 was a brutal month in Austria-Hungary—cold and hungry. As noted, Charles had his prime minister create a Ministry of Social Welfare—the first in Europe, or anywhere else—to try to deal specifically with the hunger and the disease which followed in its track. The deputies from Bohemia and Moravia in Parliament issued an "Epiphany Declaration," which asserted their right to "a free national life and self-determination." Strikes broke out and spread throughout the empire, followed by a naval mutiny in February. While this was put down, it did allow Charles to cashier some older officers and to appoint as commander the man who had been his adjutant at his wedding, Nicholas Horthy. But the language and flags used in strikes and mutiny bolstered Charles's fears of what was happening to his east.

On the surface, things there appeared to be going well. A month after the Russian Revolution, negotiations were opened with Lenin's new regime at Brest-Litovsk. Although the Soviet strategy was to spin out the negotiations as long as possible, the Central Powers were impatient; indeed, Czernin, who envisioned countless grain-filled wagons from Ukraine ending Austria's food shortage, was almost desperate. But he was also very much a junior partner, a position of which the Germans forcibly reminded him from time to time.

During their occupation of Russian Poland, the Germans and Austrians had collaborated in creating a Polish State out of it, which, as we have seen, Charles was willing to offer complete control of to the Germans—with Galicia—if it would bring peace. Toward the end of 1917, independence-minded non-Communist Ukrainians had also begun to emerge out from under Russian control. In Austrian Galicia, where the western section was inhabited by Poles and the eastern by the Ruthenians, close kin of the Ukrainians, the Habsburgs had always had to balance between the two mutually antagonistic peoples. When, in February of 1918, the newly proclaimed Republic of Ukraine (which had declared independence from Russia) asked for recognition of their sovereignty—and their rights over an ethnic Polish area—in return for grain, the Germans and Czernin jumped at it. Moreover, it allowed the Central Powers to pressure the Soviets to come to an agreement more quickly. The downside was that it turned a large part of Polish opinion in

Galicia against the emperor. Double eagles were torn down, and pictures of the emperor defaced—very troubling in a people whose loyalty to the dynasty had been unquestioned. At least one Pole remained loyal to Charles his entire life, however: an obscure NCO in the Imperial Army named Karol Józef Wojtyła. Although he and his emperor shared a name, it was actually Emperor Charles he would have his young son named after when the child was born in 1920; that infant, of course, grew up to be St. John Paul II. About these events, the wife of a well-known Polish politician, Prince Zdzislaw Lubomirski, said:

> Horror! We, a nation with a past, with a mature right to life, dedicated to a vague, non-crystallized Ukrainian creation, which without boundaries, without social classes, emerges from the flood of Russian anarchy. Our fertile land, built-up, throws himself on the booty of Bolshevik robbery destroying the past of the earth. The feeling of injustice spreads—internal rebellion strengthens hatred. . . . The forceful protest against committed crime has taken on a sizeable scale covering all classes and all states. . . . The image of Christ martyred on the cross between two rogues: Charles and Wilhelm supposedly is hung in the Cloth Hall.

Indeed, the bad blood between Poles and Ruthenians/Ukrainians went back for centuries, and as with other such ethnic blood-feuds within the empire, it made impartial governance of the type Charles sought to practice very difficult. Certainly, many Poles to this day believe that from 1914 to 1918, he definitely favored Ukrainians at their expense. His remarks to Czernin about the Treaty of Brest-Litovsk are cited: "Sir, you have made me the most pleasant day in my—so far full of concern—reign." His opinion about the inhabitants of Ukraine was: "I am and will remain impressed by the faithfulness of the Ruthenians to the monarchy. I met this people during my many-week stays in Eastern Galicia and I learned to love them. The Ruthenian is faithful, without a lie, and he is lost in life only because of Polish rule."

Charles's remarks in exile are considered to represent a change of view:

> The rebirth of the Polish state was only an act of justice, because there is no more patriotic nation than the Polish nation, and in history there was no greater injustice than the partitions of Poland. The Polish enemies—Russians and Prussians—are also the enemies of the Entente, and the Entente has no safer outpost in the East than the really extraordinary Polish soldiers. From a Catholic perspective, there is no more a believing nation than the Polish nation, and no nation has suffered so much for its faith as the Poles in recent times. The Polish state has only one negative feature: it is too exposed, it has too many enemies and a very bad military position. In the east the Russians, in the west the Prussians, in the north the Lithuanians, in the south-west the Czechs—and they are all enemies of Poland. Poland must defend itself like a hedgehog on all sides.

But one cannot help but wonder if these two views were really contradictory or simply the witness of a neutral party observing and loving each on their own merits.

Tired of Soviet delaying tactics, the Germans declared that they would simply begin occupying as much as they could until the Soviets were willing to sign a treaty. The Germans marched eastward virtually unopposed until Lenin sent an emissary to sign the treaty on March 3. The Soviets recognized the independence of Finland, the Baltic States, Poland, Belarus, Ukraine, Georgia, and Armenia. Although an occupation force was maintained in the liberated areas, half a million men were freed for service on the western front and elsewhere. This "peace dividend" was unleashed upon the armies of the entente on March 21 in the famous "Spring Offensive"—one of the most massive such assaults in history. Initially, the enemy fell back in disorder.

At such a time, when victory seemed within reach, no one—except Charles—wanted to speak of ending the war peacefully. When the efforts through Prince Sixtus failed in 1917, Charles immediately looked for another outlet, and this time he was not concerned about Germany's views. On January 18, 1918, in a speech to Congress, Woodrow Wilson set forth his famous fourteen points as the formula by which heaven would be brought down to earth. They were these:

> I. Open covenants of peace, openly arrived at, after which there shall be no private international understandings of any kind but diplomacy shall proceed always frankly and in the public view.

II. Absolute freedom of navigation upon the seas, outside territorial waters, alike in peace and in war, except as the seas may be closed in whole or in part by international action for the enforcement of international covenants.

III. The removal, so far as possible, of all economic barriers and the establishment of an equality of trade conditions among all the nations consenting to the peace and associating themselves for its maintenance.

IV. Adequate guarantees given and taken that national armaments will be reduced to the lowest point consistent with domestic safety.

V. A free, open-minded, and absolutely impartial adjustment of all colonial claims, based upon a strict observance of the principle that in determining all such questions of sovereignty the interests of the populations concerned must have equal weight with the equitable government whose title is to be determined.

VI. The evacuation of all Russian territory and such a settlement of all questions affecting Russia as will secure the best and freest cooperation of the other nations of the world in obtaining for her an unhampered and unembarrassed opportunity for the independent determination of her own political development and national policy and assure her of a sincere welcome into the society of free nations under institutions of her own choosing; and, more than a welcome, assistance also of every kind that she may need and may herself desire. The treatment accorded Russia by her sister nations in the months to come will be the acid test of their good will, of their comprehension of her needs as distinguished from their own interests, and of their intelligent and unselfish sympathy.

VII. Belgium, the whole world will agree, must be evacuated and restored, without any attempt to limit the sovereignty which she enjoys in common with all other free nations. No other single act will serve as this will serve to restore confidence among the nations in the laws which they have themselves set and determined for the government of their relations with one another. Without this healing act the whole structure and validity of international law is forever impaired.

VIII. All French territory should be freed and the invaded portions restored, and the wrong done to France by Prussia in 1871 in the matter of Alsace-Lorraine, which has unsettled the peace of the world for nearly fifty years, should be righted, in order that peace may once more be made secure in the interest of all.

IX. A readjustment of the frontiers of Italy should be effected along clearly recognizable lines of nationality.

X. The people of Austria-Hungary, whose place among the nations we wish to see safeguarded and assured, should be accorded the freest opportunity to autonomous development.

XI. Romania, Serbia, and Montenegro should be evacuated; occupied territories restored; Serbia accorded free and secure access to the sea; and the relations of the several Balkan states to one another determined by friendly counsel along historically

> established lines of allegiance and nationality; and international guarantees of the political and economic independence and territorial integrity of the several Balkan states should be entered into.
>
> XII. The Turkish portion of the present Ottoman Empire should be assured a secure sovereignty, but the other nationalities which are now under Turkish rule should be assured an undoubted security of life and an absolutely unmolested opportunity of autonomous development, and the Dardanelles should be permanently opened as a free passage to the ships and commerce of all nations under international guarantees.
>
> XIII. An independent Polish state should be erected which should include the territories inhabited by indisputably Polish populations, which should be assured a free and secure access to the sea, and whose political and economic independence and territorial integrity should be guaranteed by international covenant.
>
> XIV. A general association of nations must be formed under specific covenants for the purpose of affording mutual guarantees of political independence and territorial integrity to great and small states alike.

All of the concessions that the points demanded from the Central Powers Charles had been willing to concede in earlier peace talks. Point ten filled Charles with joy, partly because it was the first firm assurance from the Allied side that Austria-Hungary's survival would be assured. As an added bonus, his federalizing ideas would be part of the peace, whether the Hungarian politicians liked it or not.

Moreover, Wilson was not bound to Italy by any treaty. But how to deal directly with Wilson without involving either his allies or Charles's? He and Czernin selected the neutral King Alfonso XIII as the ideal go-between. Then, on February 11, in another speech to Congress, the oracle at Washington delivered a sort of philosophical meditation upon his more concrete fourteen points. These were the famous four principles:

> The principles to be applied are these:
>
> First, that each part of the final settlement must be based upon the essential justice of that particular case and upon such adjustments as are most likely to bring a peace that will be permanent;
>
> Second, that peoples and provinces are not to be bartered about from sovereignty to sovereignty as if they were mere chattels and pawns in a game, even the great game, now forever discredited, of the balance of power; but that
>
> Third, every territorial settlement involved in this war must be made in the interest and for the benefit of the populations concerned, and not as a part of any mere adjustment or compromise of claims amongst rival states; and
>
> Fourth, that all well-defined national aspirations shall be accorded the utmost satisfaction that can be accorded them without introducing new or perpetuating old elements of discord and antagonism that would be likely in time to break the peace of Europe and consequently of the world.

The fourth point was particularly welcome to Charles and Czernin, because while emphasizing national aspirations, which was congruent with Charles's personal program, it also forbade "introducing . . . new elements of discord and antagonism" which would surely occur if the dual monarchy were broken up.

On February 19, Czernin sent a telegram to the Austrian ambassador in Madrid asking him to ask the king for his aid in opening up a private channel. This done, Charles sent Wilson a note which focused on his agreement with the four principles, while pointing out that most of the population of the areas the Italians claimed did not want to become Italian, and that this would not help build a stable peace. Wilson's response was to ask for detailed responses to each of his fourteen points, and specifically proposals regarding the Adriatic coast, Serbia's outlet to the sea, and Trentino. This arrived in Vienna on March 1.

By the time a conciliatory response might have been drafted, the spring offensive had effectively ended Czernin's interest in the negotiations. He sent back a sharp note rejecting categorically any concessions to Italy; it was so sharp that the Spanish effectively lost it. What no one knew at the time was that Czernin had wasted the last chance Austria-Hungary had to emerge from the war intact.

He then proceeded, unwittingly, to drive a few more nails in the coffin in a speech he delivered at Vienna on April 2. After making a number of inflammatory statements, he declared, "Whatever happens, we shall never abandon German interests just as Germany will never leave us in the lurch." This appeared to signal an end to any separate peace.

He went on to say, "The wretched Masaryk [Tomas, leader of the Czech nationalists in exile] is not the only one of his sort. There are Masaryks within the frontiers of the Monarchy as well." Although this played well to the Pan-Germans in his audience, it did not go down well amongst the Slavic subjects of the empire. But what caused his, Charles's, and ultimately the empire's undoing was his assertion that the only obstacle to peace with France was France's "unreasonable" insistence in the return of Alsace-Lorraine. It was this intransigence and Clemenceau's unwillingness to negotiate on the issue that had brought about the current offensive.

Of course, the problem with this was that Charles had already one year before agreed—in letters held by the French Foreign Office—that France's claim to Alsace-Lorraine was reasonable. Had Charles been allowed to see a copy of the speech before it was given, he would have excised those references, but Czernin only sent the draft after he had delivered the speech. In a response of April 6, Clemenceau hinted obliquely at the Sixtus affair; Czernin asserted that in all their negotiations, the Austrian side had refused to consider the cession of Alsace-Lorraine. On April 9, Clemenceau asked why Czernin always claimed that it was France's unjust claim to Alsace-Lorraine that blocked negotiations. "For, it was actually the Emperor Charles who, in an autograph letter of March 1917, gave his definite support to the just claims of France relative to Alsace-Lorraine. A later letter establishes the fact that the Emperor was in agreement with his minister. The only thing left for Count Czernin to do is to make a full admission of his error." Without consulting the emperor (and mindful of the untruth he was shooting forth) Czernin sent out a communique declaring that Clemenceau's claims were lies from beginning to end.

It should be recalled at this point that the Sixtus negotiations had had to be conducted in the utmost secrecy—not least because of German spies. Poincare, Briand, and then Ribot had all been sworn to secrecy, and no copy of Charles's letters were supposed to be left in French hands. It was agreed that should some word of the negotiations become public, Charles would send a letter to Kaiser Wilhelm denying it, and this would be a signal to the French to drop the issue. Charles did, but Clemenceau had a copy of the letter that had been quickly copied by a secretary. This second letter, moreover, had been accompanied by a note from Czernin endorsing the note's comment on Alsace-Lorraine.

Charles duly sent a telegram to Wilhelm, assuring him of Austria's undying support; the German Kaiser sent back a warm reply. But rather than dropping the issue, Clemenceau had the letter published. Czernin at this point was anxious to disengage himself from the affair, and on April 12, he arrived in Baden, demanding that the emperor sign a release disavowing the second letter which Clemenceau had published. The emperor had a mild heart attack the next morning and could not be disturbed for the moment, so Czernin raged at the empress, declaring that Charles must sign the release or Germany would invade (which was a real possibility); alternately, he said he would be chancellor in a German occupation government or else commit suicide. His ravings were so mad that Charles (having recovered sufficiently to contract business) called the chief of police in Vienna to see if he could be arrested before he did something terrible. The response was classic: "No, Your Majesty, I am afraid not. We can only arrest him *after* he has done something." Finally, Czernin having promised that the affidavit was purely a personal matter which he would never publish, Charles signed it, knowing it was a lie. Sure enough, that very night, Czernin had it published; Clemenceau responded with indisputable proof, and Czernin resigned on April 14.

The damage done to the emperor's reputation was enormous. But beyond that, the affair was a strong reminder of just how far apart the German and Austrian real needs and concerns were. The truth was, despite the conflation between them that wartime propaganda on both sides had pushed, Germany's aims could not help but be different from Austria's. The German "Second Empire" was based upon nationalism, pure and simple; in this respect, Bismarck was Napoleon's heir. When Germans in 1914 spoke of the war as a "fight to the finish between Germans and Slavs"—meaning the Russians—they were revealing a world view: the same which had earlier expelled the Habsburgs from Germany. But for the Habsburgs, half their subjects were Slavs, and keeping them reasonably contented alongside their German, Magyar, and Romanian co-nationals were all any Habsburg emperor wanted. From the time they became Holy Roman emperors—and especially after Charles V and his world-wide dominions—the Habsburgs were bred to think in multi-national terms. This attitude was reinforced by their Catholic faith. Where the Protestant British and Prussian kings and the Orthodox Russian tsars could focus on exalting "Great" Britain, "Greater Germany," or "Holy Mother Russia," the Habsburgs could not. They could only hope to administer the peoples God had given into their care as well as they could.

The revelation of the Sixtus affair did several things at once. The Pan-Germans in Austria turned against the emperor; the German high command were resolved to snuff out any independence on the part of the dual monarchy; and Charles's own cabinet ministers begged him to come to any possible arrangement with their more powerful ally. On May 12, he went with some of his ministers to meet with the kaiser and his generals at Spa. When Charles met Wilhelm on the train platform, he told him point-blank that the Sixtus letters were in fact the negotiations that he had told him about at Homburg. Charles reminded him that he had offered to sacrifice Galicia if the Germans would give up Alsace-Lorraine; since they had refused to consider it, they had nothing to speak of now. That satisfied Kaiser Wilhelm.

"His" generals were another matter entirely. They presented Charles with a three-point memorandum requiring a political, military, and economic alliance that would amount to annexation. The Austrian side, however, added a fourth point which made the other three contingent on settling the Polish issue, which effectively delayed the political and economic issues until after the end of the war. But the German generals wanted and received an immediate military accord which essentially put the Austrian armed forces under German control. During the negotiations, Kaiser Wilhelm—at one point annoyed by the Austrian delaying tactics—shouted out, "What's wrong about it? Bavaria has already signed the same convention with us and is quite happy with it!" Given that Bavaria was a state of the German Empire, there was an embarrassing silence. Later in May, Charles and Zita made state visits to Sofia and Constantinople; enjoyable as these visits were, they underlined to Charles that those allies would not be able to hold out much longer either.

None of it mattered, however, as much as the perception by the Allies that Austria was now simply a German puppet. Apparently, Wilson was annoyed at Clemenceau's revelation of the letters, correctly presuming that it would bring about a German backlash. At any rate, all thought of preserving Austria-Hungary as a Central European counterbalance vanished from the Allied calculations. On June 29, 1918, France recognized the Czechoslovak National Council headed by Tomas Masaryk as the government of "Czechoslovakia," thus committing herself to the breakup of the empire.

Shortly thereafter, however, the imperial couple travelled down the Danube to Pressburg (Bratislava) in what is now Slovakia, bringing Otto and his sister Adelheid with them. The crowds cheered, troops were reviewed, and for all anyone might guess from appearances, things were much as they had ever been. But Charles and Zita were entirely too aware that things were not as they appeared. The German advance had stalled in the west, and the Americans were now coming over in appreciable numbers. Everything Charles had feared from the beginning of his reign was coming to pass.

On August 8, the reinforced Allies began their last offensive. By the time Charles reached Spa on the fourteenth, it was apparent that the war would not be lasting much longer. He explained to the Germans that his military advisers had warned him that country could not hold out beyond the end of the year. Charles then suggested a meeting be called with allied leaders at some neutral territory. But the Germans delayed, preferring to find some neutral intermediary. While they dithered and delayed, their military position worsened.

Charles returned to the Villa Wartholz, to celebrate his thirty-second birthday on August 17. In the morning, there was a small military ceremony, whereby several soldiers received the Maria Theresia Order, while Zita and the children watched. None of them could know that the end of their world would begin in earnest within a month. In September, the Austrians sent a request for a separate armistice to Wilson, who ignored it.

On September 15, the Macedonian front, which had been static since the fall of Serbia three years before, erupted with a new Allied offensive. Over the next two weeks, the Bulgarian army collapsed, and on October 2, King Ferdinand abdicated and fled the country (leaving his son, Boris III, to deal with the allies). Bulgaria surrendered, thus opening up the entire southern front to Allied penetration.

Things were sufficiently desperate in Vienna that even the politicians were beginning to listen to their emperor. A cabinet meeting on September 27 finally accepted Charles's plan for federalization. But no concrete proposals were ready when the chancellor, Hussarek (who had replaced Seidler in July) read his vague proposal to Parliament on October 2. Despite all the unrest that day in 1918 was filled with, Charles never lost sight of what, in the final analysis, is most important. It was the feast of the Guardian Angels, whom Charles no doubt was invoking frequently, and the first Communion day for the six-year-old crown prince, Archduke Otto. The family gathered in the castle chapel at Villa

Wartholz. The emperor himself prayed the formula of consecration to the Sacred Heart with firmness and fervor and put his whole soul into these words as, you may remember, he had first done as a boy in that very chapel back in 1899. The chronicle of the parish of Reichenau states:

> All the schoolchildren from Reichenau went to Holy Communion at 8:30 in the chapel in the imperial castle of Villa Wartholz. Bishop Ernst Seydl offered the Holy Mass. Cardinal Piffl was present. Dr. Heinrich Giese of St. Gabriel assisted as catechist of the Crown Prince. The Empress had taught him herself and prayed with him the act of virtue. The whole Imperial family went to Holy Communion: first the Prince, then the Emperor and the Empress. The whole court staff had given retreats and communicated the same day. Pastor Goldstein also had the honor of being able to assist. At this festival, the statue of the Sacred Heart was consecrated, and the Imperial family were also consecrated to the Sacred Heart.

In her testimony during the course of the beatification process, Empress Zita stated on record that on this day Charles also included all the peoples of the monarchy in the consecration. He was also determined to repeat this act officially and publicly but was stopped by the November Revolution. At that time, he had even thought of declaring the celebration of the Sacred Heart of Jesus to be a public holiday after the peace. It did not come to that, but he renewed this act of consecration with his family every first Friday. One cannot help but be reminded of King Louis XVI, who in his imprisonment also planned to consecrate all France in a solemn act to the Heart of Jesus and to make the feast of the Sacred Heart a holiday. Louis XVI, too, was unable to fulfill his plans.

The following day, the German generals demanded that their government request an armistice of the allies; on the fourth, both Austria and Germany sent notes to Wilson asking for an armistice. In the Austrian note, a promise was made that the system would be reformed; would America give the imperial and royal government sufficient time to do so? No response was forthcoming, and so, on October 16, Charles issued his "Imperial Manifesto":

> To My faithful Austrian peoples!
>
> Since I ascended the throne, I have constantly endeavored to achieve for all my peoples the peace they long for and to show to the peoples of Austria the paths along which they may, unhindered by obstacles and conflict, bring their powerful national identities to richly beneficial fruition. The terrible struggle of the world war has hitherto impeded the work of peace. . . . In accordance with the will of its peoples, Austria is to become a federal state in which each nationality shall form its own polity on the territory on which it lives. . . . This reshaping, which shall in no way affect the integrity of the lands of the holy Hungarian crown, is intended to give each individual national state its independence.

The national councils envisioned began forming in the Austrian lands. The German-speaking regions of Austria did not even have a name for themselves; when they convened—by imperial authority—it was 205 self-proclaimed members of the "Provisional National Assembly of German-Austria," a national name coined for the occasion.

Croatia was in a peculiar position. Just as the Kingdom of Hungary was in a personal union with Austria, the Kingdom of Croatia was in one with Hungary; Charles was king of Croatia by virtue of being king of Hungary. Many Croatians and non-Croatians had been in favor of replacing Austro-Hungarian dualism with Austo-Hungro-Croatian Trialism, whereby Croatia would both become an equal partner with the two other nations and annex Dalmatia from Austria as well as Bosnia. Knowing that Charles had long supported this idea, the Croatian National Council's representatives approached him on October 21 asking him to sanction such a move. Charles signed the decree but pointed out that as he was bound by oath to uphold Hungary's territorial integrity and that they would need to get the approval of the Hungarian government. Going on to Budapest, they were able to get the prime minister, Wekerle, who succeeded Tisza, to sign the following day. The Allies, including the Serbs, were pushing ever closer to Hungary, and the Hungarians hoped the Croats might stop them. On October 23, the proclamation was read in Zagreb, announcing Croatia's new status as an equal realm with the other two and her annexation of Dalmatia and Bosnia.

The very day that Wekerle signed the decree, Charles and Zita were on the train to Budapest en route to Debrecen to inaugurate the newly founded university there. On the twenty-third the imperial couple was greeted by a cheering crowd; this strangely normal act accomplished, they moved on to the royal residence at Godollo. There their children joined them, while Charles tried desperately to find some group or other of politicians who would take responsibility for the government and deal with the Slovaks, Romanians, and other nationalities on a basis of equality. As in Vienna and every other major urban center within the empire, the people of Budapest were desperate for food and fuel. Every family had lost fathers, sons, or other relatives, and the prospect of another winter was fast approaching. The "Red Count," Count Karolyi was the favored candidate for prime minister as far as the mob were concerned; Charles took Karolyi along with him and Zita on the train back to Vienna on the twenty-sixth.

In the meantime, the Americans declared that the manifesto was too little and too late. Having been reinforced with French and British and American troops, the Italians launched a major offensive on the Tyrol front on the twenty-fourth. "For three days the motley legions of the Dual Monarchy held firm. Austrians, Czechs, Poles, Magyars, Croats, Romanians, Slovaks, and Ukrainians stood together and fought together for every ridge and ravine as though weakened neither by privations nor by political propaganda; as though indeed a common fatherland still existed just as solidly behind them. The achievement impressed—and probably surprised—even the German liaison officers attached to Field Marshals and Kovess and Boreovic. Yet this last feat of defiance of the 300-year-old joint army was as unnatural as it was splendid."[1] On October 26, Magyar and Slovak units began to return to their motherlands.

On October 27, Charles telegraphed Wilhelm that he was suing for a separate peace within the next twenty-four hours; this effectively ended the alliance. But while this action freed Austrian diplomacy, it also removed the last factor that menaced declarations of independence.

So it was that the following day, the Czech National Council in Prague declared independence. On the twenty-ninth, the Croatian National Council followed suit, and declared their unity with the Slovenians and the Serbs. October 30 saw the Provisional Assembly in Vienna arrogate to itself the right to decide on "German-Austria's" future form of government and name a State Council, which would, after swearing allegiance to the emperor, form a sort of cabinet. Chairman of this council would be the Socialist leader Karl Renner (1870–1950). Renner was a most remarkable man—in many ways, the architect of modern Austria. As we shall see, he was able to betray his country three times and end his days as president of the Republic of Austria. In any case, on the thirty-first, the Poles, Ukrainians, Romanians, and Slovenes had joined the exodus. Habsburg rule was confined to Austria and Hungary, and its frontiers were vague; moreover, although units drawn from the newly independent nationalities were melting away, there was still fighting on the Italian front. Just prior to cessation of hostilities of the Balkan front, a unit of Croatian Serbs were engaged

---

1 Gordon Brook-Shepherd, *The Last Habsburg* (Weidenfeld & Nicolson Ltd., 1968), 192.

against a detachment of their co-ethnics from Serbia. The latter declared that since the empire was collapsing, they should surrender. But the emperor's men replied, "You of all people should know, we Serbs never surrender!" Thus, were the strange contradictions of that time.

Budapest, in the meantime, after Charles appointed his cousin, the Archduke Joseph (from a branch of the family long resident in Hungary) as his viceroy, collapsed into anarchy. Charles had been reluctant to appoint Karolyi as prime minister and chose someone else, Count Hadik, who after decreeing the separation of the Hungarian from the Austrian army, resigned. Archduke Joseph appointed Karolyi to appease the mob. From now on, Hungary was separate, and on November 16, Karolyi would be elected the first president of the People's Republic of Hungary.

Meanwhile, on the Italian front, despite desertions and confusion regarding what was going on in what we must now call their various home countries, the emperor's men were still putting up resistance to the Allied assault when the Austrians asked Italy for an armistice on October 29. The Italians played a rather cruel trick on their opponents; they gave them a vague answer regarding the time that they should lay down their arms. When they did, the Italians advanced, maintaining that the ceasefire had not yet arrived. Virtually unopposed, they rushed up to the Brenner Pass by November 4, in the meantime capturing a large chunk of the Austrian army who were under the misapprehension that the ceasefire had taken effect.

The news of this debacle did nothing for the spirits of the mob in Vienna, nor did the rumors about Charles and

Zita that Allied and nationalist propaganda had been spewing since the summer. One bright note for the emperor and empress was the safe return of the children from Hungary on October 31. Whatever happened from this point on, they would face it as a family. They had much to face. Charles had appointed Professor Lammasch on October 30 as Austrian prime minister, but Lammasch was finding it very difficult indeed to find anyone to form a cabinet with him. The angry, hungry mobs began to talk of abdication, and as in Budapest, Communist agitators made their appearance.

As it happened, Field Marshal Boreovic had managed to pull a large number of troops from the wreck of the Italian front, and twice wired army headquarters in Vienna offering to bring his troops to Vienna to restore order and forestall any revolution. The commander of the garrison did not forward those messages to Charles, to whom they were addressed, but did decline the offers in the emperor's name. This was a signal act of betrayal, but among so many, it would go unnoticed for a long time.

The bulk of the guards protecting Schoenbrunn at that moment were Hungarian. On November 2, they were ordered by Count Karolyi to return to Hungary. They marched off, leaving the palace and the imperial family unguarded. At that juncture, anyone could have entered the palace. But then, a column of troops arrived: cadets from the military academy at Wiener Neustadt. Shortly thereafter, another contingent of cadets from the artillery school at Traiskirchen reinforced them. However, Charles had no desire to risk the young men's lives; when the chief of the Vienna police, Dr. Schober, called to say that the threat to the palace was such that the imperial family must leave, there was a great deal of consternation. But at 6:00 a.m. the following morning, Schober called back to say the threat had receded and they could stay.

Over the next several days, it became apparent as Renner's State Council took control of the infrastructure of government that the emperor's chancellor and ministers had lost control of everything. The only hope they had was that the two parties who held the majority of seats in the assembly had been ostensibly monarchist when it convened. On November 4, Charles's name day was celebrated with a Solemn High Mass at St. Stephen's Cathedral, offered by the cardinal archbishop; packed though the cathedral was, few if any of the Mass-goers wore imperial uniforms and decorations. When they sang the imperial anthem, most were weeping.

Two days later, the demobilization of the army agreed on as part of the Italian armistice came to pass. Soon Vienna's mobs were augmented by unemployed soldiers, some of whom retained their weapons. On November 8, Woodrow Wilson wired the State Council in Vienna and the governments in Budapest and Prague, congratulating them that "the constituent peoples had now thrown off the yoke of the Austro-Hungarian Empire." Lammasch and his fellow ministers returned to Schoenbrunn asking to resign, but Charles convinced them to stay.

The following day, Kaiser Wilhelm abdicated and fled to the Netherlands. Renner's Social Democrats called for a "democratic socialist republic of German-Austria." On November 10, Charles sent one of his advisers into the city to see if the two majority parties retained their monarchist allegiance. He returned saying that the Pan-Germans were wavering, but the Christian Socials would follow the lead of the Church. The emperor sent a message to Cardinal Piffl, who had just a few days earlier celebrated his name day Mass, asking for his support. A note was returned saying that it would make it easier for the Christian Socials to support his cause if he "agreed to put aside his rights and place the constitutional decision in the hands of the people." During the afternoon of the tenth, Charles had several visitors. One of these was Admiral Horthy, who had come from Croatia to discuss turning over the fleet to the new authorities there. He could not restrain his grief over what was happening; so overwrought was he that Charles asked Zita to offer him some comforting words. Pulling himself together, he raised his right hand and said to the imperial couple, "I will never rest until I have restored Your Majesty to his thrones in Vienna and Budapest." Both Charles and Zita would long remember those words. In any case, the National Assembly voted for a republic.

Those around him at that time have left two sets of assertions. One is that he appeared resigned to whatever happened. Having tried his utmost from the beginning of his reign to bring both peace and reform to the empire, he was all too conscious that his predictions from the beginning were being fulfilled—though those that had impeded him were now nowhere to be seen. The second was his constantly repeated refusal to abdicate or to leave the country.

On the eleventh, Lammasch came to Schoenbrunn with another minister and a document that had been worked out by the State and Crown Councils. The latter wanted Charles to abdicate; the former knew he would not. So the paper that they brought him was designed to remove him from power without abdication. A remarkable document, it reads thusly:

> Ever since my accession I have tried ceaselessly to lead my peoples out of the horrors of a war for whose inception I bear no trace of blame.
>
> I have not hesitated to restore constitutional life and I have opened up for the peoples the path of their development as independent states.
>
> Filled, now as ever, with unwavering devotion to all my peoples, I do not wish to oppose their free growth with my own person.
>
> I recognize in advance whatever decision that German-Austria may make about its future political form.
>
> The people, through its representatives, has taken over the government. I renounce all participation in the affairs of state.
>
> At the same time, I relieve my Austrian Government from office.
>
> May the people of German-Austria, in unity and tolerance create and strengthen the new order! The happiness of my peoples has, from the beginning, been the object of my most ardent wishes.
>
> Only an inner peace can heal the wounds of this war.

Charles signed this document in the Blue Chamber of the palace. After Charles distributed some awards and titles to the bearers of the bad tidings, these went off and immediately had the emperor's manifesto published.

All of that having been accomplished, some hard choices had to be made. Not only mobs but groups of Red Guards were roaming the city—and the example of the Russian imperial family's murder the previous July 18 was very much on their minds. Moreover, Schoenbrunn, with many reminders of imperial pride, was growing simply intolerable—and there was the safety of the cadets to consider. Of the options available to them, the Castle of Eckartsau seemed the best proposition. A hunting lodge, it was surrounded by woods and marsh, in the northeastern corner of the country, near where the new borders of Austria, Hungary, and Czechoslovakia came together. Thus, were there any momentum for restoration in any of the three "core countries," the family would be nearby.

After saying prayers in the palace chapel that they might one day return, the family and those staff accompanying them got into the caravan of cars that would take them away. The teary-eyed cadets, sixteen- and seventeen-year-olds, drew up smartly and saluted. The little caravan made its way out of the palace park. They drove through the night to their destination. At last, the little party arrived.

That next day, November 12, the Austrian republic was proclaimed; the Communists celebrated by unsuccessfully attacking the Parliament building. Except for the three Christian Socials who had voted against the republic (one of whom, ironically, was Wilhelm Miklas, later to be president) the fight had gone out of the party for the moment. The Assembly also voted to unite the country with Germany.

On the following day, a delegation from Budapest, including the prince-primate, came to Eckartsau at the behest of Karolyi asking Charles to abdicate. Just as with Austria, he refused to do so point-blank: he was the anointed and crowned apostolic king of Hungary. The most he would concede was signing another somewhat ambiguous document: "I do not wish to stand in the way of the evolution of the Hungarian nation, for whom I still feel the same unchanged love. Consequently, I resign my part in the business of state and accept this decision as regards the new form of Government in Hungary." With that, Karolyi would have to be content.

The "court" at Eckartsau over the next six weeks varied in number between fifty and one hundred. Apart from the family and the small number who had come with them from Vienna, there was a detachment of Vienna policemen who were supposed to protect them, as well as the employees of the estate and a constant flow of visitors and refugees from Vienna. Other than the game in the woods, there was little food to be had. Trucks loaded with supplies from the city were often pilfered or stripped entirely, and bands of Red Guards and ex-soldiers roamed the neighborhood.

The Spanish influenza hit that winter; the emperor and all the children got it; the youngest, Karl Ludwig, the eighteen-month-old, almost died. Christmas of 1918 was not as somber as it might have been; they found a trunk full of the small sorts of gifts the imperial couple would give out on trips around the country—watches, cigarette lights, and the like. These and things like chocolates they had been saving, the family gave to the servants and other folk in the castle. Even today a few of the gifts are still cherished possessions of local families. They had a Christmas tree, and the emperor got out of his sick bed for a little while. Though they did not know it at the time, all over Vienna that Christmas Eve, people toasted the emperor's health, causing an exasperated Renner to remark, "Austria is a republic without Republicans!" A week later, with the horrific old year behind them and an extremely uncertain new one ahead, Charles insisted on singing the "Te Deum" on New Year's Eve in thanksgiving.

As long as they remained in the country, Charles and Zita were a burr under Renner's saddle blanket. Already he had raised the matter of the Habsburgs in the State Council and wanted to talk to Charles about going into exile on December 22. He was dissuaded then. But in the first week of the New Year, he showed up unannounced at Eckaersau demanding to see Charles. Since he had not made an appointment, the imperial couple declined to see him; they did have him served the best lunch their meagre resources could afford. The aide who was assigned to keep him company heard the burden of his message: the area was unhealthy for the family and there were security problems. The aide, knowing Charles's attitudes, said that the air was fine and that they had no worries about security, seeing that Renner was responsible for it. With those responses, the head of the government had to be content for the moment.

Meanwhile, the indefatigable Bourbon-Parma brothers, Princes Sixtus and Xavier, had been extremely worried about the well-being of their brother-in-law, sister, nieces, and nephews. While the Habsburgs had no news of the outside world, their plight and the worsening situation was well known to Zita's brothers. As part of the peace settlement, the entente had token military forces in Vienna. The brothers reasoned that these could be used to guarantee the family's safety. Trying the French president, Poincare, without success (he declared himself powerless), they sought an audience with King George V and Queen Mary. Explaining to them in detail the plight of the imperial family, Sixtus likened it to that of the Romanovs, about whose fate King George felt a great deal of guilt. The result was that both king and queen were quite disturbed, and George replied, "We will immediately do what is necessary." His Majesty was as good as his word.

The result was the appointment of a British officer to look after their welfare in the immediate, who arrived on February 16. He would be replaced eleven days later by an individual who would become a dear friend of the family: Lieutenant-Colonel Edward Lisle Strutt, D.S.O., a highly decorated veteran of both the Boer War and World War I, peacetime adventurer, and devout Catholic. He proved to be precisely the man for this difficult task.

Strutt became extremely fond of the imperial couple and of their children, whom he could see were suffering from malnutrition. He arranged for a lorryload of British army supplies to be brought up from Vienna to feed the over one hundred people now encamped there, amongst which was the first white bread any of them had seen since 1916. He also organized the defense of the locale, played bridge with

Charles and Zita, and in general set things to rights in the immediate area.

What he could not do was affect the course of events in Vienna. There, an election having been held, a new Parliament was returned on March 16, with a Socialist-Christian Social coalition; since the former was the larger party, Renner was chancellor. He was determined to deal with the Habsburgs once and for all. The following day, Strutt received a telegram from his government declaring that it was "highly advisable to get the Emperor out of Austria and into Switzerland at once," adding helpfully that "the British Government can in no way guarantee your journey."

Keeping this news to himself, the intrepid officer went into Vienna to find out what was happening. There he found that Renner and his cabinet had decided to give Charles three choices: if he abdicated all his family's rights, they could live in Austria as private citizens; if he refused to abdicate, he must go into exile; if he refused to either abdicate or leave, he would be imprisoned. Strutt then arranged for a special train to leave from the Westbahnhof at his signal and called the Swiss to get their approval (since the British Foreign Office had not). It took three days to convince Charles and Zita of the necessity for departure, but he managed to do so.

A new obstacle arose in the portly form of the irascible Renner. Strutt had visited him on March 20. Knowing the kind of man with whom he was dealing, the Briton knew he had to overawe him. When he stepped into the chancellor's office, Renner was lolling behind his desk. Strutt peremptorily yelled at him in what he called his "best Boche style:" "Please stand up in future when I enter your room!" Renner leapt to attention, although he exhibited what Strutt called "nervous twitching," more in anger than fear, Strutt believed.

On the twenty-first, Strutt returned and ordered the Austrian railway authorities to reassemble the imperial train as it had been and to bring it up to Kopfstetten, the nearest station to Eckartsau. He then arranged for a British military police escort of one sergeant and six men. He returned to Renner's office to find him already standing up. Despite this outward show of respect, Renner had demands. He began by saying that the emperor and empress would have to be searched before they could leave. Strutt said that would not do, and he swore "in the name of the British Government" that they would take nothing that was not their own property. The little chancellor then declared that he would send a "High Commissioner" to oversee their departure. Strutt saw this as an attempt by Renner to exert his authority over his erstwhile sovereign at British expense. The colonel calmly replied that he could send his representative if he liked, but at the first sign of difficulty, he would personally shoot him! That was the end of that.

The next day, Strutt had returned to Vienna to make various final arrangements when he received a telephonic summons to see Renner once more. As it happened, Strutt had taken Renner's measure well; he drafted a telegram to London and put it in his pocket. When he reached the chancellor's office, Renner declared that Charles must abdicate at once or he would not be allowed to leave but be thrown into prison. Strutt said nothing but pulled out the draft and laid it in front of the chancellor, who read, "Austrian Government refuses permission for departure of Emperor unless he abdicates. Consequently, give orders to re-establish blockade and stop all food trains entering Austria." It was a complete bluff, of course; the British would never have done such a thing, and if they would have, Strutt was hardly in a position to order such a measure. Fortunately, the bully is usually a coward as well: Renner shrieked, "*Grosser Gott*!" Then the chancellor said, "All right, he can go!" "Without any conditions?" "Yes," Renner said sulkily. As Strutt left, he saw the self-proclaimed father of the Austrian republic staring out the window in a pout. Charles was leaving as emperor. Years later, Charles's eldest son, the Archduke Otto, was asked if he hated the British given the role they had played in his father's downfall. Smiling, he responded, "Well, I could, but then, there was Strutt!" The last dinner the imperial family enjoyed at Eckartsau—and indeed, in Austria—featured an official menu, as every dinner there had. Despite the elegance thereof, the listed main dish bore witness to the catch-as-catch can diet the family had lived on there: *Filets de gibier variées* (filets of assorted game).

The following day, March 23, the party at Eckartsau attended Mass in the castle chapel, with Otto as server. The imperial train arrived at 3:45, right on time. Crowds had gathered to bid them farewell. It took several hours to load the train, and at 6:35 p.m., the imperial couple came down the great staircase, and behind them Charles's mother. There were four cars waiting for them, the children, and the staff who would be accompanying them into exile. They set off and reached Kopfstetten station twenty minutes later.

Waiting was a crowd of about two thousand, standing in the rain, many of whom were audibly weeping. By the entrance to the emperor's saloon car were the British escorts and a group of wounded soldiers, who had suffered in his service. Charles, in his field marshal's uniform, saluted the soldiers and shook hands with the veterans. He and Zita entered the train, and then Charles leaned out of a window and said simply, "*Meine Freunde, Auf Wiedersehen*," and the empress curtsied. The train started up, and as Strutt reported in his diary, "As we steamed off a sort of low moan went up from the crowd." The three went to the middle saloon car, and Charles said sadly, "After 700 years," followed by, "Sacred Heart of Jesus, I trust in you!" Later, Zita said, "My family has been exiled from France, Italy, and Portugal. When I married, I became an Austrian subject, and am now an exile from Austria. Colonel Strutt, tell me, to what country do I now belong?" To that the usually unflappable officer had no response, and the couple retired for the night.

The next morning, the court chaplain offered Mass on the train. At Innsbruck, they stopped briefly. At Imst, they stopped once more to get a mountain train attached, and a small squad of British soldiers (Honorable Artillery Company) presented arms on the platform. It was feared there might be trouble with passports at Feldkirch, since no one had any, but they were assured there would be no problem. The emperor changed into civilian clothes, they crossed the Rhine into Switzerland, and at 3:45 steamed into Buchs. There, Swiss Army troops were arrayed and presented arms, while Swiss government officials welcomed the party. The imperial family and their party were driven to a Bourbon-Parma castle on the shore of Lake Constance, Schloss

Wartegg. Their long exile had begun; for Charles, it would never end.

Chapter 12

DOUBLE THROW

Receive this sword, in the name of the Fa+ther, the + Son and the Holy + Spirit, and may thou use it for thy defense, and that of the Holy Church of God, and to the confounding of the enemies of the Cross of Christ, and of the Christian faith: and as far as human frailty shall permit, may thou harm no one with it unjustly. And may He deign to grant this to thee, Who with the Father and the Holy Spirit etc.

—Blessing of the Sword, Roman *Pontificale*

Schloss Wartegg, on the shores of Lake Constance, was inherited by Zita's grandmother in 1860, the year after she and her son, Robert, had been forced to leave Parma. Sixtus had been born there. So the imperial family's arrival was a bit of a family reunion, with Zita's mother and many of her brothers and sisters gathered to meet them. For a large family long separated by war, this was a joyous time, despite the somber occurrences which had brought it about. But they could not stay there permanently, as the Swiss authorities required them to settle further away from the Austrian frontier. Thus they settled at the Villa Prangins, on Lake Geneva—ironically built by the exiled nephew of Napoleon

Bonaparte, but at the time owned by a Swiss (and now the clubhouse of a golf club). Here was born their sixth child, Archduke Rudolph, and here ensued Charles and Zita's happiest days together since they lived at Hetzendorf, as heirs to Franz Ferdinand. To think that all of that had ended less than five years before!

The rest of the year passed by in domestic tranquility; the family attended Mass every day and offered their devotions together; Charles enjoyed helping with the education of his children—especially in religion—and playing and going for walks with them.

> In the chapel of the Villa Prangins on Lake Geneva, where the imperial family had found asylum, there is then a statue of the Sacred Heart of Jesus in front of which a lamp is constantly burning. The Sacred Heart Friday is celebrated in solemnity: in the morning, the Holy Mass is missa cantata, celebrated by Bishop Ernst Seydl and with the two Archdukes Otto and Robert as ministrants. Little Karl Ludwig then loudly speaks his prayer: "Most Sacred Heart of Jesus, I trust in you. Have mercy on the Fatherland, keep close all your loved ones in your heart and bring us all back home happy soon!" In the evening, during the blessing devotion, the litany is prayed and consecration prayer is spoken. Then the national song sounds: up, to the oath, people and country! In addition, every Friday there was a dedicated Sacred Heart devotion in the house chapel.

> In the nursery we find a small house altar and on this a picture of the Sacred Heart of Jesus, in front of which the children performed their prayers. But not only the children found help through the display. The Emperor himself had a picture of the Sacred Heart of Jesus on his desk, as well as near his bed. He also painted images of the Heart of Jesus for his mother-in-law, for his brothers-in-law and sisters-in-law, and framed them in silver, using them as Christmas gifts.[1]

They selected Disentis in the Alps—home of the famous abbey of that name—as their winter vacation home at the suggestion of one of the monks there. On December 30, 1919, this Fr. Carnot celebrated a Mass in the crypt of the abbey's Marienkirche in commemoration of the third anniversary of their coronation. All of this was fitting because Disentis had been an imperial abbey since the time of Charlemagne and had enjoyed particularly close relations with several emperors over the centuries.

Indeed, no matter how enjoyable their life was in the immediate, they could not forget their God-given imperial and royal vocation—exceedingly easy and pleasant as it would have been for most of us to do in their position. Just before his arrival in Switzerland, Charles signed a declaration called the "Feldkirch Manifesto." It is important to read

---

1 Ildefons Maria Fux, "Der selige Karl von Österreich und seine Beziehung zum Heiligsten Herzen Jesu," January 22, 2005, https://www.stjosef.at/artikel/sel_karl_v_oesterreich_herzjesu.htm.

because it expresses Charles's view on the political situation both in Austria (to which it referred) and in Hungary:

> The German-Austrian Government has put aside my proclamation of 11 November 1918, which I issued in a dark hour, in that on the same day it decided to lay before the Provisional National Assembly a resolution proclaiming the transformation of German-Austria into a Republic, thus pre-empting the decision which, according to my proclamation, should only have been taken by the whole German-Austrian people. . . .
>
> What the German-Austrian Government and the provisional constituent National Assembly has decided and done in this regard since 11 November 1919, and what it resolved to do in the future, is therefore null and void for Me and My House. . . .
>
> And so I leave German-Austria. . . . It was in war that I was called to the throne of my ancestors. It was to peace that I sought to lead my peoples and it is in peacetime that I have desired and still intend to be their just and faithful father.
>
> Feldkirch 24 March 1919

But after some reflection, the emperor decided not to publish it. There were two reasons for this. On the one hand, his many supporters in Austria might well be victimized by the vindictive little fellow Karl Renner; without anyone around to overawe him, like Colonel Strutt, there was no way of knowing what he might do, especially with a mob behind him. Reminding the chancellor in such stark terms of his betrayal of his country's people (the first, thus far!) would imperil the safety of Charles's supporters.

Things were even worse in Hungary. On March 21, even before Charles and Zita had left Austria, the feckless Count Karolyi was overthrown by the Communists under Bela Kun. During the autumn unrest in Budapest the previous year, Communists had murdered Franz Ferdinand's and Charles's old nemesis, Istvan Tisza. The new Soviet Republic would do much more of the same. All private land was nationalized, and secret police were created to round up and murder opposition. In such an atmosphere, Charles decided instead to send copies of the manifesto to the pope and various friendly sovereigns privately for the historical record.

Nevertheless, the knowledge that the imperial family, even in exile, were happy was a bit much for Chancellor Renner. In April of 1919, he pushed a bill through Parliament without opposition: the Habsburg Law. It had three provisions: 1) No Habsburg in line for the throne could ever enter Austria unless he renounced his rights and swore allegiance to the Republic; 2) No Habsburg could ever be elected president of the Republic; and 3) All private properties of the main line of the House of Habsburg were seized by the government (this last did not apply to state properties, such as the Hofburg or Schoenbrunn, which the government already had, nor to properties owned by younger branches of the clan, such as Persenbeug and the Kaiservilla at Ischl; only such places as Laxenburg, Eckartsau, the Villa Warholtz, and various rental properties were covered). This was inserted into the Constitution.

At the same time, Renner pushed through an Abolition of the Nobility Law, which purported to abolish both the nobility as a class and their titles. So if someone were, say, Franz, Count von Lindner von Kustein, he was now legally Franz Lindner, and if he dared to use his hereditary title in public, he was to be fined two hundred crowns. The pettiness of the law may be gauged by how the contemporary Socialist government in Germany handled the same issue. Abolishing class privileges, they nevertheless declared that the title became part of the individual's legal name, thus at once burning incense on the altar of equality while leaving the citizen's private heritage intact. Amusingly enough, recently this legacy of Renner's has come up in the news. Charles's senior grandson, the Archduke Charles, has a website: "Karl von Habsburg." He was taken to court under the law and found guilty. But since the law has remained unchanged for a century, and the crown subsequently replaced with the Groschen and then the Euro, they could not initially figure out what to fine him. Eventually, the Austrian solons came up with the sum of ninety euros; the case is on appeal at this writing. In any case, even at the time, annoyed as the nobility were by the move, it did lead to a great deal of levity at Renner's expense. The well-known joker, Adalbert Count von Sternberg, ever after had his visiting cards inscribed:

> Adalbert Sternberg
> Ennobled by Charlemagne 798
> Disennobled by Karl Renner 1918

Although the emperor was in no position to affect those measures, he did concentrate upon those Austrian issues in which he could intervene; one of which was aid to returning POWs all over the former empire. Another was preventing the absorption of the rump of Austria by Germany, which most Austrian politicians favored at the time, given the state of national finances.

> To him, the idea of nationalism based on language was unacceptable, and this was the basis for his opposition to an "Anschluss" of German Austria to Germany. In the Emperor's view, Austria could never be defined in terms of Germanism. That would be, he believed, an impossibility, because Austria was something altogether different. It was not confined to one language, or one ancestry. An Austrian, he believed, could also be a person whose mother tongue was Slovak, Czech, Croat, Italian, German, Hungarian, or, for that matter, any other European tongue. The common denominator was to him, a union of Christian peoples whose aim was the betterment of their lot and that of humanity—a sort of commonwealth of nations. High ideals perhaps, but good ones, for they had sustained the Empire for over 640 years. They had to work too, he sincerely believed, for post-war Austria.[2]

As Gordon Brooke-Shepherd put it, "In as much as any man of the Dual Monarchy could think and feel with eleven minds and eleven hearts—one for each of his peoples—that man was Charles, as Archduke, and as Emperor."[3] And, one

---

2 Leo J. Hammerschmid, *Zita: The Last Empress of Austria*(Meridian Press, 1989), pp. 106–7.

3 Gordon Brook-Shepherd, *The Last Habsburg* (Weidenfeld &

might add, as exile. Having more foresight then Renner and the rest of the politicians that were running Austria, he understood all too well that annexation by Germany meant an end to the Austrian soul—no matter how much money might be realized by the sale. So it was that Charles used all of his contacts in Washington, London, and Paris to expound on his view that an Anschluss would do neither Austria nor the entente any good in the long run. In this, he had some success.

Amusing as Renner's antics might have been, the news coming out of Hungary—and brought by an endless train of visitors to the Villa Prangins—was simply horrific. To try to woo the farmers, Bela Kun had abolished agricultural taxes, but since the cities were starving, he sent gangs out to the countryside to requisition crops from the same farmers, free of charge; at least, if the farmers did not resist, they were not killed. In April, an opposition government was formed in Szeged, which town was still under French occupation—the French having marched up from Salonika in the September campaign the previous year, which had knocked Bulgaria out of the war. No peace treaty having been signed between Hungary and the victorious allies, they were still there. Moreover, this opposition government was monarchist and soon established a pipeline to Charles. So, too, were a group of Hungarians training surreptitiously in Austria under the command of Colonel Anton Lehar, brother of the famous operetta composer Franz. Admiral Horthy, although high on Bela Kun's liquidation list, managed to escape Budapest and

---

Nicolson Ltd., 1968), pp. 316–17.

hid out on his in-laws' estate, close to Arad (now Oradea, Romania). When Charles found out that he was alive, he appointed him minister of war in the Szeged government; from this position, Horthy made himself commander-in-chief of the growing anti-Communist army.

The Romanians, who had occupied Transylvania and eastern Hungary, had finally tired of Bela Kun's bloody antics and advanced on Budapest. Kun and his minions fled the city, and Socialists traded governments in quick succession. On November 16, 1919, the Romanians withdrew from Budapest, and two days later, Horthy, the "Admiral on Horseback," rode into the city at the head of a column of monarchist troops. The admiral was supposed to be the emperor-king's man, and on that basis, the majority of Hungarians, having experienced alternatives, supported him in that capacity. But there was a clique of politicians who dubbed themselves "Free Electors;" these maintained that while Hungary remained a monarchy, the throne was empty and could be filled by whomever the nation chose. In January of 1920, an election returned a coalition of Legitimists (who supported Charles) and Free Electors. This decided that a regent would be appointed to exercise the king's powers, whomever he might be, provisionally. On March 1, Admiral Horthy—believed by the public to be Charles's man, and by the cognoscenti to favor the Free Electors—was appointed regent.

After his appointment, he duly sent a message to Charles at Prangins notifying him of his new position, assuring his king of his loyalty and his intention to see him restored and to keep him informed of all government acts in the meantime. He also asked his permission to live in part of the royal palace in Budapest. But Charles began to notice a gradual change in the tone of Horthy's administration. He would send proclamations to be published in Budapest; they were received but went no further. Requests for dates upon which, or methods whereby, the king might return received evasive responses, or none at all. The final straw was when Horthy required the officers of the army to take an oath to him personally rather than to the king.

Because of these disturbing omens, Charles resolved as early as the late summer of 1919 that he must return to Hungary. But to do so, two obstacles must be overcome. The "Successor States" of Czechoslovakia, Yugoslavia, Romania, and Poland had formed, under French aegis, the "Little Entente." This grouping had three major points: 1) to bloc Soviet expansion into Central Europe; 2) to act as a counter to Germany, should it ever prove resurgent; and 3) to prevent a Habsburg restoration. This was not merely out of a fear that the broken Austrians or Hungarians could either singly or together overwhelm them. Each of the successor states still had large or small groups of Habsburg loyalists, who might prove destabilizing. Most embarrassingly for president Masaryk of Czechoslovakia, their number included his son, Jan, who had remained a serving and loyal cavalry officer in the imperial army all the while his father was agitating against the empire. After his accession to the presidency, the elder Masaryk was hosting a party in the Prague castle. He asked Jan, a noted pianist, to play something for his assembled official guests. The younger Masaryk fulfilled this request by playing the imperial anthem, much to his father's chagrin and the guests' amusement or anger. In any case, the only way to avoid immediate action against Hungary should he return, Charles needed to secure the cooperation of the French; their client states would not move without Paris's assent. The second issue was simply one of getting there. Charles had no passport or any other travel documents, and the Swiss watched his every move whenever he left the gates at Prangins.

In the meantime, "his" regent was consolidating his power in Budapest, going so far as to name himself "duke" and settling into the throne room in the royal palace. Charles realized that time was not on his side; the longer he took to return, the harder it would be to regain his throne. As it stood, he hoped that his mere return would be enough to secure the kingdom. By September of 1920, he had decided that he must go back by the following spring.

Fortunate for Charles, Aristide Briand, who had been so favorable to Charles's peace feelers in 1917, was once more prime minister and foreign minister in Paris. Through a number of intermediaries, an agreement was struck. Briand made it plain that "if the attempt goes well and the Emperor looks secure in Budapest, then we shall support him officially and keep Hungary's neighbors quiet. If the attempt fails, we can of course do nothing."[4]

In the event of success, a seven-point agreement was concluded:

1. Immediate recognition of the emperor as soon as he had taken over as king of Hungary.

4 Brooke-Shepherd, *The Last Habsburg*, p. 257.

2. Immediate setting up of economic links.
3. Immediate granting of French state credits.
4. French military aid, should the emperor need it, in Hungary against foreign attacks.
5. A pledge, on the other hand, that no French troops would be forced on the emperor if he did not require them.
6. An undertaking to "look again" at the large territories of Hungary allotted to her neighbors and to "readjust the position to some extent."
7. A promise, as regards those same neighboring states, to keep them in check and to cut off all the French credits on which they so heavily depended should they give any trouble.

All of these points were important, but the agreement to look into a revision of Hungary's borders would be some balm to the devastated Magyar soul. Moreover, they meant that Charles would come back with something more to offer Hungary than Horthy or anyone else.

For Briand and other of Charles's supporters among the French, including the redoubtable Marshal Lyautey, a Habsburg restoration in Hungary and possibly Austria under French sponsorship would create a reliable French ally in Central Europe; one to counter not only Germany and the Soviet Union but Italy, which, even before Mussolini, was seeking to expand its influence in the Balkans. And many in the French military, including Lyautey, were devout Catholics and Royalists themselves. At any rate, with French guarantees, Charles was ready. Colonel Strutt, at Charles's request, spied out the routes this super-secret mission must take and assisted with gathering fake travel documents.

On March 24, the emperor slipped across the Swiss frontier on foot into France. A car met him and drove him to Strasbourg where he boarded the Orient Express. Disguises, false papers, decoys, avoiding unexpected acquaintances, and everything that one might expect in a Grahame Greene or Agatha Christie novel occurred, until Charles got off at the Westbahnhof. He grabbed a taxi and took it to Landskrongasse 5, the home of his old friend Count Thomas Erdödy. He rang the bell and was given a warm welcome. This would be the last time the emperor would ever sleep in his Austrian capital.

The next day, with Charles still disguised and bearing false papers, they crossed the border at a gate where the count was well known (he often passed it en route to his Hungarian home). They ate a meal on the way, stopped in a town where the Easter Procession was passing, and dropped to their knees before the Blessed Sacrament. A bit later on, the car broke down. They continued their journey toward Szombathely, whose bishop, Janos Mikes, was renowned for his legitimism. Arriving about 10:00 p.m. in front of the bishop's palace, Erdödy knocked on the door. As it happened, the bishop was having a dinner party, at which was one of Horthy's cabinet ministers, a priest named Msgr. Vass. The count sent the servant who answered the door up to the bishop to ask for overnight accommodation for himself and another gentleman. Mikes himself came down and greeted them. The count asked if he did not recognize the other man, and when the bishop said he did not, Erdödy declared, "It is

His Apostolic Majesty, the King!" The bishop was overjoyed and rushed to bring Msgr. Vass. That gentleman in turn said to the king that he was a cabinet minister no longer, as "the Cabinet of the Regent ceased to exist the moment the crowned King set foot again on Hungarian soil!" The party was joined by Anton Lehar, now a major general and commander of the troops in western Hungary. He immediately assured Charles of his allegiance.

As it happened, the prime minister, Paul Teleki, was staying at an estate nearby. Lehar sent an office to summon him back to the bishop's palace at 4:30 the following morning. Teleki had absolutely no idea what had happened or why he was being called so early and was absolutely flabbergasted when he saw his rightful king. Murmuring, "too soon, too soon," he was not as forthcoming as Msgr. Vass. But he gathered his wits and told Charles that he must either go on to Budapest or back to Switzerland; there could be no middle way.

Of course, Charles had stopped in western Hungary because he knew he had support in the person of General Lehar, his troops, and may of the churchmen and nobility. But the question that the whole party debated was the best way to proceed to Budapest. Should Charles lead Lehar's army to the capital, risking civil war, or should he go to Horthy, assuming "his" regent would voluntarily surrender his office? Teleki claimed to believe that Horthy would do so, and even Lehar thought it unlikely that he would resist. It was arranged that Teleki and Vass would leave an hour early, drive to Budapest, alert Horthy, and make everything ready for the king. At 7:30, Charles set out, accompanied by

Count Sigray (with whom Teleki had been staying) and two of Lehar's officers. In hindsight, even a platoon of soldiers would have helped.

In the event, Teleki never arrived in Budapest that day. When Charles arrived at the royal palace, there was no honor guard, and no one seemed prepared to receive him. Count Sigray went in to announce his presence to the regent and returned saying, "You shall have to be very forceful." As you may recall, the last time we saw Horthy, he was tearfully declaring that he would never rest until Charles had his thrones back in Budapest and Vienna. But at this meeting, in Charles's own study, Horthy said, "This is a disaster. Your Majesty must leave at once and return immediately to Switzerland." The emperor-king's response was that it was impossible, and he had burned all his bridges. Charles thanked him for what he had done for Hungary and then formally called on him to return the government to him. This began two hours of wrangling, with Charles reminding Horthy of the various oaths he had taken and Horthy whining as to how they no longer applied, of Charles offering rewards and Horthy haggling over them. Finally, Horthy warned of the reprisals of the neighboring countries, at which Charles told him under a vow of secrecy of the French support. This led Horthy to suggest an attack on Vienna.

Charles had not slept properly in days, and he was already coming down with an illness. Colonel Gombos, one of Horthy's most fanatical supporters, had arrived at the palace—neither Count Sigray nor the two officers were anywhere in sight. Charles had not even brought his revolver. The upshot was that after warning Horthy that he expected him to join him in three weeks at Szombatheley, the king left. Horthy immediately summoned the French high commissioner and gave him a suitably doctored account of what had happened, claiming the emperor was already on his way out of the country. The commissioner wired Paris for instructions, and as Briand had warned, the French denied having made any such assurances. Instead, all of the high commissioners of the entente powers formally issued a warning that a restoration would not be tolerated. Moreover, while the 1,500 men Lehar had at his command could easily have secured Budapest in a lightning strike—and Briand would have provided Hungary's defense hereafter—they could not withstand the armies of the Little Entente by themselves.

Nevertheless, although Teleki had not managed to reach Budapest, he rejoined Charles in Szombathely on Easter Monday, the following morning. He brought a message from Horthy, saying, "under certain conditions," he would hand over power, until which time he would continue to run things. But in reality, the regent was organizing the army against Charles and mobilizing both great and little ententes against him. Charles's health broke down on April 1, and he took to his bed, but a bit of hope came from the British mission in Vienna to look after Charles in his sickness. He bore an unsigned telegram from Paris, which advised Charles to "stand firm" because Hungary's neighbors were going to "calm down." But during the days of the king's illness, the Serbs mobilized on their border, and Horthy sealed off the western Hungarian "monarchist zone." Even Lehar advised Charles that this attempt had failed.

But the emperor-king, having reconciled himself to a defeat on this occasion, made two personal resolutions: he would come back in a more militant manner, as befitted the treachery of "his" regent, and that while he had arrived as a thief in the night, he would leave like a king. He therefore demanded three things from Horthy, which were duly promised: the publication of the manifesto to the nation which he had written, a regal departure to Switzerland under the same terms as he had previously enjoyed, and the immunity from arrest or other annoyance of his supporters. In true Horthy-like fashion, only the second was honored. Before Charles left, however, he entrusted his field marshal's uniform, from the collar of which he pulled off the rank insignia. He told the loyal officer that when the message "sew the insignia on the collar" arrived, that would be the signal for the return of the king.

Certainly, as he appeared on the terrace of the bishop's palace for the last time, a huge mob waved and cheered at Charles, shouting, "Long May He Live!" and "Until Next Time!" The court train that took him to the border stopped at every station, where he received loyal addresses and cheers. At the Austrian border, three officers of the entente—British, French, and Italian—awaited him. They in turn led Charles onto a special train as part of the guaranteed transit to Switzerland. When they reached the Swiss frontier at Buchs, there were two surprises awaiting Charles: the pleasant one was Zita, who had just arrived, driving all the way from Prangins to meet him. The unpleasant one was the deal that Horthy had made with Switzerland without telling the king. The Swiss assumed that Charles had accepted the requirements since he had in fact returned. Swiss newspapers had already featured the five points of his asylum that it was claimed Charles had already accepted. Three of them dealt with his place of residence: he could not live in the Canton of Vaud, where Prangins was located, nor could he dwell in Zurich, Basel, or Berne. He and his entourage must "refrain from all political activity." Lastly, Charles must inform the Swiss Parliament forty-eight hours before leaving Switzerland. The Swiss further intimated to the imperial couple that they would need to find a new place of exile. They were not allowed to stay at Schloss Wartegg but were rushed to the Hotel National in Lucerne.

They were definitely not going to able to stay there very long, as the couple's money, such as it was, was running out. So they took a lease for a year on the nearby Schlosshotel Hertenstein (demolished in 1943) at only half the rent of Villa Prangins. The above-mentioned statue of the Sacred Heart of Jesus was moved to the house chapel in Hertenstein that Charles instantly set up and on whose wall the embroidered inscription was to be read: "Most Sacred Heart of Jesus, I trust in you!" Again and again, in good times and bad, the emperor's deep recollection was striking when he prayed.

He negotiated further with the Swiss government, qualifying his need to inform the Swiss Parliament should he move to "another place of exile"—obviously, Hungary, his own country, would not qualify as such. In July, he wrote both to George V and to the president of France asking them to use their influence to persuade their governments to help the bankrupt Austrian republic with financial assistance. As always, he was repaying betrayal with kindness.

In the meantime, it became apparent that the strategic considerations that had led Briand to back the first attempt remained intact. In April, the query came from Paris as to how Briand's support for the affair had gotten out in Budapest; Charles responded with what had happened; this satisfied Briand. The French asked Charles to appoint someone to represent him in Paris, and he duly sent a Hungarian diplomat. So as far as French support went, all was well. But how to get back to Hungary a second time? This attempt, of course, would be all or nothing.

How to get there indeed. The Swiss, Austrians, and Hungarians would all be extremely vigilant as far as border crossings went. One idea was to cruise down the Danube, but while this would reduce the danger of being discovered, it had its own peculiar difficulties. In the end, there was nothing for it but to fly.

This was a far-riskier proposition then than it is today. Colonel Lindbergh's flight to Paris was six years in the future, and any forced landing or crash could be an utter disaster. The emperor had never flown before, let alone the once-more-pregnant empress who had resolved to come along on the expedition. Lehar recruited two extremely loyal pilots, and a plane was secured through cloak-and-dagger purchase. They would fly in to a pre-arranged location.

The question of how being solved, the next question was when. Initially, they would have preferred the spring of 1922. But Horthy was doing his best, despite outward signs of deference to Charles, to isolate or remove the king's partisans scattered in political or military roles in the establishment and replace them with creatures of his own. Several of these—the foreign minister, the speaker of the National Assembly, and even Teleki's replacement as prime minister, Count Bethlen—began pressuring him to stop this activity and declare himself openly for the king. Although Horthy responded to this pressure by writing a fulsome letter full of loyalty to Charles, he occupied the royal summer house at Godollo and stepped up his anti-legitimist campaign. What determined the date in the end was the regent demanding the return to Budapest and disbanding of a legitimist unit from western Hungary on October 23. This would sap the strength of Lehar's monarchist enclave, which had to serve as the springboard for the retaking of the capital. So Charles resolved to return to his country that very date.

The plan was for Charles and Zita to land on the estate of Count Sigray. They would move on to Sopron and join the Ostenburg Battalion on its train trip to supposed disbandment at Budapest. Once they arrived, Charles would lead them on to the castle and take over; meanwhile, Charles's supporters would have arrested Horthy's top loyalists. But the timing had to be perfect and everyone true to their promises if it were to succeed.

On October 20, Charles and Zita left Hertenstein having told all and sundry that they were on their way to Wartegg to celebrate their tenth anniversary with their relatives. One wonders what they spoke about: the tremendous changes that had taken place in their lives over the previous decade? On their wedding day, they had been the most favored couple of a nation of some 51,390,223 inhabitants and doted upon by the most revered monarch in Europe. They were young and had every assurance of a brilliant and happy future. Now, only one of those things were true: they were still very much in love. That, their piety, and their senses of humor had seen them through thus far; they would need them all.

They turned off the main road to an airfield, and at 12:15 p.m., they took off. Flying over Austria, the pilot pointed out features familiar to them, and the couple were quite giddy with the flight. They had taken the statue of the Sacred Heart of Jesus from the chapel of Hertenstein with them; this statue would follow the family in all their subsequent adventures. After a landing in Hungary, they managed to make their proper locale before nightfall (in those far off days, planes avoided flying at night). But there were no torches lit. In the event, it turned out that several things had already gone awry; crossed communications had given Lehar the impression they were not coming until the following day, and so the troops had been sent back to their barracks. A key supporter of Charles in Budapest's political circles, Count Julius Andrassy, had somehow not been informed at all. Fortunately, he was in the neighborhood for a party and was easily summoned. But he was horrified because he was on the verge of launching a new legitimist party with Count Bethlen; the prime minister would be giving a speech the next day stirring a middle course between a coup d'état and dethronement. Andrassy's involvement in the new attempt would be seen by Bethlen as betrayal and deceit. (One of the amazing things in this tale is how scrupulous about their honor Charles's partisans tended to be, a trait seemingly unknown to their opponents.)

In any case, while the twenty-four-hour delay might mean added difficulties, the enterprise was far from doomed at this point. The railroad cars had to be regathered (local peasants had appropriated them for the beet harvest). The imperial couple were driven to Sopron and made their headquarters at the Osternburg Battalion's barracks. Charles appointed his prime minister, Rakovsky, and a few other political figures joined them and were duly appointed to posts. Lehar's 1,500 infantry, cavalry, and artillery were reviewed and renewed their oaths to their king. Meanwhile, the railroad cars were reassembled. Charles and Zita drove to the station through streets lined with cheering crowds, and even more awaited them as they reached the platform and mounted the train.

The train journey itself was triumphant. At every station, crowds cheered and threw flowers. Reaching Gyor at noon, they found that the garrison had already in place a guard of honor. Trumpets blared, and the crowds cheered, "Long live the king!" This was, however, deceptive. Neither the troops nor the populace knew that the garrison commander, General Lorinczy, was two-faced. Prior to bringing his men to the station, he had alerted the regent in Budapest that his king was en route.

This warning gave Horthy just enough time to prepare. He ordered the railroad track torn up all along the way, though few garrisons obeyed; none followed the command to shoot on the train. Komarom saw the garrison turn out and then join the king's men. Horthy sent Dr. Vass—whom you'll remember from the Easter enterprise—with an escort to Komarom to negotiate. But they were brought aboard and had to try their delaying tactics as the train kept moving forward; through Tata, Toris, and Bicske, all of whose garrisons declared for the king upon his arrival. By the time Charles and Zita awoke at six the following morning, they had reached Bia-Torbagy; the next station, Kelenfold, was the suburban station; from there, the troops could march to the castle hill on the Buda side and take the royal palace.

However, Horthy, although panicky, was not idle. He sought regular troops, but none would fire on the king. The day was saved for him by his right-hand man, Colonel Gombos. He had spent the evening and night recruiting students from the university by telling them that there was a party of Czechs on their way to attack Budapest. Thus it was that three hundred deluded students set out. In the meantime, Lehar's men advanced from the train to Buda-Ors, where an infantry battalion awaited them; it declared it would not only not oppose them but join them in the march on Budapest. Two of Horthy's artillery batteries joined the advancing Royalists, and two others gave no resistance. However, when Ostenburg's men tried to advance and join the regiment ahead, they were attacked from the flank by the students. A few of the men were killed, and a few more wounded, and they retreated to the train to take stock of the situation.

This was a mere delay, but it led to catastrophe. Although the loyal Lehar had skillfully conducted the situation thus far, out of modesty, he felt that he, as a mere colonel, should be replaced by the more senior General Hegedus. Unbeknownst to Lehar, but suspected by Charles, this gentleman, who as commander of Szombathely had welcomed the king with open arms and sworn allegiance to him, was in reality on Horthy's side. Lehar, although promoted to general by Charles the previous day, had been serving under Hegedus, who was commander of the western region. So with the action caused by the students, Lehar wanted Hegedus to take command. Charles suspected Hegedus of treachery, but the bluff and loyal Lehar had worked with him for months and insisted that he could be trusted. So Lehar became "chief of staff."

While this was going on, Horthy used the delay to replace the "disloyal" officers of the Budapest garrison. At 10:00 a.m., Hegedus offered to go to Kelenfold and convince the regiment there to come over to the king. Charles agreed, but sent one of Lehar's most trusted men to tail him; Hegedus was able to evade him, cross the line, and go straight to Horthy and Gombos; he joined them in planning Charles's defeat. He returned to Charles at 2:00 p.m., declaring that he had been in cease-fire talks with Horthy, whose troops were ready to fight. He then claimed then that if the truce was accepted, it would give him time to bring in more troops from the west for a thrust the following day. Charles decided that it was time to go to the front himself and lead from there.

The troops at Torok-Balint declared that Horthy's envoys were on their way to discuss the truce. At this point, Charles told his loyal officers, Ostenburg, Lehar, and the rest, that they should withdraw and regroup the troops and that he would personally lead them in a night assault on Budapest. So he intended to refuse the truce, but the officers said their men were exhausted after two nights without rest and could not go on. His political staff said that if Charles refused the truce, it would look as though he wanted bloodshed. Thus Charles agreed to the truce.

When Horthy's envoy arrived, it was agreed that the truce would last until 8:00 a.m. the following morning, after which the political talks would be held just inside the king's lines. At this point, a huge error was made on the part of Charles and his advisers. They left the traitor Hegedus to work out the terms of the armistice, while the train returned to Torbagy. Hegedus assigned the surrounding heights to Horthy's men and agreed that they would break the truce three hours early so as to catch the king's men sleeping. His treachery accomplished, Hegedus went back to Torbagy and asked to be relieved of his command, claiming that he had found both of his sons were serving on Horthy's side.

The next morning, although some of Ostenburg's troops escaped, many were captured while they slept. At 8:00 a.m. on the twenty-fourth, Graz and Lehar went to hear Horthy's terms. They came back with them; Charles must surrender and abdicate and his soldiers must surrender and lay down their arms. As the king read this note, shots rang out, several of which hit the royal train. Lehar and Ostenburg leapt down from the platform, calling for a last stand. Charles yelled at them, "Lehar! Ostenburg! Stop and come back here! I forbid any more fighting. It's all quite senseless now."

The emperor-king was quite correct; they were surrounded, with very little ammunition. He ordered the train to steam backwards in the direction they had come. Count Ezterhazy, who had joined the train before Budapest, invited the imperial couple to stay at his palace in Tata, which was on the way. When the train pulled into the station, the ten most elegant carriages the Ezterhazys owned were waiting to take the company back to the palace. As Charles and Zita descended from the train, soldiers, peasants, and servants all shouted, "Long live the king! Long live the queen!" And the traitor Hegedus threw his hat in the air, cheering with the rest of them. As soon as the carriages departed for the palace, he called Horthy from the station, put himself under the admiral's command, and asked for orders.

That night, six assailants passed through the guards and attempted to murder Charles and Zita; they got to a few yards from the bedroom door when the count, clad only in his nightshirt, shoved one down the stairs. They fled. But it was underlined that Tata was not really safe.

As promised, Briand again denied any knowledge of Charles's activities. The three entente powers discussed what to do with the imperial couple. It was decided that they would be placed aboard a ship of the British naval flotilla in the Danube. This would take them down to the Black Sea, where a Royal Navy ship was expected at Galatz; they would be transferred to that ship, which would set sail for . . . where? Various islands were discussed: Malta? The Balearics? The Canaries? But no choice was made in the immediate.

In any case, Horthy had decided to move Charles and Zita to the more secure lake location of Tihany Abbey, a Benedictine monastery. But Charles refused to budge until those of his supporters who had been arrested were released. That being agreed to by the regent, on October 26, at six o'clock in the morning, Charles and Zita left Tata aboard a special train to Aszófő. From there, they went to the abbey of Tihany. There they spent a few days wondering what would happen, until, on October 30, they were informed that the Hungarian government would hand them over to the commander of the British Danube fleet at the request of the little and great ententes. Charles wrote a protest letter to this effect, declaring that "according to the Hungarian law I have an indisputable right to reside on Hungarian soil."

While there, the primate of Hungary, Cardinal Csernoch, visited them. He recalled his visit later: "I went to his room with anxiety. I had expected to find a broken, fearful, suffering King, for whom one could find no words of consolation. . . . I had been deceived. The storm had passed over the King. His hair had gone white, his face was lined by anxiety. His appearance was solemn and serious, that of a man who has taken a full consciousness of his suffering. He was fully and clearly in charge of his position and required neither explanation nor consolation. He accepted final consequences yet still kept his trust and hope."

Charles told the cardinal very frankly, "I have done my duty, as I came here to do. As crowned King, I have not only a right, I also have a duty. I must uphold the right, and the dignity of the Crown. . . .With the last breath of my life I must take the path of duty. Whatever I regret, Our Lord and Savior had led me."[5] These sentiments, even at this bleak hour, were in keeping with what he had always held:

The Emperor always testified to the truth of the love of Jesus through unlimited faith in His help. When he

---

5 Joanna and James Bogle, *A Heart for Europe: The Lives of Emperor Charles and Empress Zita of Austria-Hungary* (Gracewing Publishing, 2000), p. 137.

spoke of Our Lady or the Sacred Heart of Jesus, he began to radiate, and on February 14, 1919 he wrote from Eckartsau to the Archbishop of Vienna Cardinal Gustav Piffl (1864-1932): "The Sacred Heart of Jesus and the Most Holy Mother of God has always protected and saved the House of Habsburg;" and in April of the same year, already in exile in Switzerland, he addressed to Pope Benedict XV, the words: "I do not lose heart and in particular have the confidence that the Sacred Heart of Jesus will not abandon the land that is consecrated to him." Invitations to give the Lord's heart unlimited trust are also found in letters to His wife Zita, in the same way in conversations with oppressed people of all kinds: "The Sacred Heart of Jesus will help!"—He said this with great conviction. . . . Or he encouraged with the words: "The Sacred Heart of Jesus will do it!"[6]

The abbot of Tihany, Cyprian Halbik, described the imperial couple's stay at his monastery in a letter to the abbot of Pannonhalma:

> I met the Royal Couple only when they arrived and when they left, when our contact was just a silent handshake. But after they arrived, they were invited, they were very graciously welcomed, sat down, and the discourse immediately began with the greeting of your dignity in Győr, and I noticed that they had been named. He was interested in home and order conditions; he said with regret that he was forced . . . only to cause us a lot of discomfort. When I offered our

6 Fux, "Der selige Karl von Österreich und seine Beziehung zum Heiligsten Herzen Jesu."

> helpful service to the Majesties, they only asked for a separate small mass. They took about 8-10 minutes.
>
> In the afternoon of their departure, October 31, they were confessed, . . . and after their dinner they went back to the chapel and left for the cars that were already on standby. At the start of the chapel, I met them again, saying goodbye to a silent but warm hand grip. Six cars started with a large number of escorts, including Count Apponyi and Count Dénes Szécheny to Ambassador Aszófő, where three trains were waiting for them.

The train took them, after seven hours, to the little river port of Bata. There sat HMS *Glow-Worm*, awaiting its illustrious prisoner/guests. Responsibility having been surrendered on the train, Charles and Zita were now wards of the Royal Navy, with no idea of where they were to go, or if they would see their children again. But trusting to God, they descended the gangplank, leaving all that they had fought and suffered for behind. Their former subjects would reap the whirlwind planted by their treasonous leaders.

Charles I of Austria/Charles IV of Hungary (1887-1922), 1917. Photo © CCI / Bridgeman Images.

Karl I of Austria in 1903. Universal History Archive/UIG / Bridgeman Images

Bridal couple Archduke Charles and Princess Zita of Bourbon-Parma at Schwarzau Palace, 1911. © SZ Photo / Scherl / Bridgeman Images

Emperor Charles I with his wife. © Arkivi UG All Rights Reserved / Bridgeman Images

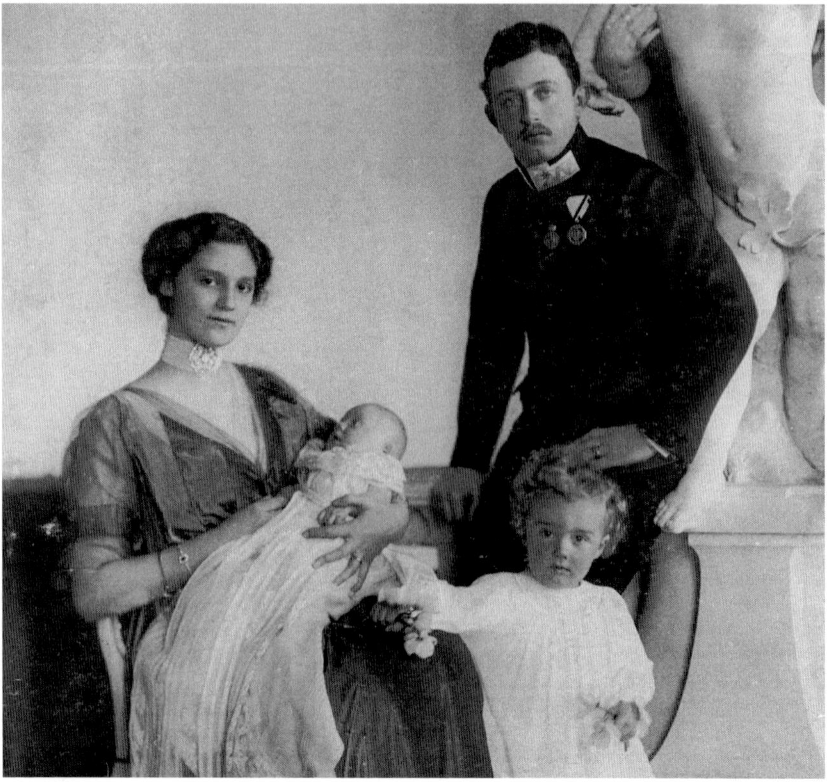

Charles I, Emperor of Habsburg, Austria, c.1914.

Portrait of Zita of Bourbon-Parma (1882-1989), Emperor Charles I of Austria (1887-1922) and their eldest son Crown Prince Otto von Hasburg (1912-2011) after the Coronation in Hungary. Universal History Archive/UIG / Bridgeman Images

Emperor Karl I and his adjutants watch the fighting, 1917. © SZ Photo / Scherl / Bridgeman Images

Emperor Karl I and his adjutants watch the fighting, 1917. © SZ Photo / Scherl / Bridgeman Images. © A. Dagli Orti / De Agostini Picture Library / Bridgeman Images

(*opposite*) After the twelfth Isonzo: The Austro-Hungarian Emperor Charles I on the way back from a visit to the reconquered Gorizia on the Italian front, 1917. © SZ Photo / Scherl / Bridgeman Images

Emperor Charles I in conversation with an invalid officer, 1918. © SZ Photo / Scherl / Bridgeman Images

Emperor Charles I in the Bukovina, 1918. © SZ Photo / Scherl / Bridgeman Images

(*opposite*) Charles I of Austria at a battle of World War I. Illustration, Hungary, ca 1914. © CCI / Bridgeman Images

© A. Dagli Orti / De Agostini Picture Library / Bridgeman Images

The return of Habsburg Karoly in Hungary - Hungarian legitimist movement - Second revolutionary attempt of Charles IV in October 1921 - Guard of Honour welcomes Karl IV in Hungary - Charles Francois Joseph of Habsburg-Lorraine (Karl Franz Josef von Habsburg-Lothringen) Charles I of Austria, Charles IV of Hungary. Bridgeman Images

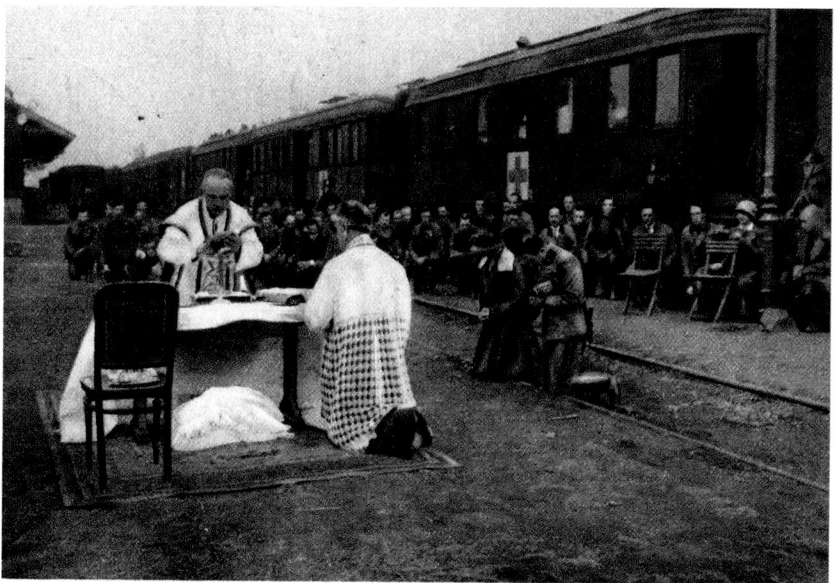

Charles I of Austria and his wife Zita kneeling in front of the altar - during the second attempt of restoration in Hungary in 1921, in prayer after having communed during their daily mass. Bridgeman Images

Former Austrian Emperor Charles 1st of Habsburg and Empress Zita leaving the church in Funchal, Madeira, 1921. © SZ Photo / Scherl / Bridgeman Images.

Karl I of Austria , by Czedekowski, B., © Arkivi UG All Rights Reserved / Bridgeman Images

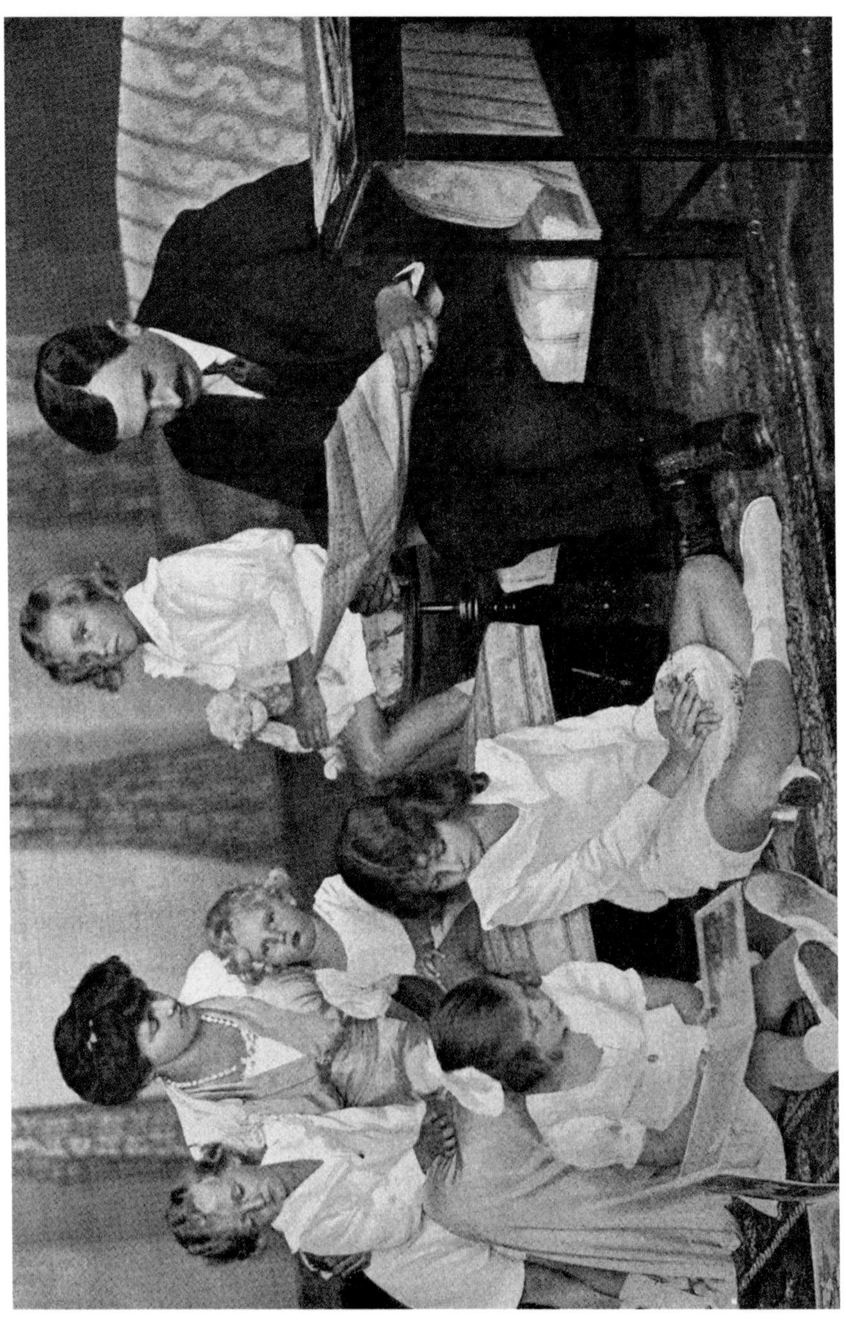

Charles I of Austria and his wife Zita and the children in Prangins castle in Switzerland, from L'Illustrazione Italiana, Year XLVIII, No 15, April 10, 1921. De Agostini Picture Library / Bridgeman Images

Emperor Charles I and his son Otto. Photo © CCI / Bridgeman Images

Ak Kaiser Otto von Habsburg, portrait, suit, son of Zita, Emperor Karl I (b/w photo).

Chapter 13

DRY MARTYRDOM

Merciful God, kind Father, our sole comfort, who wills that no one who believes and trusts in you should perish, in your boundless love look favorably on your servant, N., whom the true faith and Christian hope commend to you. Come to him (her) with your saving power, and by the suffering and death of your only-begotten Son, be pleased to grant him (her) pardon and remission of all sins. Let his (her) soul at the hour of its departure find in you a merciful judge, and cleansed of every stain in the blood of your Son, let him (her) be found worthy of passing into everlasting life; through Christ our Lord.

—Apostolic Blessing for the Dying, Roman *Rituale*

HMS *Glow-Worm* was led by the unfortunately named Captain Snagge. He asked for Charles's word of honor in writing that there would be no escape attempts made while the emperor-king was aboard ship. If he would do this, Snagge would be able to treat the couple as honored guests. Otherwise, they must be confined as prisoners. This was agreed to for as long as the ship was en route to Galati, where Charles and Zita would be transferred to another vessel. But early on, they encountered a major problem. Most of the pilots on the Danube were Croats; when they realized that the ship was taking the emperor and empress away, they refused to pilot the ship, no matter how much money the British offered. They finally found a Hungarian Serb, who made it clear he was only doing it for the pay. On November 3, they passed Belgrade and came to Moldova on the Romanian side of the river. At this point, the Danube was too shallow for the ship to proceed. After a day in which the entente leaders sent telegrams back and forth, it was decided that the pair, their companions (Count Ezterhazy and Boroviczeny), Captain Snagge, his aide, and twenty royal marines would drive to Orsova further down the Danube; there, they would take the train to Galati to make the rendezvous with the ship that would take them to their unknown destination.

Early on the morning of the fifth, they set off by car; locals were cheering them with shouts of "Long live the king! Long live the queen!" The same cheering, saluting, and dropping to knees as they passed happened all along the route during the three-hour drive, much to Captain Snagge's pleasant surprise. Detached from Hungary by the treaty, these areas were now Romanian. But the almost festive air belied that. In Orsova itself, the streets were lined with cheering crowds, so it was decided against departing from the main station, which would have attracted an enormous number—perhaps sufficient for some sort of break-out attempt. So they went instead to a smaller station just outside of town, where a fair number of people managed to catch up with them. But they boarded the train without incident and left with the cheering of their former subjects in their ears.

The train trip across Romania took about twenty hours, and the news was brought to Charles and Zita that Count Esterhazy and Baroness Boroviczeny would be replaced by Count Joseph Hunyadi and his wife at Galati. They arrived at the port at 9:10 a.m. to find the Hunyadis' awaiting them. Quick farewells were said, and the whole party boarded a Romanian steamer, the *Princess Maria*. They were served lunch, and to Charles and Zita's surprise, it tasted much like one they might have had in the palace before the war. It turned out that the chef had in fact worked at the kitchens there before 1914 and for Charles's younger brother, Archduke Max, at the front. He had done his best to console the imperial couple for their plight by making the meal as much like one they might have had before as possible.

The ship arrived at the port of Sulina by 5:30 p.m. to find the cruiser HMS *Cardiff* awaiting them. They transferred to the ship; Charles and Zita said farewell to Captain Snagge and hello to their new host, Captain Lionel Maitland-Kirwan, to whom Charles also gave a written oath that he would not try to escape. The following day, November 8, they set off for Constantinople, which, at that pre-Kemal Ataturk time, was still hosting Sultan Mehmed VI, who would not be deposed for almost another year. But there was no question of seeing their former ally; the entente controlled the city, which was occupied by British, French, and Italian troops. Anchored off the oldest part of Constantinople, Charles and Zita looked at Hagia Sophia and the other monuments and reminisced about their state visit there in May of 1918. It could not have escaped them that this city too—like Rome, St. Petersburg and Moscow, and of course,

Vienna—was a city where once the double eagle had symbolized a Christian empire. A telegram arrived from Colonel Strutt to say that the children were alright in Switzerland, which allayed a tremendous fear; with the endlessly capable Strutt on the watch, they feared little in that quarter. It was only at noon the next day that the order finally came: they were sail to Gibraltar. The empress told Captain Maitland-Kirwan that she presumed this meant they would be going to Madeira; the Captain responded that he hoped so; he had heard rumors it was to be Ascension, a South Atlantic island even more remote than Napoleon's St. Helena.

After six days, they made Gibraltar, where the governor and his lady were forbidden from meeting them, although they had wanted to do so, by London and had to content themselves with sending a lavish basket of flowers and fruit instead. The Hunyadis were also forbidden to go ashore to buy anything. Charles asked if a priest could be brought aboard to say Mass, and the Captain agreed. An English naval chaplain was brought on but had already offered Mass that day. He arranged to return the next day with everything required for Mass and duly showed up thus equipped on the following day, November 17. It was the imperial couple's first Mass in seventeen days, and they were both overjoyed. Afterwards, Hunyadi attempted to give the priest some money; he refused it, saying, "If the Emperor were still where he ought to be, I would accept it gladly; but not here." To that the count replied that it was for the poor. "That I cannot refuse. But I will tell them that it is the Emperor who sends it." Shortly afterwards, the chaplain left, and the *Cardiff* set out for Madeira.

On the nineteenth, they arrived. The captain went ashore to turn over the imperial couple to the Portuguese authorities. The mayor of Funchal came aboard with him to be presented and decided that they should wait until the heavy seas subsided for Charles and Zita to go ashore. When they made ready to leave, the ship's officers gave them champagne and said that they hoped they might soon be able to come back and take them home. When asked if they might accompany them ashore, Captain Maitland-Kirwan and the British consul were told by the mayor of Funchal that they could not—"they were no longer Britain's affair."

Despite deliberately putting out a false time, the Portuguese authorities were unable to fool their subjects, and so a large number of local citizens turned out to greet the imperial couple. They and the Hunyadis were driven to Reid's Palace Hotel—then, as now, the finest and biggest hotel on the island. The management gave them the use of the neighboring annex, the Villa Vittoria. There was an unconscious irony in all of this in that Charles's great aunt, the empress Elizabeth, had arrived at the then newly opened hotel on Christmas Eve, 1893—she would stay until the following February 6. Where Franz Josef's consort had come to Madeira to avoid the requirements of her state in life, her great nephew would be sent there for the crime of pursuing them.

In any case, there were other pressing issues, and one of them was how the imperial family was going to live. On November 16, 1921, the Ambassadors' Conference in Paris came to the conclusion that to live in Madeira would require £20,000 per annum—roughly $1.4 million in today's money. This was certainly a most generous sum, especially given that all of Charles's properties in the empire had been sequestered for their own purposes by the politicians of the new governments. But who was to pay this princely sum? The entente decided that it would be neither themselves nor the former combatants—Austria and Hungary. Instead, they would assess each of the successor states—Poland, Romania, Czechoslovakia, and Yugoslavia—£5,000 a year, which would be paid to Portugal. Nice as this arrangement would have been, it had one flaw: those four governments simply refused to pay. For their part, having acknowledged the problem, the entente powers simply refused to help.

It was actually worse than that. The Hunyadis had to return home, but the entente refused to allow other supporters, such as Count Revertera and Baron Hye, to join their master in exile. This was a two-fold problem, because not only would they be without a staff, they would thus be unable to receive any funds from such would-be helpers. Only one man already resident in Madeira, Dom Joao d'Almeida, who had served in the Austrian army, was allowed to assist the illustrious exiles. Only at Christmas would a cook, a maid, and a housekeeper be allowed to join them.

But what to do about money? On November 1, 1918, Charles had sent Leopold Count Berchtold to Switzerland with some of the family jewelry, including the famous "Florentine Diamond," the largest yellow stone of that type ever known. These were deposited in a Swiss bank in Zurich. To deal with and sell them if necessary, Charles hired a man named Bruno Steiner, an Austrian resident in Switzerland, who had been one of Franz Ferdinand's advisers and helped with the settlement of his estate. As needed, Steiner had negotiated the sale of some of these jewels, which had financed both the rentals and expenses in Switzerland and the monoplane in which Charles and Zita had flown to Hungary. Charles presumed there would be something like half the hoard left. No doubt the poor and childless Christmas and New Year's reinforced these thoughts.

Speaking of the children, not only were they still in Switzerland, but the six-year-old Archduke Robert needed an appendix operation. Charles and Zita applied to the Allies to allow Zita to go and oversee the operation, after which she would bring all the children to Madeira. The entente were fearful, lest the empress should somehow use this opportunity to overthrow either the Austrian or Hungarian governments; in the end, as long as she travelled alone under strict supervision and accepted a police presence every moment that she was in Switzerland, she could go. Whilst there, however, it was planned that she should also bring back with the children the remaining jewels.

Zita met her brother Xavier in Zurich, and he agreed to fetch the jewels, only to find that Bruno Steiner had vanished with them. Making enquires, the resourceful prince was able to track him down to a hotel in Frankfurt, where the shocked Steiner had holed up with his family. He told Xavier that if he returned at 8:00 a.m. the next morning, he would have the jewels. Even though Xavier turned up an hour early, the bird, his family, and the jewels, if any were left, had flown the coop. No sign of them or their thief has ever resurfaced since.

When Zita and the children (save Robert, who would return after his recovery) arrived at Madeira on February 2, Charles raced down the gangway to meet them, tears in his eyes. But he was already only too aware that he had no means of supporting himself, let alone them. So, on February 16, he had Dom Joao write his lawyers a letter, directing them to pursue the Ambassadors' Conference for funding, as he was out of money, and "the Ambassadors' Conference brought him here against his will and is thus under obligation to meet itself the costs of his stay."

The conference sent back a note admitting their obligation on their part and asked for an estimated annual sum necessary for his existence but then followed that with what amounted in the event to a death sentence: it required a detailed list of everything he considered to be his assets and "all payments which His Majesty considers to be owing to him from any source." The next month, the emperor told his lawyer to ask for £60,000 a year as the minimum needed. (He did so, presuming whatever figure he submitted would be cut by at least half.) Charles also instructed the man to draw up a comprehensive list of the strictly private and family properties in Austria and Bohemia. The other bit of business he attended to concerned the matter of the treasury of the Order of the Golden Fleece in Vienna. Due to the Burgundian origins of the order, there was some talk in Belgian government circles about seizing it. Charles successfully forestalled this move by writing to King Alfonso XIII of Spain as head of the other branch of the order (this division being a result of the War of Spanish Succession) to prevent this, which he did.

There was nothing more to be done except move. He could not afford to stay any longer at the villa. The problem was that Charles could not afford to move anywhere else either. Offers of alternative housing poured in, each with a prohibitive price tag. A local banker offered him free use of his summer house on the cool, steep, high hill overlooking Funchal, its name was the Quinta do Monte. Originally built by an Englishman in the 1820s, it was a wonderful respite from the summer heat, always cool and misty. This was a definite disadvantage in the winter and early spring, however! But no matter, there was no money. So before February had passed into March, the servants brought a great deal of lent furniture, linens, and much else up from the villa to the quinta.

There was no hot water, no electric light, and not enough food. The servants were volunteering and crammed into a one room cottage. Zita was expecting once more—this time a May birth, but there was no money for either prenatal care or for a midwife when the baby did come. There *were*, however, fogs, rain, and fungus growing on the damp walls. In a letter home, after enumerating in great detail the hardships involved, the maid wrote, "Their Majesties won't complain and they wouldn't even murmur if they were locked in a cellar with bread and water. . . . Sometimes we do get very low and depressed, but when we see how patiently their Majesties accept all these ills, we carry on again courageously."[1]

[1] Gordon Brook-Shepherd, *The Last Habsburg* (Weidenfeld & Nicolson Ltd., 1968), p. 327.

How long this could have gone on is anyone's guess, but it came to an end. On March 9, Charles took Otto and Adelheid on the long walk down to Funchal and back to buy some toys for Karl-Ludwig, who was turning four the next day. The emperor refused an overcoat, as it would be warm in town. So it was, but on the way back up, they entered a chilly mist, which had descended in the late afternoon, as was usual. Now, since his bout with bronchitis in Hungary, Charles's lungs were weakened; moreover, he was showing the effects of malnutrition. Perhaps, had he had decent food and housing, things might have been different, but they were what they were.

Charles caught a cold, which he could not shake; after five days, he took to his bed with fever and a bronchial cough. Initially, he refused to allow a doctor to be summoned, because of the expense. But by the twenty-first, his state had so declined that there was no choice; a doctor was called, examined him, and brought in a second. They agreed that one of his lungs was already infected and ordered him brought from the dank bedroom he had been in to a much larger airier room downstairs that would capture whatever sunlight might be available.

Despite the change of scene, pneumonia was setting in. On March 25, his coughing became almost constant, and his temperature soared to 104. Today, antibiotics would be used to kill the bug, but they did not come along until the 1940s, and this was 1922. All the doctors could throw at the infection was what mankind had always thrown at them: turpentine injections, camphor and caffeine injections, linseed and mustard plasters, and lastly, cupping the back. All of these treatments ranged from annoying to downright agonizing. Moreover, they were ineffective. What did help were the primitive oxygen bags that could provide his labored breathing seven minutes of blessed relief at a time.

During all of this torture, he never murmured or complained. Part of this was due to the constant presence of his wife. Although three of the children and most of the servants were sick by this time and she treated them, she somehow always managed to be at his side when he woke. To manage to keep the household running under these circumstances must have required an iron will; the empress had shown she had one before this sad time—she would need all of it later. During this time, Zita would try to bolster his spirits by talking with him about the future of the family and their children.

> [His] trust in the almighty goodness of Christ reached its perfection in Madeira. Charles hoped to find in the heart of his master the longed-for peace, in that heart which had always been his refuge, his trust, his absolute hope. He prayed daily the rosary and the three litanies: the Sacred Heart of Jesus, of Loretto, and of St. Joseph; also the Te Deum and Psalm 90 (91). One always heard how he called during his last illness on the Heart of Jesus. He recommended his children individually and especially to the love of the Sacred Heart. Under the head cushion of the dying man lay a picture of the Sacred Heart of Jesus, and again and

> again he kissed this picture when it was held to his lips.[2]

Much of Charles's thought during these last days turned to them, and especially Otto, his heir. What was he leaving him? Not money, that was sure, nor was he bequeathing power. All he could leave the future head of the House of Habsburg were his ideals and his example. Clutching the crucifix as he had been doing, Charles had Otto brought to him on March 27 (although he had not wanted the children near him, for fear of infection). They spent some time together. Charles told his wife the next day, "The poor boy. I would gladly have spared him that yesterday. But I had to call him to show him an example. He has to know how one conducts oneself in such situations—as a Catholic and as Emperor."

These horrific days were cushioned by the practice of his Catholic faith. When Charles was installed in the room downstairs, he was able to see and hear Mass in the next room every day, offered by Fr. Paul Zsamboki, a Hungarian priest who had become their permanent chaplain. He heard Charles's confessions, gave him Communion, and attended to his spiritual needs. Frequently, Charles would say his Rosary, praying in Latin or German.

His last few days, Charles had bouts of delirium, but in the midst of them, he would become quite clear. During the

---

2 Ildefons Maria Fux, "Der selige Karl von Österreich und seine Beziehung zum Heiligsten Herzen Jesu," January 22, 2005, https://www.stjosef.at/artikel/sel_karl_v_oesterreich_herzjesu.htm.

evening of March 31, when his imminent death had been foretold by the doctors, he declared calmly, "I declare yet again that the November Manifesto is null and void since I was forced into it. And no man can take away from me that I am the Crowned King of Hungary." But even in this terrible extremity, it was not only his rights but his duties that were paramount in his mind. During another lull, he told those around him in very calm tones, "I must suffer like this, so that my peoples can come together again."

The following morning, April 1, it was obvious that the emperor's life was ebbing away. Although he had rallied and his temperature dropped, it roared back with a vengeance. Fr. Zsamboki offered Mass and gave him Communion. Then the fever returned, and his wife held him in her arms for the last three hours of his life. At one point, Charles whispered to Zita, "Let's go home, let's go home together—we are already so near. Why won't they let us go home?" He then publicly forgave all of his enemies. Charles then turned to his wife and said she must go to King Alphonso XIII for aid; she thought that odd, since neither of them had seen the Spanish monarch in years. But he added, "He is chivalrous . . . he has promised me." He then mentioned each of their children's names, including the unborn Elizabeth, and said, "Protect their bodies and souls."

At one point, as Zita was saying one short prayer after another into his ear, he said the last words he would ever speak to her in this world, "I love you so much." Charles tried to lift the crucifix he was holding to his lips, but he was too weak, and let it down, sighing. He then said, "I can't go on," after which, "Thy will be done. . . . Yes . . . yes. . . .

As you will it . . . Jesus," and died with the holy name on his lips. Nine-year-old Otto had already been called in. He later recalled, "I began the death prayers. . . . At the moment of death, April 1, 1922 at noon, 12:23 minutes, the sun broke through completely. I prayed in the deep silence of the dying room: an Our Father, into which the others gradually joined." So passed from this earth, Charles I, Emperor of Austria; Charles IV, Apostolic King of Hungary; and Charles III, King of Bohemia.

It was noticed by onlookers after Charles was laid in his coffin that the face of the dead emperor appeared to be getting younger and younger. News of the death of the "holy emperor" spread quickly through Funchal. The evening of his death, he was embalmed and laid out in uniform. One onlooker recalled, "There were streams of people passing by the coffin. The people touched the corpse with their rosaries, with little pictures. Many have kissed the corpse. The funeral of the [emperor] was also attended by many people." There were several thousand present at the funeral which took place on April 4, 1922 in the presence of the bishop of Funchal. The body was then entombed in the side chapel of the church of Nossa Senhora do Monte.

The people of Funchal had grown to sincerely love the man they were already calling "their saint." Such sincerity was perhaps not universal among the mourners in his former realms. At Budapest, the requiem for the dead king in the Matthias Church, where Charles had been crowned with such pomp, took place on the same day in April. According to the papal nuncio to Budapest, Lorenzo Schioppa, "The funeral ceremony was . . . imposing, solemn and sad as never before. All have grasped the tragic fate of the unfortunate ruler. . . . Carlists and anti-Carlists stood around the imposing catafalque, . . . on which lay the four royal crowns: those of the Emperor, the King of Hungary, the King of Bohemia and those of the House of Habsburg. There were also two white flower crowns, one from Governor Horthy and one from the Government."

Horthy, who had already proven himself a master of the empty gesture, truly exceeded himself on this day. On the throne he sat as regent, representative of a king whom he claimed to have deposed! Around the bier, officers and soldiers of the same army who had fought their king; a dense group of legitimists, including Andrássy, Rakovszky, Gratz, who yesterday had been arrested for high treason and would possibly be sentenced to prison tomorrow for participating in the abortive restoration of the king. On the left, Bethlen, Bánffy, and the whole government, which had approved in November the deposition law of the Habsburgs.

The primate, who had secretly legitimated Horthy on the day of the king's deposition, now boasted of the steadfastness and divine trust of the pious king, the model who had faithfully endured all fateful blows. "He lived briefly, but fulfilled much in his time. . . . Although the bitterness of human life overwhelmed him, he died peacefully and left us so that we wished to have him back, and even time cannot extinguish this desire. *Vale pia anima Martyr Regni et Coronae Sancti Stephani, vive aeternum in pace Christi*."

Fewer crocodile tears and more sincerity was to be found in Prague. On the same day there, the former adjutant general of the emperor, Prince Zdenko Lobkowitz,, had a Low Mass offered at St. Kajetan. "It was quite well attended. That's all that could happen to the deceased King of Bohemia!"

At Vienna, Cardinal Piffl celebrated the funeral as a private service on April 6, 1921 in St. Stephen's Cathedral with Mozart's "Requiem." Among the mourners were Chancellor Schober (Renner's government had fallen in 1920, but he was still looking for opportunity), four ministers, the president of the National Council, Richard Weiskirchner, and Christian Social National and Federal councilors.

> From the middle of the crowd, which surrounded the cathedral, after the end of the service, the receiving of God, the old, solemn manner, which for generations had been the expression of Austrian patriotism and loyalty, was celebrated. Now she struck again, a torrent of enthusiasm, from the heart of the Imperial city. I [Friedrich Funder] witnessed the scene that suddenly brought the traffic of the city center to a standstill. Many people cried. In the song voices mingled from the windows of the high houses, it was a waving and greetings as with a loving farewell. Once more the face of Vienna had been revealed.
>
> There was no memorial service in the National Council.

On April 8, at 10:00 a.m. in the Vienna Deutschordenskirche, the Knights of the Order of the Golden Fleece held their requiem for the deceased sovereign, their grand master.

Chapter 14

THE LONG WATCH

Comfort, O Lord, this your handmaid who is bound by the sorrows of her widowhood, as you undertook through the prophet Elijah to comfort the widow Zarepheth. Grant her the fruit of chastity, that she may not remember the fleshly pleasures of the past. May she not even know the stirrings of lust, so that she may accept the yoke of belonging only to you and that through these great trials she can more fully bring forth the seed sixtyfold, an acceptable gift of devotion. Through Jesus Christ.

—"Prayer for the Blessing of Widows,"
Gelasian Sacramentary

It might well be argued that Charles was killed by the neglect of the entente, the pettiness of the successor states, and the treason of Renner and Horthy. But Zita had no time for recriminations. In the immediate, she was penniless, pregnant, and had seven children and a small staff to feed. Beyond those short-term challenges, she had the future and education of the heir to the throne to arrange for, and the preservation for him and his, perhaps, future peoples of the legacy of the House of Habsburg. The day her husband was entombed, it must have seemed impossible. But Zita had endless faith in God and an implacable sense of duty. The Archduke Otto remembered that he never saw his mother in any color but black after his father died.

Rather than wait for the entente to cease their endless dithering in Paris, she followed her husband's dying instructions and contacted King Alfonso XIII. He in turn, in a public letter to Pope Benedict XV, appealed to the pontiff to join him in an appeal to the rulers of Europe for aid in solving the empress's predicament. The British government, despite having essentially dumped the family there in Madeira, refused to lift a finger. But on April 20, King George V's secretary sent a letter to the Foreign Office of one line: "The King asks whether any progress has been made in Paris about the arrangements for the ex-Empress Zita." The response was that the Foreign Office had replied to the king of Spain that if Zita promised not to work for a restoration, he should offer her asylum; that is to say, if she gave no such pledge, she and the family should stay where they were—and presumably starve.

Enraged by this, the Spanish king told the Ambassadors' Conference in Paris on May 17 that he would be taking the family away from Funchal regardless of their approval or not. At that, they gave in; a week later, the *Infanta Isabel* arrived at the island and the Habsburgs embarked. A few days later, they arrived in Cadiz and took the train to Madrid, where Alfonso awaited them at the station. The king made them welcome, giving them the palace of El Pardo, northwest of the city. A beautiful place, originally built by Emperor Charles V, it became the birthplace on May 31, 1922, of the

Archduchess Elizabeth, whose name had been chosen by her father.

Apparently, the king had an odd experience when he heard the news about Charles's terminal illness:

> King Alfonso related to her, how in the night before the death of the Emperor Charles, he was overcome with a feeling that, in the event of the Emperor's death, if he, the King, would not take his widow and the children under his protection, his own wife and his own children would suffer one day the same fate. He only found peace, after he had firmly resolved to give the bereaved family a home in Spain, as the death of the Emperor seemed to be certain. King Alfonso was not less overcome than the Empress Zita, when she then told him what the Emperor Charles had said before his death.[1]

The family's hosts had problems of their own. Alfonso's mother, Queen Maria Christina, had herself been born a Habsburg archduchess. The last king, her husband, had also died when she was pregnant, so she understood Zita's predicament completely. She had been regent then and when her son was born, so she had remained after her son's birth in 1882, and remained so until his twentieth birthday. Moreover, the queen had had to try to steer her country through the war waged against Spain by the United States in 1898; that debacle had cost the country its last major

---

1 Joanna and James Bogle, *A Heart for Europe: The Lives of Emperor Charles and Empress Zita of Austria-Hungary* (Gracewing Publishing, 2000), pp. 150–51.

colonies—Cuba, Puerto Rico, the Philippines, and Guam. She served as a wise councilor to her son.

But the atmosphere at the court in Madrid was not a happy one. Alfonso's queen, Victoria Eugenia was a granddaughter of Queen Victoria (and named after her and her other godmother, Empress Eugenie, widow of Napoleon III). From her grandmother—as with her cousin, the Tsarina of Russia—she passed on to two of her five sons the gene for hemophilia. Although theirs had been a love match, with the ardent Spanish prince pursuing her, this ruined Alfonso's affection for her—he was no Nicholas II in this regard. In addition, Communist agitation was rising in the cities and the Spanish army was being mauled by Arab rebels in Morocco. Zita needed a refuge of quiet in which to raise her children and keep in touch with events in Central Europe. It would need to be a more affordable and cooler place than Madrid. The Austrian ambassador in Madrid suggested the Villa Uribarren, in Lequeitio on the Bay of Biscay, in the Basque country. As it happened, Alfonso XIII's grandmother had stayed there; it was in a beautiful location, and the pilgrimage routes that took many Central Europeans to Compostela, Limpias, and elsewhere went right by it. Despite their hosts' requesting that they stay in El Pardo (which would one day be Francisco Franco's residence as chief of the Spanish state), Zita's mind was made up. On August 18, 1922, the imperial family moved on.

With the help of the abbot of Pannonhalma in Hungary, the empress assembled a stellar cast of teachers for her offspring. Zita's day began at 5:00 a.m. She went to Mass at the Basilica of Lequeitio a half hour later and returned to join the children. Their day began at 6:30, winter and summer. At seven, the family attended Mass together (it being Zita's second); then, breakfast and a horse ride; and then classes until dusk, alternated with breaks and lunch. Otto and his brothers mixed with the locals of their age, so they picked up some Basque. At home, to improve their languages, they used a different one each day: German on Mondays, Hungarian on Tuesday, French on Wednesday, and so on. Their education was comprehensive and Catholic to the core.

The local area had always been a center of Carlist sentiment, so the inhabitants felt honored at the presence of their illustrious guests, who mixed quite naturally among them. From time to time, they asked the empress to forward their requests to the king; the most remembered in the area was their successful bid to keep the local nautical school open. From time to time, the king, queen, and/or the queen mother would come to see them. And so it was that the next six years passed happily for Zita and her children.

But things in Spain were deteriorating; the queen mother had a heart-to-heart chat with her in which she revealed that the monarchy in Spain would end six months after her death (in the event, it took twenty-two). This was not the only sign, however, that it was getting time to move on. Otto was coming of age and needed to go to university; the same would soon be the case for the others in succession. Moreover, Zita wanted to move the clan closer to Central Europe and the center of things in general. Various considerations eliminated most European countries as another home in exile—even Luxembourg, where her brother Felix had married the reigning grand duchess. Belgium, at the crossroads of Europe, seemed the best possibility, and it had the University of Louvain, at the time one of the best in Catholic Europe. Her brothers Sixtus and Xavier—who, as you shall remember, had served alongside King Albert during the war—made the arrangements. King Alfonso XIII sadly authorized their departure; he and his family, whatever their own problems, had become quite fond of their cousins. In September of 1929, they left for Belgium.

After a bit of house hunting, in January of 1930, the family settled at Ham Castle in the Flemish town of Steenokkerzeel. It was close to Brussels and Louvain, and while Otto went to the university, his siblings would continue the intensive program of education their mother had developed with her panel of experts. In the decade they would live here, Zita, too, was able to live a bit more freely, taking part in local cultural and church events. Due to Belgium's location at the crossroads of Europe, friends, family, and supporters of all kinds were able to drop by.

On November 20, 1930, a very important occasion took place. It was the Archduke Otto's eighteenth birthday, and coming of age. Legally, Zita's regency over the "invisible monarchy" came to an end; although practically speaking, it would continue another four years, when Otto would have finished the law studies he was just beginning. Guests had come from Austria and Hungary, and Bishop Seydl—the court bishop who had said Mass for the family in their days of glory in Eckartsau and in exile in Switzerland—offered Mass that morning in the castle chapel. Following the Mass, there was a ceremony in the grand salon of the castle, wherein the empress declared that, in keeping with the wishes of Charles, her son had become "in his own right, sovereign and head of their reigning house." She then bowed to her son and signed a written proclamation. This was then signed by Otto's next oldest brother, Robert; his Uncle Max, Charles's younger brother; his grandmother Archduchess Maria Josefa; and various other figures from Austria and Hungary.

Zita was as convinced of the possibility of restoration as she had ever been. The Depression had hit the uneasy republics of Central Europe hard. Communists on the one hand and Brown- and Blackshirts on the other were a hammer and anvil between which sane people would surely look for sanity. All the parliamentary republics could offer was growing feebleness and indecision, as party politicians showed themselves incapable of dealing with the crisis. So the empress began a series of tours to meet with various figures in hopes of easing her son's way forward: in 1931, she visited both Pope Pius XI and King Victor Emmanuel III and Queen Elena of Italy. At that time, Mussolini attempted to set up a marriage between the Italian royals' youngest daughter, Maria, and Otto. This went nowhere, although the then sixteen-year-old girl did marry Zita's brother, Prince Louis of Bourbon-Parma.

Meanwhile, events in Austria became increasingly interesting from a monarchist perspective. As in many European countries, the postwar political instability had inspired the major political parties to arm paramilitary organizations—this was true of Christian Socials, Socialists, and Pan-Germans alike. The Christian Socials, while historically pro-Habsburg (and still harboring a monarchist minority when Otto came of age) were committed to the republic. But while the priest-chancellor, Msgr. Seipel, had brought stability to the republic, Karl Renner's Socialists became ever more militant, as did the government and its supporters in response. Seipel resigned over the violence in 1929, being replaced by Ernst Streeruwitz. In quick succession a few more governments followed, and as the Depression kicked in, politics got even worse; in 1931, the Credit-Anstalt Bank collapsed. Then, in 1932, Engelbert Dollfuss took over the unpleasant job. Then, Adolf Hitler became the ruler of Germany, and there was no question what he had in mind for Austria. In May of 1933, Karl Renner, who was the president of the lower house of parliament as head of the largest faction, resigned so he could vote on a bill; the two vice-presidents, leaders respectively of the Christian Social and Pan-German parties, resigned to do the same. This meant, effectively, that Parliament could not function because there was now no one who could legally preside over its meetings.

Dollfuss could have called for new elections. But he feared that the Nazis would win about 25 percent of the votes; *Time* magazine analysts at the time thought it would be more like 50 percent, and Communist influence and militancy was spreading. So like Franz Josef before him, Dollfuss chose to shut down Parliament and rule by decree. He banned the Communists on May 26, 1933 and the Nazis on June 19. He then vowed to replace the failed "democratic state with something new."

In the complex of failed states that was Depression-era Europe, Dollfuss's plan for economic and social regeneration was not particularly unusual—even the United States was attempting something similar with the New Deal. What made Dollfuss's corporate state different from many was his attempt to base it on Catholic principles as enunciated in *Rerum Novarum* and *Quadragesimo Anno*. In their hatred of his principles, academics have dubbed his regime "Austrofascist" in order to pre-provide it with opprobrium, which would be a bit like dubbing Franklin Roosevelt's economic program "Americofascism"—intentionally biased and inaccurate. In any case, Otto had established contact with Dollfuss, who apparently became interested in restoring the Habsburgs as a way of further bolstering Austrian independence. But he was murdered by the Nazis on July 25, 1934, before he could anything much about it.

The following year, Otto's schooling finished, and he assumed effective control of Habsburg policy. Dollfuss's successor, Kurt Schussnigg, began to dismantle the Habsburg Law; initially, their private property was released to them so that, once again, there was a decent income. But the unhappy push toward the Anschluss on March 12, 1938 drowned all progress, although it did give Karl Renner the opportunity to betray his country a second time by ordering the Socialists to vote for the Nazi takeover. For Otto's role in resisting all of this, we shall wait for the next chapter.

Zita, in the meantime, had a personal fright: her children Adelheid and Felix were in Vienna when the Nazis took over. Fortunately, a friend furnished a car, and they were able to drive to Hungary. From there, they were able to get back to Belgium. Felix moved to Washington in 1939 and began to push for Austria's cause with various American government figures. Archduke Robert moved to London to represent his oldest brother before the British government. Then came September of 1939 and the outbreak of World War II.

On May 9, 1940, the Empress Zita's fortieth birthday, a family party had been organized for her. Otto was in Paris, Robert in London, and Felix in America, but the remaining five were there, alongside four of their cousins—the prince and princesses of Luxembourg, the children of Zita's brother, Felix of Bourbon-Parma. On that afternoon, that Felix and his wife, Grand Duchess Charlotte, had also come over. There was a great deal of tension; since the outbreak of the war, all of the family's private documents had been sent to her brother Xavier's Chateau de Bostz, near Moulins in the Province of Auvergne. This would serve as the Habsburg refuge if the Germans overran Belgium. The empress had already set plans in order, should it be necessary.

That evening, King Leopold III called from Brussels to say that an attack was imminent; at 1:00 a.m., Prince Felix called to say the Germans had crossed the border into Luxembourg. It was time to go. The packing of five cars—four for the Habsburgs and their staff and one for the Luxembourg children—proceeded apace. At 4:30 a.m., aircraft flew overhead, dropping bombs nearby. The five cars finally set out at nine and drove west, on a route intended to bypass Brussels and onto the coast, then southwards into France. Refugees were everywhere, bombs were being dropped, and they could only suppose St. Christopher himself was guarding them. They made it over the French border and spent the night near Dunkirk. The next morning, they drove on to the Chateau de Fourdrain, near Laon, where their friend, Baron Coppee, put them up for a few days while the imperial party evaluated their situation. While they were there, Belgium capitulated, and the front moved ever south; so must they.

The party drove on to the Chateau de Bostz and Prince Xavier. Deep in the heart of France, they all thought they would be safe, but it was illusory. As the front pushed southward, the American ambassador suggested they send their secret papers and anything else of importance on the last American ship due to sail from Bordeaux. That task done, Archduke Robert returned to the chateau, as did Otto, having left Paris.

They then drove south of Bordeaux, as the news came that Paris had been surrendered. They stopped at the Chateau de Bergerac south of the city to pick up the Luxembourgs, who were reunited with their children. The whole band (which kept getting larger as friends, acquaintances, or just Austrian refugees joined them) set off. The plan was to get to Lisbon and apply for American visas. But first they had to cross the Spanish border.

When the caravan arrived there on June 18, it was accompanied by at least a hundred or more refugees. The Archdukes Otto and Karl Ludwig went up to the border to see if they could somehow talk the mob's way in. As it turned out, the officer in charge at that crossing had been the Colonel of the Civil Guard in Lequeitio when they arrived there; he let the entire mob in. It was now clear sailing all the way to Lisbon.

Staying with a friend near Lisbon, the family waited until mid-July for the visas and then flew the Transatlantic Clipper to New York, while their servants and staff came on by ship. Finally, the clan settled in a large house lent to them in Royalston, Massachusetts, for the rest of the summer. Zita still had four children to educate: two boys and a girl for university and young Elizabeth needed a high school. But where to find such an education in a setting that would be sufficiently Catholic? Fortunately, Professor Charles De Konick, formerly teaching at Louvain University, was now in charge of Philosophy at Laval University in Quebec and was completely familiar with the programs the imperial students had been studying at Louvain. Zita felt this to be an answer to her daily prayers. They would move to Quebec.

Quebec in those days was perhaps the most Catholic city in North America—and in many ways, the most European. By October 20, the family, at least the empress and the four who would be going to school there, were in place. The following day, the archbishop, Cardinal Villeneuve, officially welcomed the empress of Austria and queen of Hungary to the city at a reception. The family settled in a home—the Villa Saint Joseph—in the suburb of Sillery. With a staff of three, Zita looked after her children for the rest of their college years.

In 1942, the three oldest graduated from Laval and went to join their brother in New York. Zita continued her daily Masses and devotions, raised money for refugees, and lobbied—sometimes visiting—American and other Allied government officials about her favorite political causes: to save Austria and the rest of the monarchy from Stalin; to restore the dynasty; to get South Tyrol and Trieste restored to Austria from Italy; and to counter the proposals of Czechoslovak prime minister in exile, Eduard Benes, who wanted national minorities exchanged between his country and Austria—he was the originator of the catchy slogan "Better Hitler than Habsburg." In September of 1945, she saw Franklin Roosevelt at Hyde Park and got from him a promise to save Hungary from Stalin, a promise forgotten at Yalta.

Her sons and daughters scattered around Europe and America—first fighting Hitler and then trying to forestall Stalin—the empress threw herself even more into the sort of charitable and religious endeavors she loved, and supported her children's activities to her best ability. When the war ended at last, Zita stayed in Quebec, while her sons tried to help Austria, as we shall see in the next chapter. But when they were unable to do much more, Rudolf and Karl Ludwig and some of the others returned to New York; their friend Calvin Bullock, who had owned the house in Royalston, procured one for their mother in the gated suburb of Tuxedo Park; she moved into it in 1950. From this town, which she loved, Zita could easily travel into New York, visit her children, shop, and do other chores. On one occasion, she stopped by her favorite cleaners to pick up some laundry. There she ran into the then famed Hungarian writer George Molnar, who had complained to the manager that he had to pick up his laundry and wanted to know why it could not be delivered. The manager retorted, "If the Empress of Austria can come and personally pick up her own laundry, why can't you?"

Starting with the marriage of one of her daughters in 1949, the empress found herself returning to Europe regularly as her children found spouses—Otto in 1951. But she moved back to Europe only in 1954, because of her mother's failing health. She lived with and looked after her mother at the castle of Colmar-Berg in Luxembourg until her death in 1959. Three years later, the empress moved into an old age home for religious, the Johannes Stift in Zizers, Switzerland. For the rest of her long life, she lived with the religious there. Now and then, she would visit the Benedictine nuns at Solesmes, France, where three of her sisters were nuns. She spent one month there annually—Zita took her status as a Benedictine oblate very seriously.

In 1982, the Austrian government lifted the requirement for her to renounce the throne, which she never had, and never would, if she wanted to enter the country. After a few short visits, on November 13, 1982, she assisted at a Mass offered at St. Stephen's Cathedral by the archbishop of Vienna. Ten thousand people attended; at the end, a band played the old imperial anthem. It was a long-delayed personal triumph.

The next few years saw an endless round of visits back and forth with family and friends. The empress's sight began to fail, but her mind did not, and she kept up her interest in world affairs. Nevertheless, the winter of 1988–89 was very hard on her, and Zita ceased to leave her apartments. After the new year, she called each of her seven surviving children to her and warned them, "I shall soon depart from this earth." In early March, she fell into a coma from which she would never awake. Zita of Bourbon Parma, Empress of Austria, Apostolic Queen of Hungary, Queen of Bohemia, and etc., passed away on March 14, 1989.

Her body was taken to the Abbey of Muri in Switzerland; there, Charles's heart had already been inurned in keeping with Habsburg custom in the dark days when there was little likelihood of any of the family ever being entombed at Vienna's Kaisergruft. Her heart was placed next to his. On March 27, her body was brought to the Marble Hall of the Augustinian monastery at Klosterneuburg to lie in state for two days. Thousands of people came to pay their respects, including those from inside the Iron Curtain (still extant at the time). On the third day, her body was brought to St. Stephen's Cathedral and placed in front of the altar. Again, tens of thousands paid their respects.

On April 1, Old Vienna saw something she had not seen since that cold day in 1916 when Franz Josef was laid to rest among his fathers: an imperial funeral, with the Habsburg mourning coach, soldiers in imperial uniforms, and the threefold banging on the door of the Capuchin church. As at Klosterneuburg, many of the mourners came from the many provinces they had ruled that were now trapped under Communist rule. That very year, the Communist empire began to collapse. But the long watch of the empress was over; it is to be hoped that she has at last rejoined the great love of her life.

So what are we to make of this imperial couple, in a worldly sense? Brooke-Shepherd's opinion is useful:

> The "weakness" of Charles was rather a gentleness of personality than a softness of character. For most people who knew the Emperor and Empress well, it was Zita, with her vivacity and her striking looks, who made the greater immediate impact. Even an English outsider like Colonel Strutt, who became equally devoted to them both, had the same reaction on meeting them at

> Eckartsau for the first time. The Emperor struck him as being good and kind and brave, but without any more remarkable qualities. Of the Empress he wrote: "As I entered the room I realized that she must always share with the Queens of the Belgians and Romania the honor of being one of the three great royal women of the war."
>
> Yet personality is linked with character only as a flower is to its roots. The two are not identical, and some gentle-looking blossoms can be deceptively well-embedded in their native soil. So it was with Charles. For if by strength of character is meant sticking to the basic aims of one's life through thick and thin; holding on to one's beliefs, however unpopular; and pursuing one's ideals, however elusive, with a dedication that nobody and nothing could ever alter, then this last of the Habsburg Emperors was no shaky figure but a solid one. His brief reign can serve in this respect as his own apologia.[2]

As the world sees these things, the emperor's brief life was a tragedy; his empress's long wait, an exercise in illusion. But the truth is that, devoted to their Faith, their peoples, their children, and each other, they saw far more clearly than those whom fortune or Providence gave more power to—more than Wilson, the kaiser's generals, Clemenceau, or Lloyd George. The pettiness of the Czernins, the Renners, and the

2 Gordon Brook-Shepherd, *The Last Habsburg* (Weidenfeld & Nicolson Ltd., 1968), pp. 315–16.

Horthys that lined their path merely serve, a century on, to underline their true greatness. Intertwined with that element, and integral to it, was their pursuit of holiness. Thus, they may be said to have left three legacies for us behind them: personal, in the sense of the work their descendants have done and are doing in pursuit of the ideals the imperial couple cherished; religious, that is the growth of their cultus since Charles's beatification and the introduction of Zita's cause; and political. We shall now look at each in turn.

Book Three

THE LEGACY

Chapter 15

UNCROWNED EMPEROR

Here and there the symbolic links with the archetypal structures of the unconscious still remain and give a measure of psychological sustenance to humanity. The Queens and Kings of England still stand as archetypal symbols of the soul of their people, their crowned and anointed heads bearing not merely earthly diadems, but the effulgence of a transcendental glory from beyond this world. The Tenno reigns in austere splendor in his vast palace in Tokyo, and as the representative of the Kami deities, performs annual sacrifices and blessings for the fertility and prosperity of the islands of Dai Nippon. But in most portions of the globe, the gods have died, and with them have passed the Kings, the earthly representatives of archetypal splendor. The old Tao has departed. As in the China of Confucius, warlords and usurpers march over the countryside and strut in palaces. The earthly city and the city of God have lost their linkage, and humanity vainly builds towers of Babel to reach heaven once more.[1]

—Stephan A. Hoeller

1 Stephan A. Hoeller, *Freedom: Alchemy for a Voluntary Society*, p. 134.

Hitler hated the Habsburgs; indeed, he was typical of those who did in the past or do so today. Why should they have inherited their rule over their empire when a man of genius like himself had literally to pander to lesser men for their votes or crawl over their bodies to attain power? How could they treat their non-German subjects, and even Jews, as though they were equals? (Substitute any of the other ethnic groups in the empire for "German" and you'll have a complaint shared by many.) They were representatives of an outdated past that held men back by denying their nature! In his way, as John Lukacs points out in the *The Hitler of History*, Hitler was, save for his obsession with the Jews, typical of twentieth-century modernist politicians. An avid secularist, he favored Christianity's—and especially Catholicism's—expulsion from the public square. Hitler was a vegetarian, anti-smoking, pro-animal rights, pro-homosexual (when he found them useful—expendable when they were not), pro-contraception and abortion (at least for some, hence his fondness for Planned Parenthood), and was for "Yule" rather than Christmas (as so many today prefer "Holiday"). He was poorly educated and resented and mistrusted those whom he feared might be better informed than he. As with so many of his breed of politician down to our own time, Hitler was fiercely egalitarian when confronted with anyone who might come of a higher social stratum to himself, and just as fiercely authoritarian with everyone else. His body-count was certainly impressive, though far less than Stalin's; it absolutely pales in comparison to Mao Zedong's. As an aside, this writer can remember when it was considered almost cute for young people to be carrying and quoting from Mao's *Little Red Book*. It ought to have caused as much disgust as the same people toting *Mein Kampf* would rightly do.

This little digression was necessary because it is important to understand that Hitler represented all that the young Archduke Otto despised—even as he and his did for Hitler. Realizing this basic enmity is key to comprehending how Otto attempted to apply the political, cultural, and religious legacy Charles and Zita had left him. His father, as heir to the imperial idea—not merely Austro-Hungarian, but in a very real sense, Holy Roman—was a symbol of how many nations could flourish equally under their own laws and customs without dominating one another or being dominated but united under a shared allegiance to altar and throne. If anything, this was reinforced by his mother's descent from princes who had fought for the traditional constitutions of France, Spain, Portugal, and the Italian States: the rights of Church and local provinces enshrined under the protection of an effective monarch. All of this was simply reinforced by the extraordinarily deep education Otto had received.

The attempt to apply those principles to whatever stage and in whatever manner he could in the changing situations the archduke found himself in throughout his long life is key to understanding both him and his parents. Commentators have often seen Otto's attempts to fulfill his imperial vocation and his commitment to Pan-European and other political causes as separate things: they were not. Both were expressions of his lifelong quest to fulfill, without any power to command, the legacy bequeathed him by his parents.

That legacy very naturally led to the first fight of his political career: the struggle to preserve Austria against Hitler.

As we saw, the archduke came of age on his birthday in 1930; his adherents in Austria hailed him as emperor, and in Hungary as king. There was even a version of the old imperial anthem composed to commemorate him. The tune, composed by Josef Haydn as an anthem for Franz II (I) is famous, and has served since for everything from *Tantum Ergo* to *Deutschland, Deutschland über Alles*. But it was intended as the imperial anthem, and its words were altered to fit successive emperors; the version sung by the time Charles came to the throne was generic. After his death, young Otto's supporters composed a new version for the exiled heir:

In Verbannung, fern den Landen
Weilst Du, Hoffnung Österreichs.
Otto, treu in festen Banden
Steh'n zu Dir wir felsengleich.
Dir, mein Kaiser, sei beschieden
Alter Ruhm und neues Glück!
Bring den Völkern endlich Frieden,
Kehr zur Heimat bald zurück!

"In exile, far from the land
You are, hope of Austria.
Otto, loyal in solid ties
We stand by you like a rock.
To you, my Emperor, be granted
old glory and new happiness!

Bring the peoples peace,
return home soon!"

It is important to remember that the rise of Adolph Hitler to power—like that of Lenin, Mussolini, Franco, Salazar, Horthy, Mannerheim, Roosevelt, or even Renner (and I am certainly not equating these figures morally or ideologically!)—was born out of desperation, a desperation difficult for most of us from North America, Western Europe, or Australasia today to understand. It came in waves in different places: the first was the end of World War I and its aftermath of civil wars and influenza; outside the Soviet Union, things then settled down, until the Great Depression. There were economic hardships (not merely lack of work, but often enough the threat of actual starvation), a sheer lack of confidence brought about by the collapse or weakening of traditional institutions (and the breakup of traditional morality as a by-product thereof), and a political divisiveness between extremes created by the ficklessness or seeming apathy of conventional politicians. In such an atmosphere, a whole universe of nostra were conceived by thinkers of greater or lesser merits: technocracy, social credit, distributism, solidarism, corporatism, guild socialism, agrarianism, and on and on. But more compelling still was the charismatic leader who radiated confidence: he would somehow set things to rights: the hungry would be fed and the jobless employed, traditions would be fulfilled and transmuted into a glorious future, and the real problems of society at last addressed by someone who claimed to know the answers to them. Often enough, those answers included certain knowledge of the villains responsible for putting us into this mess, be it national minorities, neighboring countries, Jews, Freemasons, or the "economic royalists" of Franklin Roosevelt's imagination. To such a personage, the struggling man who had feared what the future would bring for so long would give all power under heaven in return for hope. Sometimes, as with Roosevelt or Salazar, the results might be fairly benign; sometimes, as with Lenin, they were not. For the sake of his peoples and all Europe, Otto needed to find out just who Hitler was.

Thus it was that the archduke enrolled in the winter of 1932 at Professor Max Sering's Agrarian Institute. Sering was not only a renowned agricultural expert; he was a member of the Prussian Landtag for the Catholic Centre Party. He and one of his colleagues in both the party and the legislature, Franz Count von Galen (brother of Blessed Clemens von Galen, "the Lion of Munster") arranged for Otto to meet a number of important people, including Heinrich Bruening, who had been Centre Party chancellor of Germany until the previous May. Otto had already read *Mein Kampf* from cover to cover. What he saw in Berlin during his time there simply confirmed what he thought. As he told *Die Presse* in a 2007 interview, "I also used the two months I spent in Berlin to keep going to the Reichstag, talking to people, making contacts. I participated in German politics. That, of course, Hitler also played a role in this was clear. If you came to Berlin at the time, you could not pass him by. What people cannot imagine today is this indescribable misery."

But Hitler was also aware that the Habsburg heir was in town. The future führer had dangled in front of the

Hohenzollerns the prospect of restoration in return for supporting him. Off in the Netherlands, the exiled kaiser was skeptical; his fourth son, August Wilhelm bought the Nazi line completely. The kaiser's oldest son, Crown Prince Wilhelm, was more hopeful than his father, but Wilhelm's son, Louis Ferdinand, completely rejected the Nazis. So it was that when Otto had lunch with the crown prince, August Wilhelm invited him to his own house for a private chat and received him in his Nazi uniform; there he conveyed Hitler's invitation. Otto simply said that he was there to study and not to have political conversations, which, of course, was not true. Nevertheless, he repeated the same lie to Goering when the latter conveyed a second invitation. Otto was convinced that Hitler wanted to use him as he hoped to use the Hohenzollerns, and he was not interested. Nevertheless, as he said in the cited interview, "In itself, I would have been interested in meeting Hitler. I have never refused an interesting conversation. That was the only time."

Just before leaving Berlin in January of 1933, the archduke met with Field Marshal Paul von Hindenburg, president of the Republic and, due to his intransigence during the war, in a sense author of both Germany's and Austria-Hungary's downfall. The president received the archduke in an Austrian officer's uniform, wearing only the decorations given him by either Franz Josef or Charles. Their conversation avoided current politics and focused on Hindenburg's exploits as a young officer in the Franco-Prussian War of 1870–1871. Otto reckoned that he must have been the last non-Nazi to be received by Hindenburg. The night he left to return to his regular studies at Louvain was January 30, the day Hitler became chancellor. The path home meant taking a train through Czechoslovakia, then back through Germany: "I was again on German soil immediately after the election victories of the Nazis but only to pass through Bavaria, going from Lindau to Munich. I had first been to Mittenwald just inside Germany where I held meetings with leading Austrian Monarchists and, during the two days I was there, I witnessed how the local Nazis took over power in the municipality."[2]

He would come a little closer to tasting Hitler's methods the following day when he stayed at a house of his paternal grandmother's in the village of Gaisl-Gastieg on the border.

> On the very evening of my arrival, a gentleman from Hitler's Gestapo came to call on us. He was a Croat who had become a German citizen and risen to high rank in the police. He came to warn me to leave at once because that same afternoon the Nazis had stormed the editorial offices of a German newspaper, *Der Gerade Weg*. It was a weekly, and ferociously anti-Nazi. I had been on very friendly relations with its editor who had just been murdered. The Croat told us that the Nazis, having seized all the editor's correspondence, would have learnt of the relationship and might well come for me. I left by the next train for Belgium and did not see Nazi Germany again until after its defeat in 1945.[3]

---

2 Gordon Brook-Shepherd, *Uncrowned Emperor: The Life and Times of Otto von Habsburg* (Bloomsbury, 2007), p. 81.

3 Ibid.

What reading Hitler's book had taught Otto was that once Germany was secured, he would come for Austria. In the very beginning of *Mein Kampf*, Hitler had written, "German Austria must return to the great German motherland. . . . One blood demands one Reich." Charles had helped defend Austrian independence against an Anschluss when the German government was relatively benign; now it became an imperative. But how? The little court at Ham had little influence and no power. The first thing to do would be to get into contact with the vehemently anti-Nazi Engelbert Dollfuss, whom we met in the last chapter. Asked in the cited interview if he had ever met Dollfuss—who, thanks to decades of socialist imprecations, remains a controversial figure in modern Austria—the archduke replied:

> No, I was supposed to have a meeting with him, but it was already too late (Federal Chancellor Dollfuss was murdered by the Nazis on July 25, 1934). But I have been very much in contact with him. Politically, we were probably more of the same opinion than with Schuschnigg. I have infinite respect for Dollfuss. The man was brave, ready to fight for Austria until the last consequence. At that time I saw everything from this perspective: we have to save Austria.
>
> And did you have no problem with Dollfuss dissolving parliament, banning parties and unions?
>
> None at all. When it comes to the good of the country, I'm ready for anything.

Dollfuss's murder and the attempted Nazi takeover was immediately responded to by Mussolini, who rushed Italian troops to the Brenner Pass, ready to invade if Germany should attempt to annex Austria. At that time, the wartime entente of Great Britain, France, and Italy was still intact; moreover, Dollfuss and Mussolini were friendly—*il Duce* saw this murder as a personal affront. He had signed, four months before Dollfuss was murdered, the "Rome Protocols" with the Austrian chancellor and Horthy of Hungary, forging a military alliance between the three countries. Italy was also allied with Bulgaria and Albania, and the following year, Mussolini would renew his alliance with France and Great Britain in the Stresa Pact. At this juncture, the Duce was the most powerful he would ever be in international affairs, and as we have seen, he was somewhat friendly at the time to the House of Habsburg. Both this friendliness and his power would wane as he became closer to Hitler.

By this time, Alfonso XIII was in exile, having been forced to leave Spain in 1931 (as his mother had foretold). But he was as well-intentioned toward Otto as ever; with Otto's uncle Sixtus, he came up with another possible area for Otto to make contacts. Since his wife—whatever their personal difficulties—was a member of the British royal family and also fond of the young archduke, why not have him come on their planned trip to London in June of 1933? He could meet the king and queen and be introduced to all the major political figures. The empress wrote a letter to the king suggesting it; Alfonso reported back that both George V and Queen Mary were delighted by the idea, but then the Foreign Office scuppered it. The king was forced to write back declining, but got a little of his own back on "his" government by addressing it as one would to a reigning empress and ending it as "Your Imperial Majesty's Good Cousin."

Otto himself had much better luck with French politicians, but as always, their support was contingent on the heir to the throne succeeding at something, at which time, and not before, they would back him up. Ironically, given that he had been a disciple of Charles's nemesis Clemenceau, Otto's biggest ally in French politics was Georges Mandel, who would later play a key role in the escape of the imperial family from France.

A meeting that would have a great effect on the archduke's life was his encounter with Richard Count von Coudenhove-Kalergi. An early advocate of the European Union, the Austro-Japanese nobleman urged "an ethnically heterogeneous European nation based on a commonality of culture" and had converted no less than Aristide Briand to his views. Briand, whom we saw last attempting to support Charles's restoration bids, served as honorary president of Coudenhove-Kalergi's Paneuropean Union, which Otto joined in 1936. One of Coudenhove-Kalergi's rather key insights was that if Europe did not unite, it would be partitioned between the United States and the Soviet Union—a dark, but unhappily accurate, prediction.

In any case, if outside help were not forthcoming, it might be that existing monarchist circles within Austria could be used to stiffen resistance against Germany and the Nazis. Perhaps in response to the growing Nazi threat, perhaps simply because of his coming-of-age, Otto was becoming more popular in his homeland at a very grassroots level. Already, on December 6, 1931, Josef Kaltenhauser, mayor of the little village of Ampass in Tyrol, and the town council, named Otto an honorary citizen of the place. The reasons cited in the illuminated proclamation were: 1) to protest against the Habsburg Law; and 2) to "give the House of Habsburg some small moral recompense for the injustice it had suffered." This example spread like wildfire throughout Austria. By 1938, there were 1,603 "Emperor Communities" scattered across the nation.

This revealed a great deal of monarchist sentiment. But then, as now, monarchism in Austria was a highly divided thing. There were and are monarchist student fraternities, and there were very many Catholics who were loyal to the dynasty for religious reasons. The Jews were deeply divided: the non-Socialists in their number adored the Habsburgs while the Socialists hated them. The nobility felt the tug of ancient loyalty but had to somehow deal with the republic to hold onto their property. Veterans were another element who were very loyal, and of course, there were (and are) many nostalgics. But how to bring these disparate groups together? How to effectively mobilize sentiment into a political force? In late 1932, under Otto's cousin (Franz Ferdinand's son) Maximillian, the Duke of Hohenberg, a political group was formed: the "Iron Ring." It incorporated as a nucleus an already authorized organization, the *Reichsbund der Österreicher*, which had been founded in 1921. Its best-known leaders were Johannes Prince von and zu Liechtenstein, Friedrich Ritter von Wiesner, and Hans Karl Freiherr Zessner von Spitzenberg. By 1938, the Iron Ring encompassed more than fifty associations comprising between thirty and forty thousand people. There were, of course, many sympathizers, but as we saw, the most important died on July 25, 1934. In Brook-Shepherd's words:

> Only a few days before his assassination, he is said to have told Ernst Karl Winter, the Deputy Mayor of Vienna and himself a passionate monarchist, that Austria could only now be saved by a restoration and that he was going to do everything in his power to bring back the dynasty as swiftly as possible. Calling on Austria's imperial past to the rescue of the republican present would have been a tough task to achieve and not simply in the face of Berlin. The only man with both the courage and the dynamism even to have attempted it was Dollfuss, and he was gone.[4]

His successor, Kurt von Schuschnigg, was definitely a monarchist as well. But he also felt Pan-Germanism very strongly. As Otto said of him in the cited interview: "Schuschnigg was an absolutely decent person. He was a good Austrian, but he had a *Deutschtum* complex. This duality saw him bounce back between extremes." For the first two years of his Chancellorship, he sought foreign aid to bolster Austria's position against Germany; his first visit was to Rome, to thank Mussolini for his support. Thence he went to Paris, London, and Budapest. Nothing concrete was achieved. When the question of Restoration came up, he told Mussolini that it was not opportune; he told Laval in Paris that it was a matter for an eventual decision by the Austrians alone; he was

---

4 Ibid., p. 88.

not asked in London; and in Budapest, he told the Prime Minister (Gombos, whom we last met lying to the students in Budapest) that it would never happen. The Regent having sat in on that meeting, he pulled Schuschnigg aside, and assured him that, should the Habsburgs be returned to Vienna, he "would walk on my own two feet . . . to offer my services again." Horthy certainly lacked any sense of irony.

Thomas Masaryk, having at last stepped down, was replaced by Edouard Benes as president of Czechoslovakia. Replacing Benes as prime minister was Dr. Milan Hodza. Where Benes had been furiously anti-Habsburg, the Slovak Hodza had actually been one of Franz Ferdinand's expert advisors. He was anxious to discuss closer relations with Austria; indeed, some believed him to favor a personal union, under Otto, of Austria, Hungary, and Czechoslovakia. But Schuschnigg had sworn off any anti-German policy, and the Reich made known its opposition to any kind of Prague-Vienna-Budapest axis, with or without restoration. The country's continued existence, then, depended on Italy.

The year 1936 was to be a crucial one for Austria. The invasion of Ethiopia by Italy the previous year had destroyed the Stresa Pact, leaving Italy isolated. While this was happening, on March 7, Hitler's army marched into the Rhineland. This unilateral scrapping of the Versailles Treaty proved to be catastrophic; had a single French battalion crossed the border in response, the German army was prepared to depose the führer. Instead, it was the first of many victories that kept Germany marching in lockstep behind him, all the way to war. But his first renewed dealing with Austria would be gingerly: he sent the debonair Franz von Papen as Germany's emissary to Vienna.

Von Papen negotiated a "Friendship Treaty" with Austria, which required Schuschnigg to release the 17,045 Nazi prisoners in Austrian jails and to admit two pro-Nazis into his cabinet. Mussolini made it clear that if he wanted Italian aid in any contingency, he was going to have to sign it. The British and French offered to meet with him at Geneva if he wanted to turn down the pact. Fearful of angering the Germans, he turned down the meeting. That Berlin saw the treaty as a means of preventing a Habsburg restoration is shown by von Papen's report to Hitler, where among other things, the ambassador declares that it would put an end to the "constantly increasing efforts towards a Habsburg Restoration."

Schuschnigg had promised Otto that he would inform him if he were to do anything that would alter the position of the Nazi Party in Austria of its relationship with Germany. He sent a courier for that purpose, but only after the treaty was signed. The archduke was now certain that Austria was en route to destruction; even so, Schuschnigg agreed to facilitate a restoration.

On January 7, 1937, Otto and Schuschnigg, accompanied by their secretaries, secretly met at the Swiss monastery of Einseideln. There they composed the "Einsiedeln Protocol," headed "Preparations for the Restoration." In it, the chancellor promises to "carry out the restoration as soon as possible in the coming year . . . even if this should eventually lead to a serious European conflagration." In that discussion, Schuschnigg expressed the hope that Hitler would approve of Otto's return. The young archduke made it clear that he knew the führer had no intention of permitting it. The chancellor ended the interview by promising, "Any form of aggressive action on Germany's part against the independence of Austria will be resisted with force of arms."

Despite "his" chancellor's stirring words, Otto did not put much stock in them: "Schuschnigg was certainly an honorable man and he was certainly loyal to the dynasty. But he was hesitant, and had none of the dynamism of Dolfuss. . . . Of course, he had a certain vision of the future but it was along the lines that the restoration would finally lead to the re-establishment of the Holy Roman Empire. In this sense, he was a romantic . . . while I, in my talks with him, stressed the reality and the priority of mobilizing resistance against the threat which was approaching."[5]

Hitler's foreign secretary, von Neurath, arrived in Vienna for talks with Schuschnigg. Still hopeful of getting Hitler's blessing on the restoration to which he had pledged himself, Schuschnigg asked the German if such an act might not quiet the domestic scene. Hitler's henchman answered, "To restore the Habsburgs would be the best way for Austria to commit suicide." As it turned out, the opposite was true.

The months passed, and German pressure on Austria continued to increase. Despite Otto pleading with him not to go, on February 12, 1938, Schuschnigg was summoned to Berchtesgaden for a ritualized bullying by Hitler; cowed, he agreed to a set of demands which would virtually end Austria's independence. When he returned to Vienna, the

---

5 Ibid., p. 104.

hapless chancellor attempted to resign, but his resignation was refused by President Miklas for the simple reason that there was no prominent figure in the country willing to take the risks that assuming the chancellorship and reneging on the treaty would require. There was one living outside the country, however; he had sent Schuschnigg a letter, in which he offered to take up the chancellorship and resist the Nazis. This was not the same as asking for a restoration, "which would require a log drawn-out process of recognition by the Powers."

Schuschnigg refused, not least because it was the president who made those choices. But the archduke's letter appeared to galvanize Schuschnigg. He gave a rip-roaring speech in Parliament vowing resistance until death. This pleased the imperial family; less enjoyable was a letter received on March 6, which indicated that there could be no restoration for the foreseeable future, because it would spell the death of Austria. Worse, Otto read this after returning from Paris where he had been garnering support for the chancellor's stand.

But on March 8, Schuschnigg gave another stirring speech, having been presented with an ultimatum by Germany in response to his earlier one. To counter them, and the Nazis in his own administration, he called for a referendum on the state. On March 10, the Fatherland Front (Schuschnigg's party) banners were everywhere: support was rolling into the Yes side and all looked well.

Hitler, however, was outraged. He ordered his generals the next day to bring up the plan for the invasion of Austria: "Operation Otto," so-called because it was intended to be used in case of a restoration. He massed troops on the border and issued an ultimatum to Schuschnigg to cancel the referendum. Initially, the chancellor called up the reserves and prepared to fight, but attempts to reach Rome and Paris resulted in finding out that Mussolini would not back him up and the French government had fallen once again. Schuschnigg ordered the troops to stand down and cancelled the plebiscite. The German army rolled in, and Austria's independence was gone.

Debate raged at Castle Ham in the meantime, as Zita urged her son to go to the Aspern airfield outside Vienna and rally whomever he could against the invaders. He pointed out there was nothing left with which to resist and reminded her that the 1921 adventure had killed his father. They must bide their time and see what could be done.

In the meantime, the Nazis announced that there would be a referendum to legitimize their takeover on April 10. This gave Karl Renner the opportunity to betray his country a second time, and he took advantage of it, calling on Austria's socialists to vote for the Anschluss. Afterwards, Renner's offer to collaborate with the new regime was rejected—surely a rarity during World War II. In fact, so little did the Nazis think of him that Renner was left unmolested in his Vienna home for the remainder of the Nazi rule.

The same was not true for the monarchists, however; all of their organizations were banned, and their leaders sent to concentration camps. The Habsburg Law was renewed, and the family's properties seized once more by Hitler's government. This is one pile of Nazi loot that has been held on to by every succeeding government. This retention of ill-gotten gains has thus far failed to prick the consciences of a government which often professes to be ashamed of collaboration with or profiting from the Nazis.

At any rate, the struggle between Hitler and Habsburg entered a new phase. On March 12, 1938, Otto issued a statement declaring himself to be "the spokesman of the ardent patriotic feelings of millions of Austrians" and calling on the nations of the world to help restore Austria's independence. He moved on to Paris shortly thereafter, working with his uncle Sixtus on a vital project. There were many Austrians in France—more than a few because of their fear of the Nazis. The German government cancelled their Austrian papers; so far as Berlin was concerned, they were citizens of the Reich; if the French recognized them as such, the danger of their being returned rose exponentially. Fortunately for all those in that situation, Otto and his allies in the French government were able to persuade Paris to create a special immigration category of "ex-Austrians."

The next logical step would have been to create some sort of government-in-exile. But the émigrés were deeply divided. Otto was, of course, the best known Austrian, but he could not head a republican government; on the other hand, the extreme Socialist exiles would never accept anyone outside their circle—while one of those outside could never accept one of them. That division, mixed with a paucity of militarily-trained Austrians in the diaspora, also scotched Otto's efforts to raise an Austrian volunteer force. Otto saw quite clearly that some show of resistance to Hitler, however small, must be made for the sake of Austria's future. The exiles were too busy reliving old battles with each other to see that a united front was necessary in the immediate. Once again, as Charles had discovered, Otto found that being right does not always help. Nevertheless, he was able to launch a newspaper and radio station to encourage unity in the diaspora and resistance at home.

On October 7, the feast of Our Lady of the Rosary, ten thousand Catholics gathered to recite the Rosary in St. Stephen's Cathedral. This is a feast and a devotion that has meant much to Austria. The feast itself commemorates the victory of the Christian fleet led by Charles V's son, Don Juan of Austria, against the Turks at Lepanto in 1571; it was extended to the Universal Church in 1716 by Pope Clement XI in thanksgiving for the victory of Prince Eugen of Savoy against the Turks at Peterwardein (Petrovaradin). It has always been an integral part of the Habsburgs' *Pietas Austriaca*, and so the Nazis rightly saw this huge gathering as an assertion of both Catholic faith and Austrian nationhood—both anathema to them. Clashes broke out between the young Catholics and the Hitler youth, and the police intervened. A number of the older lads were sent to concentration camps.

This was the only external manifestation of opposition at the time, but it showed several things, most notably about the resistance in Austria. The Socialists and Pan-Germans were in favor of the Anschluss, and most of the Church hierarchy were simply trying to continue functioning under it. That meant that resistance—and so the country's future claims to independence—fell to the rank and file of Catholics, be they clerical or lay, and to the monarchists. Between 1938 and 1942, 4,000 to 4,500 of the latter were arrested;

800 to 1,000 of them were executed or murdered in concentration camps. Much of their resistance lay in gathering information about what was really happening in Germany and Austria. The archduke was soon receiving information from such circles in both countries. Otto had contacts in Germany with whom he worked:

> I had had many contacts with a resistance group that was still relatively important in Germany back then. It had two elements: senior officers and the Church. I got a lot of information about the Church.
>
> I would like to find out, but I did not succeed: at the time there was someone in the top leadership of the NSDAP[6] who worked absolutely against Hitler. And I am a witness of that myself, for the following reason: I was told that there was some important information about the church resistance that went through Holland.
>
> I arranged the transfer on the border between Germany and Belgium over the Ardennes. It was a kind of jungle right on the border. And there the rendezvous took place, in a house belonging to a friend who was half Belgian and half Czech. I met a young seminarian, Rudolf Graber, later bishop of Regensburg. He brought me a very interesting document: Hitler's talks with the leaders of the NSDAP about their step-by-step plans for the future.

---

6 Nazi Party.

It is interesting to note that intrepid go-between was just as brave when he was a bishop, authoring the stirring *Athanasius and the Church of Our Time*. In any case, Otto brought the information to the only place he thought might use it: the American embassy in Paris. The archduke had gotten to know Ambassador Bullitt and trusted him to get the information to FDR. The president saw the papers and invited Otto to come to Washington.

On March 10, 1940, the archduke found himself at the White House. His impression of Roosevelt was interesting: "Roosevelt was a big, well-meaning man. He had weaknesses, his biggest: he was a poker player. He always thought you could solve things with play and that was not the case. But I always had strong support from him concerning Austria." At that meeting and at another before Otto returned to Europe, Roosevelt reminisced about bicycling through Hungary and Transylvania before World War I. The major point of discussion, however, was the future of the Danubian area once Hitler was defeated. As to his own future and that of his House, "I made it quite clear at the outset to Roosevelt that questions concerning the constitution or the economic regime of any country could only be decided by the people of that state, once its own sovereignty had been firmly established." It was there in particular that he asked for Roosevelt's aid. The United States were still neutral, of course, but Otto had already begun to push for the recognition of Austria and Hungary as victim states. Between those two discussions were a flurry of speaking engagements, wherein the archduke pushed the idea of a future Danubian Federation. When the archduke said farewell to the president the second time, FDR offered his protection, should the family ever need it.

As we saw in the last chapter, that need arose very quickly. As the Habsburgs made ready to leave Lisbon for the United States, they were faced with a daunting task: "to persuade the New World to restore something of the shattered order of the Old: to repair ravages started by an American President in the recent past, continued by a Nazi dictator in the present, and finally threatened by a Soviet tyrant in the near future."[7]

When President Roosevelt met once more with Otto in 1940, he suggested the formation of a "Free Austrian Battalion" to be recruited out of the thousands of Austrians living in exile in the United States. In late 1942, it was set up as the 101st United States Infantry Battalion at Camp Attenbury, Indiana. Otto's brothers, Archdukes Karl Ludwig and Felix, were among the first. But after a few weeks, most of the men left, and the numbers dropped from 650 to 90. What had perhaps been forgotten was the bulk of Austrian exiles in the United States, at least of fighting age, were Socialists. The sort of man who would have rallied to Otto's cause had either been drafted to the Russian front to fight the Soviets or else were in Austria—either under arrest or doing what they could do in the resistance. Interestingly enough, the largest resistance movement in Austria, primarily monarchist, was called "O5." This mysterious name, which would appear on walls as a taunt to the Nazis, had multiple meanings. *E* is the fifth letter of the alphabet; Oe was a code word

[7] Ibid., p. 154.

for "Oesterreich"—the name of the country, which the Nazis had replaced with "Ostmark." But the five could also stand for the five vowels, *A, E, I, O,* and *U.* The letters had been used as personal code by Emperor Frederick III (1415–1493) who enjoyed putting it on buildings as his mark. It has been variously interpreted: *Austria est imperio optime unita* (Austria is best united by the Empire); *Austria erit in orbe ultima* (Austria will be the last surviving in the world); *Austriae est imperare orbi universo* (It is Austria's destiny to rule the whole world); and on and on. But whatever the mystic symbol may mean, it is for the elevation of Austria, not Germany. There was, however, one other possible meaning for O5. As emperor of Austria, the archduke was Otto I; had he been Holy Roman emperor on the other hand, he would have been Otto V. There were indeed no shortage of men willing to fight for the archduke; the problem was that they were not safe in exile, nor in front of newsreel cameras, as were so many of their ideological opponents. Nor were they simply tolerated as harmless nullities, as was Karl Renner.

No, it was on the political front that the archduke was forced to wage World War II. Once again, as in Paris, it was necessary to try to put together a united front of Austrian refugees. Once again, the Socialists and the Right could not agree on anything. Worse still were the anti-Habsburg machinations of Eduard Benes, who had also made his way to the United States. He had several advantages: he had taken Czechoslovakia's gold reserves with him to London, he led a country expressly created by Woodrow Wilson (at least in American eyes, which gave it a cachet equaled only by that of Yugoslavia), and he was pro-Soviet at a time when that was becoming ever more popular in White House circles.

But Otto was not without advantages, of which his charm was an important one, as was his Faith. Many major Catholics in the United States, such as Cardinal Spellman, joined his team, as it were, so did several leading members of Congress. Without the Socialists, a Free Austria Movement was set up, which Otto was close to, though he avoided any official position. The Czechs and Soviets set up a common propaganda office at Rockefeller Centre in New York, and a constant barrage was kept up against the Habsburgs therefrom.

The archduke's major advantage in this struggle was his friendship with Roosevelt, which was further cemented after the latter met Zita. This was helpful in a number of ways. Immediately after Pearl Harbor, most Austrians were sent to internment camps while their bank accounts and other assets were frozen, as were many of the German Americans and most of the Japanese. Otto lobbied the Justice Department to reclassify them as friendly aliens, which was done; Socialists benefitted as much from this as anyone, but gratitude was not overwhelming. Otto was also able, when the Post Office issued a series of stamps commemorating the occupied nations, to prevail upon them to issue one for Austria. It was a reprint of a 1917 Austrian military stamp with Charles's face on it!

But the archduke's struggle was to gain recognition for Austria as a separate nation after the war and to secure for her different treatment than would be meted out to Germany, and he had won Roosevelt to that view. On November 1,

1943, in Moscow, Roosevelt, Churchill, and Stalin agreed that Austria had been the first "free nation" to fall to Hitler, and so they wished to see its independence restored. But as part of the Third Reich, many Austrians had assisted the German war effort. So it was that "in the final settlement, account will inevitably be taken of her contribution to her liberation." While this was certainly in accord with Otto's hopes and wishes for his people, the Danubian Federation idea, of which FDR was initially so fond and which Churchill championed, began to fade as FDR and Stalin became closer and closer.

Meanwhile, Hungary was realizing that her alliance with Hitler would ruin her—that is to say, Horthy wanted out. Otto was at the center of these negotiations in Washington, having introduced the Hungarian envoy round. He sent his brothers Rudolf and Karl Ludwig to Lisbon to negotiate with Horthy's prime minister, Kallay, via his ambassador there. But the Germans, aware that Horthy was trying to escape the Axis, overthrew his government in March of 1944. What was needed for Austria and Hungry to escape the clutches of the Soviets—regardless of landings in France, Italy, Greece, or anywhere else—was a campaign by the Western allies to somehow reach the Danube basin before the Red Army. The great advocate of this amongst the Allied leadership was Churchill, who argued for a landing of six Allied divisions in Trieste that could make a "lunge" at Vienna and Budapest, liberating them before the Soviets could arrive. But in the end, FDR sided with Stalin, and the Soviets would seize both cities.

This is not to say that Otto was entirely without any military influence in Washington.

> I have dealt with concrete things, mainly that Austria would not be so badly bombed. For a long time, a lot has been saved by connections I had with Bomb Target Command in Washington.
>
> You prevented bombings?
>
> Yes, if I had specific information. As about Bad Vöslau. Some embittered Austrian emigrant, who was evidently badly treated in Bad Vöslau, said that this was one of the centers of scientific research on German extermination bombs. One must therefore extinguish Bad Vöslau. I heard that. And there I gave Roosevelt evidence that it was nonsense. I have achieved that Bad Vöslau was not bombed.

Meanwhile, Otto's brothers, Rudolf, Felix, and Karl Ludwig, having both their military attempts in America and their diplomacy in Lisbon ended by events, resolved with his permission to enter the Austrian resistance. The French Underground provided each of them with false papers, and one by one they made their way through France, Switzerland, and Austria, mostly on foot and by night. Rudolf, who at twenty-three was carrying false papers identifying him as "Johann Weber," was picked up by the German MPs near the Austrian border with Liechtenstein. As a young man out of uniform, he was very likely a draft-dodger at the very least! But while waiting to be interrogated, the intrepid archduke jumped through an open window and ran as fast as he could;

he eventually found refuge at the Capuchin monastery in Feldkirch. Waiting until the search was called off, Rudolf eventually made his way to the Resistance. He was joined shortly thereafter by his brothers.

The Resistance in the Tyrol with whom they fought were in large part monarchists, fighting in both North and South Tyrol, which word from London led them to believe would be returned to Austria after the war. In the beginning, they primarily performed acts of sabotage; they stepped up the attacks after June of 1944 and the Normandy invasion. But in May of 1945, when German tactics changed to blowing up bridges and other strategic facilities, the archdukes and their comrades-in-arms fought to save them.

Early in 1945, the France of General de Gaulle had been admitted as a full partner into the Grand Alliance—the Big Four (the United States, the Soviet Union, Great Britain, and China) were now the Big Five. Tyrol was assigned to the French to liberate. When the archdukes and their comrades made contact, they were immediately arrested, as the French had no idea that there was any resistance in their zone. But Ambassador Bullitt vouched for them to General de Lattre de Tassigny, who released them all. After the German collapse, the archdukes made their way to Vienna to work with monarchists there. The French occupation also allowed Otto to set foot once more on their native soil. He set up his headquarters at the Hotel Kreith in Innsbruck. With the four of them on Austrian soil—and all having done their part for Austria in the war—surely the future looked bright?

It was at this juncture that Karl Renner was able to emerge from his comfortable wartime obscurity to betray his country one last time. Making contact with the incoming Soviets, he offered his services to Stalin in a fawning letter that even today is embarrassing to read. Fortunately for him, Stalin was no Hitler, and recognized his talents. Renner was made chancellor of what was intended to be a puppet government. The Western Allies combined to force Renner to hold an open election, and to everyone's surprise, the Austrian People's Party (successor to the pre-war Christian Socials) won a clear victory. Renner was out as chancellor, though the Soviets made sure he got the presidency as a consolation prize. The Austrian constitution was restored, and the Soviets insisted that the anti-Habsburg laws be reinstituted. Despite the best efforts of the French commander, General Antoine Béthouart, to negate the law in his zone, Otto and his brothers were rewarded for all their wartime efforts with expulsion and renewed theft of their property. Their homeland closed to them once more, they had somehow to carry their family legacy into a new and very different world.

For one thing, most of Europe in those first years after the war boasted heaps of ruins, cold, and want, and innumerable bereaved and shell-shocked survivors. Over all, the specter of Soviet domination loomed. The horrible forecast of Coudenhove-Kalergi had come true. How to recover? How not only to recover but ensure that the horrors that had engulfed the Continent since 1914 would never occur again? For many thinkers and statesmen in Europe, the answer was to be found in a return to the traditions that had built Europe in the first place —Christianity and especially Catholicism, classical learning, and the vast and varied matrix of local and national cultural traditions these had produced. These were what made Europe stand apart from either the Soviets or the Americans. For such as these Charlemagne and his crown were powerful symbols of the state of affairs they sought: some looked to the old Holy Roman Empire for inspiration, others to the Burgundians, and still others to the multi-national Habsburg Empire. A dizzying number of alternatives were considered by different schools of thought, but most agreed at the very least on the religious and cultural foundations of Europe. So Schuman the Frenchman, Adenauer the German, and de Gasperi the Italian created the beginning of today's European Union, which de Gaulle signed on to. Coudenhove-Kalergi soldiered on with his Paneuropa Union.

As early as 1946, the journal *Neues Abendland* was founded in Germany and funded by Erich Prince von Waldburg-Zeil, who had funded *Der Gerade Weg* before Hitler's takeover. "Abendland" literally means "Evening Land" because of the sun setting in the West, but it refers to Christian Europe as opposed to the pagan or Muslim East. The French would call it the *Occident*. The introduction to the first issue explains the term:

> The concept of the Occident, in the modification of its historical significance as a unified concept of culture in Western and Central Europe, made possible and interpreted only one interpretation: the Christian one. Neither the geographical nor the national composition of Europe, but a spiritual attitude gave it the essential meaning. Antiquity and Christianity, Juno

> and Ecclesia, humanitas and caritas coined it; it was realized in medieval universalism.
>
> Whoever examined the causes of the "decline of the Occident" after the destruction of Western unity came to the same conclusion, namely, that the destruction of Western universalism has already begun in the addiction of the Ratio to explain things which only in faith can be seen and found: Faith stands before the ratio, the latter leads, absolutized, the separation of knowledge and belief.[8]

These ideas gathered a large following not only in West Germany and Austria but in France, Italy, Spain, and Portugal. For people who held such ideas, who best symbolized them in his person then the son of Charles of Austria-Hungary and Zita of Bourbon-Parma?

In the first years after the war, Otto was busy making a living—lecturing first around the world and then in America. In 1950, he went on a lecture tour of refugee camps along the German border, encouraging the Hungarian, Czech, and Sudeten German inmates. There he met an aid worker, Regina, Princess von Sachsen-Meiningen. They married the following year in Nancy at the church of the Cordeliers. To the church had been brought from Mariazell the image of the *Magna Mater Austriae*, before whom Charles and Zita had prayed after their wedding. As they left the church, the crowds yelled, "Vive le duc!" as Otto's ancestors had been

---

8 Johann Wilhelm Naumann, *Neues Abendland,* foreword to the first edition.

Dukes of Lorraine. The happy couple settled in Germany in the little town of Poecking bei Starnberg.

But with his homeland closed to him, how and in what way could he continue the struggle for the ideals bequeathed to him by his parents? The year 1952 saw the birth of two organizations somewhat interconnected by views and membership with each other, Neues Abendland, and the Paneuropa Union: these were the Abendländische Bewegung and the Centre Européen de Documentation et Information (CEDI). Varying in nationality and specific emphases, the membership were united in their basic outlook, forged of their Faith and shared experiences of resistance to Nazism and Communism. In a way, they wished to apply to Europe as a whole the solutions that Franz Ferdinand and Charles had sought for Austria-Hungary—in a real sense, a modern version of the *Reichsidee* we explored in the beginning. The attempt to bring this about would take up the rest of the archduke's active career. Neues Abendland and the Abendländische Bewegung both closed in 1958, but the other two continued.

Seeing his role as more European in scope, Otto sought to reenter Austria in 1958 by officially recognizing the republic, but the hatred of those who hated the Habsburgs was too strong. In 1961, he very reluctantly gave up his rights to the Austrian throne (though not the Hungarian) for himself (but not his descendants). This, too, was not enough to appease those who, like Hitler, could not be appeased. But that same year, as a sort of consolation prize, he was offered the throne of Spain by Francisco Franco. In deference to both Alfonso XIII (whose son and grandson were the immediate heirs) and his uncle Xavier Bourbon-Parma, who had been taken by the Carlists as their candidate, he declined.

At last, in 1967, the Socialist chancellor of Austria, Bruno Kreisky, was able to allay the hatred of the Rennerites sufficiently to allow Otto to finally reenter his homeland and regain his citizenship. In return, the archduke directed the Monarchistischen Bewegung Österreichs to reorganize as Aktion Österreich Europa. Six years later, when Otto was elected head of the International Paneruopa Union, in succession to Coudenhove-Kalergi, it simply became the Austrian branch. Having become friendly with the leaders of the Christian Social Union in Bavaria where he lived, in 1979 Otto ran successfully for the European Parliament. There for two decades he pursued a number of agendas, fighting waste and inefficiency in the parliament itself, standing up against secularist tendencies, pushing for a single European passport. But above all, he struggled in a hundred ways, from symbolic measures to open debate, to keep alive in his fellow parliamentarians the memory of their fellow Europeans sequestered behind the Iron Curtain.

The death of his mother Zita in 1989 could not help but affect Otto deeply. Nevertheless, the great shadow that had loomed over him and all of Europe since 1917 began to buckle and break in that very year—many wondered if perhaps the empress's intercession was involved. Certainly, her son was; on August 19 of that year occurred the Paneuropean picnic. Organized by the Paneuropean Union and the opposition Hungarian Democratic Forum, its patrons were Otto and Hungarian opposition leader Imre Pozsgay. It was supposed to be simply a tearing down of the border fence in one small section between Austria and Hungary. Instead of, or in addition to, the "picnic" per se, a huge number of East German refugees poured out and, given on the spot financial and other assistance, made their way to West Germany.

The rest of Otto's parliamentary career centered on bringing the post-Communist states—especially but far from exclusively those over whom the Habsburgs had ruled—into the European Union. He worked hard as well to garner support for Slovenia and Croatia during the breakup of Yugoslavia, and he travelled extensively through the newly liberated lands. In all his parliamentary endeavors, he was a rare—often enough, lone—voice for sanity. He had, after all, by the time he retired, lived through three major European dramas—the two world wars and the fall of Communism. Given the wealth of training, knowledge, and experience he possessed, it is perhaps a cruel irony that those talents were not allowed to benefit the people of Austria and his other countries by those who constituted themselves the representatives of the people. But then, they had been deprived of his father and mother in the same way by the same cast of characters. In his later years, there were legal attempts to regain for his family the properties the occupiers had stolen in 1938; in the end, the courts were of the opinion that the constitution might crumble if the Nazi loot were returned to its owners.

It would be a mistake to see the archduke's service to his peoples and to Europe as purely political, or as purely parliamentary. He had a keen understanding of the fact, as his father and great uncle had had, that the unity and well-being of a people or peoples is not primarily political or economic, essential as those things are. Rather, they are spiritual—that is to say, religious—and cultural. So it was that in addition to his more explicitly political work, he acted as patron to many non-political organizations. The European Shooting Fraternities, the Dignitatis Humanae Institute, European Wine Brotherhoods, and a host of other worthy causes received his patronage.

After his retirement from Parliament in 1999, he began to cut back on his responsibilities. But in 2004, he and his entire family were in Rome for the beatification of his father. Although he had been present at Charles's grave on April 1, 1972, when the cognitio that discovered that his father's remains were incorrupt, he had very deliberately not taken an active role in promoting the cause so as to avoid tainting it. But it was surely a joyful vindication of a father whose reputation had been more or less continuously assaulted since he sat on the throne.

Unfortunately, he also saw the corruption of the European idea underway, especially through secularism. In 2007, he declared in an interview with Aid to the Church in Need:

> The struggle for the soul of Europe is the struggle for the reference to God in the constitution. If human rights, which are one of the essential elements of Europe, should have meaning and content, it must logically be a God. After all, human rights are based on the idea that man, as a creature created by God, has his own rights.
>
> For this reason, I advocate that the reference to God be included in the European Constitution. There is

> great resistance in Europe to everything that has to do with faith and Christianity. In the European Parliament, we have a prayer room for all religions. It took more than three years for us to reach a Catholic mass until it was over. The other side is more active than ever today. The devil is always near where God is—because he is the adversary of God. The antichristian and antireligious forces are well prepared, which on our part cannot be maintained. There is still much to do for Christians here.

That same year, he retired as head of the House of Habsburg in favor of his eldest son, the Archduke Karl. His beloved wife died in 2010, after which he retired completely from public life; he joined her on July 4, 2011.

If his mother's funeral rites were extraordinary, Otto's were even more so. His body was brought from Pocking first to the Theatinerkirche, the old Court Church of Bavarian kings in Munich; then to Mariazell for a requiem before the *Magna Mater Austriae*, who had been brought to his wedding. In Vienna, he had a state funeral, combining the old imperial customs his mother's obsequies had known with the current Austrian state adding its assistance. As with her, the triple knock at the Kaisergruft signaled the archduke's arrival among his ancestors. But although his body is entombed there, his heart is in Hungary, at the Benedictine Abbey of Pannonhalma, from whence Zita had summoned tutors so long ago.

For many commentators, particularly those of a shallow disposition, the funeral of the archduke was seen as a burial of all that he and his parents—his whole House—represented and represent. But the enthusiasm of the crowds that descended upon Vienna that day, the ardor of the organizations involved might suggest that, as with his mother's rites, there might be more of a beginning here than an ending. Certainly, Otto never wavered in his belief that the principles he incarnated would one day triumph. Asked once how he could be so sure that Europe would one day return to Christianity, he said very simply, "Because we have the truth." Without a doubt, his parents would have said precisely the same thing.

Chapter 16

BLESSINGS OF A BLESSED

O God, through the adversities of this world You led Blessed Charles from this earthly realm to the crown reserved for him in heaven. Grant through his intercession that we may so serve Your Son and our brothers and sisters that we may become worthy of eternal life. Through our lord Jesus Christ, your son, who lives and reigns with you in the unity of the holy spirit, one God, for ever and ever.

—Collect for the feast, *Missale Romanum*

The Emperor Charles League of Prayers for Peace Among Nations (*Kaiser Karl Gebetsliga für den Völkerfrieden*), the "Gebetsliga" for short, is the organization that shepherded the cause of Emperor Charles through the beatification process and is currently assisting the Church with his canonization; it is also in a sense the guardian of his *cultus*. It is an interesting organization because, as we saw, it was founded when Charles was just a boy in western Hungary. Normally such organizations are only founded after a person has lived a life of heroic virtue, died a holy death, and then begun to answer prayers and collect a following. A cause for their beatification is opened by the diocese concerned, and the process begins.

As you shall remember, when young Charles's father was assigned to Odenburg (Sopron), the young archduke was tutored by a Dominican priest, Fr. Norbert Geggerle. Charles impressed him with his openness to the truths of the Faith and his zeal for the practice of religion. At the same time that he was teaching Charles, Fr. Geggerle was also teaching religion at the Ursuline Institute. One day, he was speaking about his imperial student to the head of the school, Mother Maria Vincentia. Her response was rather peculiar: "Yes, you have to pray a lot for him, because he will one day be Emperor and he will have to suffer a lot. He will be a special target of Hell."

Of course, as earlier noted, Mother Vincentia was hardly an ordinary religious and academic. Born on June 18, 1852 as Aloisia Fauland in Graz, she had the stigmata as well as the gift of prophecy. Her predictions, like the one regarding Charles, were often obscure when first given but proved to be true in the distant future. Fr. Geggerle thought this prediction bizarre, but reported it to Count and Countess Wallis, who superintended the archduke's education. The idea that Charles would ever be emperor seemed most unlikely.

But the count and countess took the other part of the stigmatic nun's prophecy seriously: that Charles should be prayed for because he had a sorrowful destiny ahead of him. So in 1895, a small prayer circle was formed among the acquaintances of the family of the little archduke by the Wallises. With them, the Ursuline convent and day and boarding schools, and the families of the students therein who brought the message home, became the first prayer circle, the beginning of the Prayer League for Emperor Karl. There was a sort of organization early on, as there is a membership card in existence from 1897.

The murder of Archduke Franz Ferdinand put Archduke Charles within one elderly heartbeat of the throne. Seeing Mother Vincentia's prophecy come so close to fruition galvanized the members of the prayer circle, who had been praying for the archduke for twenty-one years. It is unknown how many people belonged to this first incarnation of the Gebetsliga before Charles's death. But we do know they followed carefully the painful events of his reign, his deposition, and his expulsion from his homeland. In the midst of betrayals and arbitrary decisions by the victorious powers that were imposed upon him, they prayed with ever-increasing zeal.

Then came the news of Charles's death and the heroic circumstances in which he had met his end. The prayer circle grew larger and received particular impetus a year after Charles died, on April 1, 1923. Future Austrian president William Miklas, at the time a deputy in Parliament, wrote to Cardinal Piffl of Vienna. In his Easter congratulatory letter to the cardinal, Miklas closed with a request for the initiation of the beatification process for Emperor Charles. The new goal of the Gebetsliga, in addition to atonement for the wrong done to the emperor and his family, was prayer for the early beatification of this servant of God, as his truly Christian virtues and the penitential nature of his death proved.

The prayer league gathered around Baron Hans Karl Zessner-Spitzenberg. He was assisted by the redoubtable Mrs. Emmy Gehrig, whose amazing organizational ability would be the heart of the league for a long time. She was assisted by her helper in the secretariat, Mrs. Alphonsa von Klinkowström. In 1925, it was finally decided that the Prayer League for Emperor Karl needed ecclesiastical recognition. This was given by auxiliary bishop and vicar general in Feldkirch Sigismund Waitz, later prince-archbishop of Salzburg. From then on a prayer recommended to the members carried the intention of the prayer league. The members and others who used the prayers were requested to report favors granted through Charles's intercession to the prayer league secretariat.

At the time, considerable material about the interest in the prayer league, its outreach all over the World, and the announcement of numerous favors granted through the intercession of Emperor Charles came about. Unfortunately, this archive which would be so valuable for the history of the prayer league was not preserved. The period after the occupation of Austria by the Nazi regime was a dangerous time for the members of the prayer league. Although the league was strictly religious, its inevitable Austrian-patriotic union side was hated by the new rulers. Baron Zessner, the champion for Austrian independence and justice for the imperial family, was arrested one week after the seizure of power by the National Socialists on March 18, 1938; he was the first martyr for Austria during the Nazi period, dying in the Dachau concentration camp on August 1, 1938. Mrs. Emmy Gehrig was also arrested at short notice. In this situation, the secretary, Frau von Klinkowström, panicked and was frightened that the prayer league archive could fall into the hands of the Gestapo. In that case, a lot of names would become known to the Gestapo, and some of the members threatened with arrest. To avoid this, she burned the archives, so we have no source material from the important time of the second phase of the prayer league, from the death of Emperor Charles until 1938. The only information about the prayer league at that time can be found in the series of Kaiser Karl Gedächtnis Yearbooks, from 1929 until 1938, which Baron Zessner-Spitzenberg issued.

The spread of the prayer league took place initially in the countries of the former Austro-Hungarian monarchy, where it was already known, and soon in Switzerland, since Emperor Charles had become well-known during his exile there and had many friends. Afterwards, during his exile on Madeira, the emperor was much revered by the population; his popularity probably shone forth when thirty thousand people attended his funeral there. He became "our saint," whose grave was venerated at the same time as the pilgrimage to Mary Monte. These folks would have to count as part of the prayer league because their intention was the same as that of "enrolled members" of the league. In southern Germany, the Gebetsliga was also able to gain a foothold, as many German Catholics knew Emperor Charles's true mettle, despite the propaganda against him for seeking a separate peace. Also, in France, Italy, England, Belgium, and the Netherlands, members of the prayer league came together. Soon followed other non-European countries who received printed matter; Austrian missionaries were informed about the personality of Emperor Charles and the prayer league. So members also appeared in the United States, Canada, and on the South American continent. Until 1938, when the activity of the prayer league came to a violent end, Emmy Gehrig estimated that there were twenty-five thousand members around the world. During the years 1938–1945, as in Austria, Germany, and other Nazi countries affected by the war, open admission to the prayer league and its further development was prevented; nevertheless, the prayer league in Switzerland and in non-European countries, where it had already taken root before 1938, continued.

Many Austrians mourned that the emperor had been entombed so far from home. Many wanted there to be at least one memorial to him in Vienna; the prayer league took this popular desire as their special task. The first question to be answered was where to erect it? The most obvious choice was the Michaelerkirche, adjacent to the Vienna Hofburg—the imperial parish church, so to speak. There, in the first side chapel to the left as you enter, a Kaiser Karl Memorial Chapel was designed. A simple memorial for the martyr-emperor was created. On the right-side wall of the chapel is a plaque of grey marble with a large cross in white marble, below which was a bronze plaque attached in a round shape, surrounded by a crown of thorns and laurel; the inscription read, "He sought peace and found it in God." The artist who designed it was already renowned in Vienna under the monarchy—Hans Schwathe (1870–1950).

On Palm Sunday, April 1, 1928, the memorial was unveiled with the enthusiastic participation of numerous guests of honor, student fraternities, associations, and a large number of visitors who filled the whole Michaelerplatz. The former court chaplain, Bishop Ernst Seydl (whom we last saw in exile in Switzerland with the imperial family), solemnly inaugurated the memorial.

At the end of the Second World War, the prayer league in Austria had been disrupted for seven years by the Nazi period. Nevertheless, Mrs. Emmy Gehrig resumed her work with unflagging zeal in 1947 thanks to her practical knowledge of the league's pre-war operations. What was most immediately required was some sort of official connection with the hierarchical Church. Karl Count von Czernin applied for recognition of the prayer league by the diocese of Gurk-Klagenfurt, but the union was not yet recognized ecclesiastically. Mrs. Gehrig was able to do a lot to rebuild the organization because of her knowledge of the previously existing groups and contacts at home and abroad. Thus, the revived league already had 9,900 members in 1950. A separate section for Italy, especially South Tyrol, had been founded in November 1947. In 1949, a separate section for the rest of Italy (separate from the section in South Tyrol) was founded, as well as one for England. Other sections were founded in rapid succession: in 1950, the sections for France, Belgium and Luxembourg, and Hungarians in exile in the United States and New Zealand; in 1952 one in West Germany and another in the Netherlands; and in 1953, Portugal and Madeira. The Swiss section, which had suffered no wartime interruption, counted in 1954 1,800 members.

From the beginning of the rebuilding of the prayer league after the war, Mrs. Gehrig once more organized events for members in the form of meetings and pilgrimages, and of course the regular meetings of the board of the prayer league. These were held at sites close to Vienna, such as the pilgrimage church on the Kahlenberg and the abbey Klostenneuburg (1948, 1950). The first general assembly of the prayer league took place in 1953 in Altötting, Bavaria. From then on, the presidential meeting and the general assembly took place every year in different places.

Beginning in 1953, the annual yearbook of the prayer league has been published, which reports on further work and events, essays on the subject of Emperor Charles, and sermons and speeches delivered at the various meetings to commemorate or reflect on various aspects of the religious side of Emperor Charles's personality. The following year, the German section reported 600 members, but among these were several monasteries with only one address but where hundreds pray. In 1957, the spread of the prayer league in the United States and Canada was notable: 250 applications were submitted; two years later, the Spanish section was founded.

With all of this organizational growth came at last ecclesiastical recognition. The approval of the prayer league by the Archdiocese of Vienna took place in 1957 and thus full recognition as an ecclesiastically approved association. Then in 1964, the Emperor Charles Prayer League for International Peace was canonically erected as a church association. The German dioceses of Regensburg and Freiburg followed suit in 1967 and the Archdiocese of Freiburg in 1970. From the time of the first establishment of the prayer league with ecclesiastical approval in 1925 until March 1, 1938 there arrived ten thousand messages from grateful recipients of Charles's intercession; unfortunately, as we saw, all of these were destroyed. But the redoubtable Mrs. Gehrig started up anew soliciting reports of this kind. By 1964, when she was appointed executive president of the Gebetsliga, Mrs. Gehrig announced 3,325 new messages of answered prayers. Listing the number of members in the individual country sections revealed a total membership of 32,210.

What the prayer league had failed to do after the death of the emperor as a result of the events of 1938, the re-founded prayer league accomplished after the Second World War in a relatively short time: since 1923, they had sought the initiation of the cause of beatification, and since 1925, ecclesiastical approbation. These accomplishments were due to the tireless effectiveness and energy of Mrs. Emmy Gehrig, who did her utmost to achieve them.

In 1949, the first phase of the beatification process began through the Archdiocese of Vienna. On November 3 of that year, Vatican Radio announced that the beatification process of the emperor and king Charles of the House of Austria started. At the end of 1952, the postulator of the cause, Msgr. von Magyary, reported that the seven diocesan processes that act as a basis (informative process) for the apostolic process in Rome had been completed. The minutes of the league's presidential meeting in 1956 are followed by the news that the translation of the process files, which were estimated to take two and a half years and encompass many thousands of pages, would be closed in July 1957, and that it was expected that the process would finally start in 1960. Each new stage and event in the continuation of the cause was reported in the annals of the prayer league.

As we saw earlier, in 1972, on the fiftieth anniversary of his death, Charles's tomb in Madeira was opened and the state of his body examined—as the Congregation for the Causes of Saints requires. This is done to see if the body is incorrupt (a possible factor in determining sanctity) and to secure possible relics. The commission performing the enquiry was headed by Bruno Wechhner, the bishop of Feldkirch. Other commission members included the bishop of Funchal and his secretary, an archaeology professor named Romoli and his crew, a notary, and two doctors. There were also on hand a large group of Austrians, South Tyroleans, Swiss, Germans, some Portuguese, and a Swede. The Gebetsliga was represented by Jesuit Father Henry Segur. Among the members of Charles's family present were Archduke Otto with his wife, Regina, and three of their daughters, Michaela, Walburga, and Gabriele, and the emperor's youngest son: Archduke Rudolph. When the coffin was opened, Charles's body was found to be remarkably well preserved despite the fact that a window in the coffin had broken, allowing in moisture and damp tropical air. Although the emperor was embalmed when he died, it was poorly done and cannot explain the state in which the body was found. While incorruption is one of the manifestations of holiness (the bodies of many of the saints have been preserved incorrupt), the Church does not interpret the manifestation as ipso facto proof of holiness. The emperor's body was clothed in a new uniform brought especially for this purpose, placed in a new coffin, and the sarcophagus resealed.

The membership of the praesidium of the prayer league and the beatification process have, of course, changed several times over the decades. The tireless executive president Emmy Gehrig worked until the end of her life for the

Gebetsliga. She was still at the annual pilgrimage and bureau meeting in 1974; on November 3, 1974, she died. In 1972, the Cistercian priest Fr. Stephan Sommer from the monastery of Lilienfeld was appointed director of the Lower Austrian group. In 1975, his office as state director of Lower Austria was extended to the territory of the city of Vienna. The archbishop of Vienna, Franz Cardinal König, appointed him in 1976 as vice president of the prayer league. The Gebetsliga archive, which had been growing again since 1947, went to the Lilienfeld Abbey until the death of Fr. Sommer on March 26, 1994. The following autumn, the archives moved to St. Pölten; this was because the archbishop of Vienna, Franz Cardinal Gröer, had, in accordance with the statutes of the Gebetsliga, appointed the Bishop of St. Pölten, Kurt Krenn, to be the new president. The cardinal also appointed new board members: Mrs. Marianne Egger and Fr. Reinhard Knittel as vice presidents and Johannes R. Parsch as executive president of the prayer league. The following decade brought the long-awaited provisional decree on the heroic virtue of the servant of God on April 12, 2003. At that point, the Church entitled the emperor Venerable Emperor Charles. The required miracle for beatification was recognized by a decree signed on December 20, 2003 by the signature of Pope St. John Paul II.

The miracle involved occurred to a Polish nun, Sister Maria Zita Gradowska, who was in charge of a large hospital in Brazil. She had severe problems with her legs and, by November of 1960, had become bedridden. After several unsuccessful operations, her legs did not heal, becoming infected and quite painful. One of her confreres suggested that she should prayer to the Servant of God Charles of Austria. The nun rebuffed the suggestion in favor of a more familiar and popular saint. However, the pain and infection only increased. Finally, in desperation, she prayed to Charles. The next day, she was completely cured. Because of the nun's work at the hospital, and numerous operations, her case is well documented by various physicians and nurses. It is said that when the empress heard about the miracle and the nun's name, she responded, "As always, he is thinking of me!" In any case, this recognition brought the beatification process to a provisional conclusion. The public announcement and elevation of the servant of God from the House of Austria to be a blessed of the Catholic Church took place on Sunday, October 3, 2004.

The week of the beatification shall never be forgotten by those who were present. In addition to the emperor, those beatified that day in Rome were Pierre Vigne, priest-founder of the sisters of the Blessed Sacrament; Joseph-Marie Cassant, priest-monk of the Reformed Cistercian Order; Anne Catherine Emmerich of the Canonesses of St. Augustine; and Maria Ludovica de Angelis of the Daughters of our Lady of Mercy of Savona. All of these had their supporters present in St. Peter's Square that afternoon, which for that very reason reflected the universality of the Church. In his homily addressing each of the newly beatified, St. John Paul II said of the emperor:

> The decisive task of Christians consists in seeking, recognizing and following God's will in all things. The Christian statesman, Charles of Austria, confronted

> this challenge every day. To his eyes, war appeared as "something appalling." Amid the tumult of the First World War, he strove to promote the peace initiative of my Predecessor, Benedict XV.
>
> From the beginning, the Emperor Charles conceived of his office as a holy service to his people. His chief concern was to follow the Christian vocation to holiness also in his political actions. For this reason, his thoughts turned to social assistance. May he be an example for all of us, especially for those who have political responsibilities in Europe today!

The following day there was a Mass of thanksgiving for the beatification at the Basilica of St. Mary Major. As described by an eye witness:

> The Basilica was filled to overflowing with devotees from all the lands of the former Empire, together with many of the Catholic crowned heads of Europe and 200 members of the Habsburg family. A beautiful portrait of the Blessed Emperor Charles occupied a dominant position near the high altar and a very fine choir sang (they were so good that the choir of the Sistine chapel that had sung the previous day at the beatification was somewhat overshadowed by it).
>
> After the Mass, the Archduke Otto and his wife Archduchess Regina led some 200 members of the Imperial family down the aisle after the clergy, led by the chief celebrant, His Eminence, Count Christoph, Cardinal von Schoenborn OP, had processed out.

> Before the Imperial family marched a contingent of Imperial Dragons and Uhlans and Hungarian Hussars who then formed a guard of honor for the Imperial family as they emerged from the Basilica.
>
> On the square outside the Basilica, and at the emergence of the members of the Imperial family, two Tyrolean bands, dressed in Tyrolean costume and the uniforms of the Tyrolean *schuetzenkompanie* with broad feathered hats, short jackets and cummerbund, and long lederhosen knitted socks and rawhide leathern shoes, struck up and played traditional and very lively Tyrolean music. The Tyroleans have ever been the most faithful defenders and protectors of the Habsburg Empire and family, not least since they were granted their own parliament (der Landschaft) in the early Middle Ages without whose consent they could be neither taxed nor conscripted.[1]

Afterwards, there was a papal audience at the Nervi Hall, where the imperial family and various other royals were received. The archduke Otto was given a special blessing, and as Col. Bogle observed in the quoted article, "It was a moving sight indeed to see these two together; the Pope blessing Otto, the son of his own Emperor, the Blessed Charles of Austria, for Pope John Paul II's father had been a subject and officer of the Blessed Emperor Charles." After the audience, this writer said to the archduke Otto, "I would

---

1 James Bogle, "The Beatification of Europe's Heart: Emperor Charles of Austria," https://www.remnantnewspaper.com/Archives/archive-2005-1015-beatification_of_europe.htm.

ask you how you are feeling, but I doubt very much there are words for it." With an enormous smile, he replied, "You are right!"

The correspondent of *Point de Vue*, a glossy French popular magazine dedicated to the doings of European Royals and Nobility breathlessly gushed that the streets of Rome that week were like the *Almanach de Gotha* (the standard genealogical reference for Europe's sovereign families) come to life. This was not an unfair assessment, but perhaps most touching to see coming to venerate Blessed Charles were Victor Emmanuel IV, grandson of the emperor's Italian antagonist, and Prince Paul Karageorgevich, representing the royal family of Serbia. This kind of reconciliation would no doubt have pleased the living Charles tremendously, and we can be assured that, in heaven, he smiled upon it.

In consultation with the Habsburgs, the Holy See decided on rather a unique honor for Charles: instead of the day of his death, April 1, the new blessed's feast is October 21, his wedding anniversary. The areas of life in which Charles was seen as a fine example to follow were several: as a Christian ruler, a chivalrous soldier, a devout layman, and as a man who suffered penitentially and without bitterness—all of which are absolutely needed today. But it was how he acted as a husband and father that was to be particularly highlighted by his feast day—even his wife and he conceiving whilst everything was collapsing around them pointed up their openness to life and their refusal to despair.

All in all, the beatification was a signal triumph for the memory of Emperor Charles, to say nothing of the Gebetsliga. It certainly infuriated the Habsburg haters, who dragged up every calumny against the new blessed in the weeks before and following the ceremony that they could. The question must be asked, why did this particular beatification arouse such ire? Archduke Otto once described this sort of hatred as a psychological complex, and he was right. Because if indeed Blessed Charles is a saint in heaven, it turns on its head a number of notions central to the current political, social, and religious arrangement of Europe and the West in general. At the very least, it means that many of those who are still considered heroes in different sectors, such as Woodrow Wilson and Karl Renner, must be reexamined; so far from being blows for freedom, their actions toward Charles become crimes, as do the actions by their successors toward Charles's memory and towards his descendants. The ingratitude toward Charles's sons and their followers, for example, after their having risked so much against the Nazis to save Austria becomes positively monstrous, as does successive governments' holding on to their stolen property in emulation of Hitler.

But that is only in the immediate. There are larger issues at stake. The very things that won Charles notice in the eyes of the Church are anathema in modern society: the ideas that a ruler can be devout, dedicated to his peoples' welfare to the point of his own death if need be, that a soldier too can be pious, and even amid the horrors of the modern battlefield be a pillar of Chivalry, that a real man can be entirely masculine, exceedingly pious, and devoted to his strong but equally feminine wife, and that such a couple can place their children's welfare completely above their own welfare, let alone pleasure. These are things that are powerful signs of contradiction to all that we are given in media, academia, and government. It would have been bad enough had these simply been the ideals held by Charles and Zita, but the imperial couple had the temerity not only to believe them but to live them.

In any case, despite the triumph, the Gebetsliga's work was far from done. For one thing, there was ever more need to answer the attacks precipitated by the Church's declaration that Charles was in heaven. But at the same time, that declaration would inevitably expand devotion to him, which had to be overseen. Besides all of that, the cause was not complete: canonization loomed ahead, and that meant that another miracle was required. To all of this work, and to extending its organization and efforts, the Gebetsliga now applied itself.

As it happened, a second miracle that was verified occurred after the beatification; as the first was in Brazil, the second was in the United States, where devotion to the emperor who was once our wartime foe has exploded in size. On January 31, 2008, a Mass was offered in the chapel of St. James Cathedral in Orlando, Florida. The Mass concluded a sixteen-month investigation of a miraculous cure attributed to Blessed Charles.

The story of how a Baptist American lady was cured of cancer through Blessed Charles's intercession is an interesting one. A few years before, Paula and Joseph Melançon of Baton Rouge, Louisiana, while travelling through Austria, met one of Charles and Zita's grandsons, Archduke Karl Peter. He in turn invited them to the beatification ceremony in 2004. The following Christmas, Mrs. Melançon gave her sister-in-law, Atlanta resident Vanessa Lynn O'Neill, a medal of Blessed Charles with a book of novena prayers to him given out at the ceremony.

As it happened, Vanessa O'Neill's mother's best friend was dying. "Thousands of miles away in the Kissimmee area of central Florida, a woman, in her mid-50s, who received a diagnosis of breast cancer began what seemed an endless cycle of hospitalization and treatment. The cancer had metastasized to her liver and bones. Medical opinion deemed the disease terminal. She was bedridden. Nothing more could be done. Nothing more on earth, that is."[2] "'I knew that when I got that novena—I knew that my mother's best friend was sick—I just knew at that moment that it was something I was going to do. And that is how I got started, I just prayed the novena,' O'Neill said."[3]

The novena was prayed by O'Neill, her mother, and a battalion of friends. "The woman recovered and medical experts could not offer an earthly explanation as to why."[4] Bishop Thomas Wenski was asked to empanel a tribunal to investigate the case. They took sixteen months to investigate it and, in the end, found it sufficiently credible to report to Rome.

According to the Florida newspaper, the late Brother Nathan Cochran, OSB, of St. Vincent's Archabbey in Latrobe (founded with the help of King Ludwig I of Bavaria, uncle of Empress Elizabeth), who was head of the American section of the Gebetsliga until his death in 2014, "I am very

---

2 Tanya Goodman, *The Florida Catholic*, February 20, 2008, www.thefloridacatholic.org.

3 Ibid.

4 Ibid.

happy that the first miracle that is being attributed to Blessed Charles (after his beatification) has been documented from the United States." Of course, there many other such miracles being investigated around the world.

At the same time, as the date of Charles's feast implied, the question of Zita's sanctity arose. Certainly, after their wedding, Charles had said to her, "Now we must help each other get to heaven." He had made it; had she?

So it was that on January 28, 2009, the Association for the Beatification and Canonization of Empress Zita, the Servant of God, wife and mother, was founded in France. The founding president of this association was Jean Sevillia, historian and journalist, expert on Austria, and author of biographies of Charles, Zita, and Andreas Hofer. The abbot of Solesmes was made an ex officio member of the board because of Zita having become an oblate through that monastery. In response to the association's petition, jurisdiction over the cause for Zita was transferred from the Archdiocese of Vienna to the Diocese of Le Mans, wherein Solesmes is located.

The trial officially opened on Thursday, December 10, 2009, at the Episcopal Palace of Le Mans. After a Mass invoking the Holy Spirit, presided over by Bishop Le Saux at 10:00 a.m., the inaugural session of the trial opened in the presence of a delegation of the association (composed of Dom Dupont, abbot of Solesmes and ex officio member of the office, Mrs. Elizabeth Montfort, secretary, who represented Jean Sevillia, Mr. Tissot, treasurer, and Mr. Peynichou) and Archduke Rudolf, who represented the imperial family.

The bishop sang the "Veni Creator Spiritus," then the postulator briefly introduced the story of the case and presented the opening request. Then the decrees already taken by the bishop and the Congregation for the Causes of Saints were read. Bishop Le Saux then questioned the three members of the court to find out if they accepted the charge that the Church entrusted to them. Then the bishop, the members of the tribunal and the postulator took an oath. Finally, the provisional list of witnesses and the list of members of the historic commission were accepted.

The reasons adduced by the association as evidence of her life of heroic virtue were adduced thusly:

> Her sense of service as Empress and Queen. On the human level she corresponded in an exemplary way with the words of the Coronation Ritual addressed to her in Budapest (30th December 1916): "Receive the sovereign's crown, in order that you may know that you are the spouse of the king and that you must always take care of the people of God. The higher you are placed, the more you must be humble and abide in Jesus Christ."
>
> Her attentiveness to others, both in her official duties, and in her ordinary life (the Cardinal Archbishop of Vienna, Monsignor Piffl, called her "the guardian angel of all who suffer").
>
> Her abandonment to God and the courage she displayed during the final illness and death of her husband Blessed Charles, and during every stage of her exile.

> Her courage when widowed with eight children. She took great care of their education, especially their Christian education. In fact, she did not differentiate between "education" and "Christian education" but wanted her children to be, above all, solid Christians.
>
> Her love for the Church, her devotion to the Sacraments, especially the Mass and the Sacrament of Penance, and her respect for Papal teaching.
>
> Her obedience: to the Pope, to the Church, and even, via Dom Prou, the then Abbot of Solesmes, to her children, when he conveyed to her on their behalf their wish that she should not become a nun.
>
> Her piety and humility, manifested in the recitation of a part of the Divine Office, of the Rosary, and in her choice of a simple life.
>
> Her union with Christ as an oblate of the Abbey of Saint Pierre of Solesmes and through her consecration, along with all her family, to the Sacred Heart of Jesus and to the Immaculate Heart of Mary at the moment of her agony.[5]

Her devotional life, too, was very much in sync with her husband's:

> The Empress, for her part, received her First Holy Communion on the feast day of the Sacred Heart, Friday, June 6, 1902, in the chapel at Pianore. When Zita was studying at the Visitation convent in Zangberg, the chapel had been dedicated to the Sacred Heart of

5 http://associationimperatricezita.com/beatification-2/.

Jesus and to Saint Marguerite-Marie Alacoque, the seer from Paray-le-Monial, the world center for this devotion. As a matter of fact, this was also the case with the small chapel in Johannesstift, Zizers, where the Empress attended private masses celebrated for her when she was unable to go to the main chapel.

Fr. Mateo Crawley-Boevey (a priest of the Congregation of the Sacred Hearts of Jesus and Mary (Picpus), and indefatigable apostle of the Enthronement of the Sacred Heart in homes), was very close spiritually to the Imperial Family. He often mentioned the Emperor as an example to be followed in regard to his devotion to the Sacred Heart, and he even personally intervened to help Empress Zita when she had to leave Villa St. Joseph in the suburbs of Québec City. He sent a letter to Archbishop Maurice Roy of Québec City to ask him to do something for them because "the misfortunes of this noble family are all the more felt by Fr. Mateo because he knows that their suffering is the result of their confessing their Faith; they therefore deserve to be treated with particular compassion." For the Empress, devotion to the Sacred Heart was not something optional. She knew it was a point of agreement between herself and her Blessed husband, who said to her just before he died: "I love you infinitely! We will meet again in the Heart of Jesus!" The Sacred Heart of Jesus devotion was therefore, part of her basic

> spirituality of marriage and an attribute of her faithfulness to her great husband.[6]

By September of 2012, thirty-five witnesses had been heard. To date, this part of the work seems to have been completed. The work of the historical commission is being collated, and of course, the association is anxious to hear of any favors granted through the servant of God's intercession. If Zita is beatified before Charles is canonized, their causes shall be combined, but until and unless that day comes, the two remain separate. There can be no doubt that if they are both beatified, they shall enjoy a joint feast day.

In the meantime, in the years since Charles's beatification, devotion to him has grown exponentially around the world. Since he has become a blessed with a liturgical feast, there has been an explosion of shrines in his honor across the globe. The Gebetsliga's national sections have grown in size and importance. At the time of writing, the international headquarters of the league and the Austrian branch of the Empress Zita Association are both located at the great Cistercian Abbey of Heiligenkreuz, which has always been closely connected to the House of Habsburg. The Emperor Charles' League of Prayers managing president is Fr. Marian Gruber O.Cist., while the head of the Austrian Empress Zita Association is Fr. Wolfgang Buchmüller O.Cist., who, with their members' assistance, plan a whole calendar year of Masses and lectures surrounding the imperial couple.

---

6 Facebook Page, Empress Zita Association of Malta.

Austria, not surprisingly, is a major focus of devotion to the imperial couple, even as it still harbors a large pool of guilt-driven antipathy toward both them and their living relations—an antipathy made all the more ridiculous by the huge amount of tourist money the Habsburg legacy continues to draw into the country. At any rate, there are four state-level Gebetsliga branches: Lower Austria (and Vienna), Upper Austria, Styria, and Tyrol. Moreover, there are at least twenty-six shrines to him scattered through the country, and the number of these keeps increasing. An official enshrinement of a relic of Charles is always quite an event, with as high a Mass as possible, reenactment units in imperial uniforms, bands, and one or more members of the imperial family in attendance. Emperor Charles's feast is on the regular calendar.

In Hungary, the situation is a bit different; in addition to Horthyite propaganda, the country suffered under decades of Communist rule, all during which, the Habsburgs were calumniated constantly by the educational system. Still, since the restoration of freedom, the cultus of the holy crown has grown once more, and of course, the memory of the last man to wear it has also revived. The centennial of Blessed Charles's coronation was celebrated with a packed High Mass at the Matthias Kirche. There are plans afoot by the current government to restore the interiors of the Royal Palace in Budapest, gutted in World War II; this, too, cannot help but serve as a reminder of the last true king to occupy them. The local Gebetsliga maintains a website which proclaims, "So far, our site is intended to spread the honor of our last Apostolic King. To this end, we publish here pictures, quotes, videos, and articles. They are related to the life of Charles." There are sixteen shrines to Blessed Charles in the country.

Czechia's section of the Gebetsliga is very active. The Brandýs nad Labem chateau is now repaired and a historical exhibition was opened to the public in 2004. Every year (since 2003), a social and historical event, "An Audience with Emperor Charles," is held here with international participation, which commemorates the memory of Emperor Charles. It is the main activity of the regional branch of the Emperor Karl League of Prayers for Peace among Nations, which was established in Czechia in 2011. In the same year, a relic of Blessed King Charles was ceremonially deposited in the Church of the Ascension of the Virgin Mary in Stará Boleslav. On 21 October 2012, the Czech texts and memorial of Blessed Charles were approved by the Holy See and Czech Bishops' Conference and included as non-binding in the liturgical calendar of Czechia.

Aside from the novena for Blessed Charles and an annual Mass at a number of important locations in the Czech Republic, the League of Prayers also supports the research and publication activities of its members. A book about the life of Blessed Charles in Bohemia (by Milan Novák, PhD) is already in its third edition. The rediscovery of the lost diary of Countess Victoria Mensdorff provided Professor Zessner-Spitzenberg (Jana Balharová, MD) with information on the last days of Emperor Charles's life in Madeira. Along with the diary, a mourning envelope containing Emperor Charles's hair, which was cut off posthumously, was also discovered. The League of Prayers arranged for this relic to be placed in the Minorite Church in Brno. Among the latest activities by the Czech League of Prayers is Czech-American spiritual cooperation on the diplomatic-military mission in Afghanistan, whose purpose is to include the peace efforts in Afghanistan in intercession by Blessed Emperor Charles I. The Czech League of Prayers sent a field reliquary to Afghanistan with a relic touched by Blessed Charles, before which the Czech military chaplain of this joint mission in Kabul will serve Holy Mass. The League of Prayers has also recently joined its efforts with the work of the newly established Order of St. George, a European Order of the House of Habsburg-Lorraine, on a number of activities in the Czech Republic. As of this writing, there are six shrines to Blessed Charles in Czechia.

Slovakia was simply a part of Hungary until the end of World War I, and Blessed Charles ruled the country as Hungary's king, something which, given the antipathy between Slovaks and Magyars, was not calculated to build up his popularity. But Charles was zealous for the rights of all his subjects, the Slovaks no less than the others. According to its website, "The Slovak branch is a firm part of the International Prayer League of Emperor Charles for Peace between Nations, which was a church organization approved in 1949, operating in the Slovak Republic and based on the Slovak language. Through its activities, it seeks to participate in the dissemination of the devotion to Bl. Charles of Austria—to seek and fulfill God's will in the service of global peace, in particular by organizing activities in his territory and informing about the common activities of the Prayer League." They organize commemorative activities and Masses in sites such as Bratislava and Piesrany, as well as an extremely informative website. There are three shrines to Blessed Charles in Slovakia.

Croatia has an interesting relationship with Blessed Charles and the servant of God Zita. Charles was king of Croatia by virtue of being king of Hungary. At the very end of his reign, as we saw, he made Croatia an equal partner in the monarchy with Austria and Hungary, and in the wake of the World War I centennial, this was remembered as the first incarnation of Croatian statehood in modern times. There is no local branch of the Gebetsliga in the country, but the very active national branch of the Empress Zita Association looks after devotion to both. There are four shrines in the country.

Southern Poland was, of course, the western part of Galicia; the eastern part is in Ukraine. In Austria-Hungary, the Poles were the fourth largest ethnic group, and the only one inhabiting one compact area. So their political significance grew, which was supported by their conservative, traditional, and Catholic views. One place in the Austrian half of the monarchy's government was reserved for Poles. In addition, at different periods, Poles held the offices of minister of foreign affairs, minister of the treasury, and even (unthinkable in other partitions) prime minister of the country. Franz Joseph I forever inscribed himself in the Polish national memory as a "good ruler." But the memory of "favoritism" toward the Ukrainians at Brest-Litovsk and interwar propaganda besmirched Charles's name with the generality of Poles. It was St. John Paul II who began to alter the Polish view of the last emperor. The Poles consider the words with which he (as the head of the Church) began his conversation with Empress Zita as extremely meaningful: "I am pleased to welcome my father's Empress." After the death of Saint John Paul II, it also began to be emphasized that the last blessed whom he raised to the altars was the last emperor of Austria. It is precisely in 2004 that the beginning of interest in the figure of Blessed Charles in Poland began to grow. It was not enough that the Polish pope beatified him, but the miracle recognized through his intercession was granted to a Polish woman. Then, for the first time, the League of Prayer began its activity in Poland led by Mr. Mariusz Kryszkowski. After a few years, however, it ceased to function completely. It was only in 2018, with the consent of the league authorities, that Marcin Kula attempted to reactivate it in Poland, for the first time making a comprehensive translation to Polish of prayers, litany, and novena through his intercession. There are two shrines to Blessed Charles in Poland.

In Italy—apart from South Tyrol, which has a section of its own—Blessed Charles's former Italian foes are second to no one in honoring him. There are eighteen provincial delegations of the Gebetsliga from Trieste to Sicily that have emerged since the Italian section was formed in 2007. There are eleven shrines in Charles's honor in Italy.

Crossing the ocean, there is a growing devotion to Blessed Charles and his wife in Brazil. This is partly because his first miracle happened in Brazil and partly because he descended from the first Brazilian emperor, Dom Pedro I, through his daughter, Queen Maria II of Portugal. There has also grown devotion to Zita; she is also a descendant of King João VI of Portugal, through his son, King Miguel I, and was also the aunt of Princess Cristina de Ligne da Orleans e Bragança. There are two shrines in Brazil.

Mexico has an extremely active branch of the Gebetsliga, presided over by Archduchess Annie-Claire von Habsburg-Lothringen. Of course, Mexico, too, was reigned over by the Habsburgs: first from the time of Emperor Charles V until the first Bourbon king of Spain, and then again briefly by Emperor Maximilian, who was Blessed Charles's great uncle. There are at least two shrines to him in Mexico.

While the other countries where the Gebetsliga is active had strong historical connections to the House of Habsburg, the United States is an anomaly. The American branch of the league, under the watchful eyes of Ms. Suzanne Pearson and Fr. Boniface Hicks, OSB, (since the death in 2014 of Brother Nathan) is extremely active. Their sophisticated website dispenses a good deal of information, and their online gift shop features an enormous number of publications, including an exceedingly fine Blessed Charles prayer book as well as rosaries, medals, pictures, third class relic holy cards, and even dolls. Their well-managed blog continually features new articles about different aspects of Charles's and Zita's lives. Moreover, there are twelve shrines dedicated to Blessed Charles scattered across the United States! What can account for the growing popularity of the imperial couple in a land with which they were at war?

Looking at the shrines themselves provides a partial answer. Two of them are Byzantine Rite Catholic churches; we have already seen that the Habsburgs in general and Blessed Charles in particular had a special relationship with them: all of the Byzantine Catholic liturgical books down to the 1950s and a few still in use today contain prayers for the emperor. One is an Anglican Use parish of the Personal Ordinariate of the Chair of St. Peter. Many former Anglo-Catholics were devotees of their own martyred Charles I before coming into the Church. The parallels between the two Charleses in every respect are striking, and switching to or adding veneration of the Austrian emperor is fairly easy for those familiar with the English king (although efforts are underway to see if he might one day be venerated as well by Catholics in the same manner as are certain Eastern Orthodox saints). Five of them are refuges of the Latin Mass, in either the Tridentine or Novus Ordo form, or both; tradition-minded Latin Rite Catholics would also be an easy fit. One is, of course, the Cathedral in Orlando, in which diocese the second miracle attributed to Blessed Charles took place, and another is St. Vincent's Archabbey, long associated with the Gebetsliga. That leaves two Catholic high schools, and this makes perfect sense, given that both Charles and Zita are eminently suitable role models for young people. So then, is devotion to Blessed Charles and Zita to be considered purely an interest of Byzantine, Anglican Use, traditional, and young Catholics? By no means; all this tells us is that the authorities who wish to host shrines generally fall into those categories. In fact, the American Gebetsliga hears from an extraordinarily diverse crowd of devotees, and not all are Catholic by any means.

So just what is the attraction? There are a number, some general for anyone living in these times, and others specific to the United States. Part of it is not monarchism in any conscious sense but a deep yearning for paternity. Without wishing to get too psychoanalytical, these United States were born of a revolution against a king, something we have had to constantly justify to ourselves and the world ever since. But despite the many advantages we associate with our form of government, it does have one signal lack: with the possible exceptions of presidents Washington, Davis, and Lincoln (each of whom were aware that he might die performing his duties, and the last named in fact doing so), it is hard for us Americans to imagine a president willing to offer his life for the American people as an integral part of the job. But in a monarchy, as shown by the last words of Charles I of England, Louis XVI, Nicholas II, and most certainly Blessed Charles, it is. That sort of sacrificial kingship inevitably looks quite consciously to the crucifixion of the King of kings for its inspiration. As with its divine progenitor, the victim in such a case lies down on the altar forgiving and blessing those by and for whom he is sacrificed. We shall never be ruled by such a man, but on some level, we crave that kind of leadership and shall take whatever substitutes we can get. This is particularly true when the going gets tough and we make unto ourselves a Franklin Roosevelt or a Ronald Reagan. So far, we have always been rather fortunate in such choices, compared to those made by some peoples overseas. May it always be so!

But apart from that, Blessed Charles symbolizes so many things we wish we had. As a ruler over eleven major squabbling peoples, he tried to lead them as a father tries to lead his children—not favoring one over the other, but reveling in each of their particular gifts, and trying to help each of them develop in their own way, albeit in concert with the others. This kind of leadership is precisely the best for the kind of multicultural people we Americans have always been to some extent, and never more so than now. He and his predecessors were a sort of living flag around which each of their peoples could gather, despite their mutual antipathies.

We have seen him as a chivalrous soldier, and neither knighthood nor modern soldiering were foreign to him. We live in a time when warfare has descended in many cases (save for the boots on the ground) into a sort of video game, where hundreds or thousands of the enemy can be eliminated at the flick of a switch (and we are speaking here of non-nuclear weapons). Against that sort of thing, Charles's response is very clear: no war against civilians, no war at all unless absolutely necessary. A leadership that asks no more of its men then it is willing to do itself, which was always the classical definition of good military leadership. Above all, care for those who serve their country, both in uniform and after. It is hardly surprising that as knowledge of Charles grows among American military men, so does his popularity. The Knights of Columbus organization among American soldiers in Afghanistan was refounded in 2019 as the Blessed Karl Kabul Roundtable. Its website explains the name: "We named the roundtable after Emperor Karl of Austria-Hungary to honor him for his prowess as a warrior, a man of peace, and being a great family man." It is also fitting that his feast is on the calendar of the Knights of Malta; he belonged to that order himself and is a great example of steadfastness despite betrayal, qualities that august order has needed at various times in its history.

As a husband, Charles was as peerless as Zita was as a wife. Theirs is an example that has long been needed, as marriage has decayed over the past century. A wife and husband who were partners in every sense of the word—personally, professionally, publicly, and parentally. Their love endured until death and beyond because they based it upon the example of the Holy Family and saw it as a vocation intended to bring them both to heaven. But in these days of massive broken homes and gender confusion, they serve an additional set of roles: Charles as a marvelous example of true masculinity and Zita as a paragon of authentic femininity, and their relationship as a sterling illustration of how the two should complement one another. These are lessons vitally needed by the young today, and there are fewer and fewer living examples to show them.

Next, we return to fatherhood—and not in any metaphorical sense, as with a monarch or an army officer. Charles's love for his children was not simply for their pleasure, their education, or their worldly futures, deeply concerned as he was for those. As all fathers should be, he wanted above all for each of his offspring to avoid mortal sin in order to attain heaven. As with his love for his wife—from which the children came, and which coming deepened that love—he saw his fatherhood also as a vocation with heaven at its end if done properly. This is an example that is also vitally needed in this day of "Baby Mamas" and "Baby Daddies." So, too, is the witness of Zita, whose long widowhood and heroic care for her children epitomize motherhood.

There is another important area in which to be mindful of Charles's example, and that is sonship. Born to a difficult marriage, with parents wildly unsuited to each other, he nevertheless loved them both. Moreover, he derived from each their best traits: his father's winning charm and lively sense of humor without his selfishness and immorality, his mother's deep piety and steadfastness of purpose without her dourness. He found himself in a somewhat similar situation between his uncle, Franz Ferdinand, and his great uncle, Franz Josef, whose political and personal differences strained their relationship and created two different centers of intrigue. Yet Charles managed to avoid falling out with either. How was this possible? Love. He genuinely loved them both, and they knew it. This may seem odd to us, used as we are to looking at both figures through the prism of their stiff (and in the case of the old emperor, seemingly omnipresent) photographs and pictures. But as their respective marriages show, both men were passionate, living beings, surrounded with people who valued them only for their position. The genuine affection and high regard in which the talented and enjoyable young archduke held them must have been a real tonic. So, how is this an example to follow today? Well, very many young people in our time are the product of marriages at least as unpleasant as Charles's parents had, if there is any marriage at all. How do you steer through the marital wreckage of our time, avoid the bad examples one's parents might have set, and yet still love them as duty commands and the Church enjoins? Here, too, Blessed Charles gives us a very fine pattern to follow.

There are many other elements of Charles's life worth meditating on and attempting to emulate: his sense of humor, his method of friendship, and on and on. But we shall close this out simply by recalling his dedication to two things in particular we moderns avoid: duty and suffering. It was his unhappy lot to have the two closely connected. He may have been entitled to wear four crowns (only one of which actually sat upon his head), but from the moment Franz Josef died, the crown of thorns was Charles's constant invisible headpiece. Wilson, Czernin, Renner, and Horthy, unjust and, in the case of the latter three, ungrateful as they were, were nevertheless symbolic of many more, lesser folk, who shared in Charles's long drawn out crucifixion: subjects, enemies, and allies. Yet he died not only not hating them but pardoning all who had done him wrong and offering his suffering that his peoples might come back together. It is to that last point that we shall now turn our attention.

Chapter 17

REDUX AUSTRIAE?

All that is gold does not glitter,
Not all those who wander are lost;
The old that is strong does not wither,
Deep roots are not reached by the frost.
From the ashes a fire shall be woken,
A light from the shadows shall spring;
Renewed shall be blade that was broken,
The crownless again shall be king.

—J. R. R. Tolkien, *The Lord of the Rings*

A century after Emperor Charles's deposition and death, Europe and the lands of former monarchy in particular are very different places. The confusion and uncertainty of the interwar years made way for the *Sturm und Drang* of World War II. This was in turn replaced in the East by the Life-in-Death of Communism. In the West, American occupation and the Marshall Plan brought about the "Postwar Miracle." By the time Kennedy was elected (on the day this writer was born!), the Europe of Adenauer, de Gasperi, and de Gaulle (despite Algeria) seemed to have reached an apogee. Despite the fall of virtually every Catholic monarchy in the world (save Liechtenstein, Luxembourg, Monaco, Andorra, and, of course, Vatican City), the Church seemed in very good shape. There were all sorts of lay initiatives, and the Christian democratic parties dominant in most of Western Europe radiated Catholic Social teaching, and never more than in the six nations of what would become the European Union. Surely the dreams of its founders—to say nothing of Coudenhove-Kalergi and Archduke Otto—would soon be coming true?

Alas, no. Without wanting to do too much chicken-or-egg questioning, suffice it to say that in the wake of Vatican II, Catholicism as an effective political or social force imploded, while the counterculture arose among the "Generation of '68," or as we would say in America, the "Baby Boomers." One of the major differences between the two, of course, is that the older Boomers tended to be spoiled folk who had been deprived of their fathers during the war, whereas their confreres in Europe were dodging bullets as children during that conflict or picking their way through rubble later. It certainly warped them and helped make many ripe for radicalization. But while that counterculture in the Anglosphere had its political side, it also possessed some gentler attributes, hence the growth of such things as Renaissance Fairs and the Society for Creative Anachronism, to say nothing of an interest in folk music and fantasy literature. As the dean of that genre, J. R. R. Tolkien wrote in the '60s, "There are, of course, various elements in the present situation, which are confused, though in fact distinct (as indeed in the behavior of modern youth, part of which is inspired by admirable motives such as anti-regimentation, and anti-drabness, a sort of lurking romantic longing for 'cavaliers', and is not necessarily allied to the drugs or the cults of fainéance and filth)." But the Continent's counterculture was more political and resulted in the revolts of '68 in France and elsewhere. One of the first rotten fruits of this movement would be the wholesale abandonment of academic dress in European universities, that outward sign of one of the bulwarks of Western civilization since the Middle Ages. But that was by no means the last thing they would destroy.

Indeed, since 1968, the emptying out of European culture and morality has proceeded apace—and everywhere else in the West—the triumph of contraception and the implosion of the birth-rate, necessitating in the minds of a profit-oriented leadership wholesale immigration to man the factories and consume what they produced. Slowly but surely as well, as the members of the Generation of '68 came into positions of power, they more or less instinctively secularized or "rationalized" or "democratized" whatever they put their hands to, from local government to marriage and family, with deleterious results.

In the meantime, as all the world knows, the Iron Curtain fell in 1989, and the captives surged forth. Due in no small part to the work of Archduke Otto, most of the regions that had been part of the empire eventually came into the EU. But it was and is an EU most unlike what either its founders or the archduke and his supporters envisioned. As the Statement of Principles of the Austrian section of the Paneuropa Union states so poignantly, "The soul of this continent is Christianity. Whoever takes it out of political action, makes Europe a soulless body, a fragile construction that is exposed to all the influences and currents of the Zeitgeist." Indeed, but that is what the '68-vintage leadership in Western Europe have done both to their individual countries and to the machinery of the European Union. This is why Belgian politico Guy Verhofstadt—a poster child for his generation of Eurocrats—before graduating from national politics to European, engineered the change of his party's name from the Christian Social Party to the Humanist Democratic Centre; why, in 2001, the Christian Democrat International altered its title to Centrist Democrat International; or why as early as 1964, the majority of the Catholic Trade Union, the French Confederation of Christian Labor, reorganized as the French Democratic Confederation of Labor.

This was the kind of West to which it was proposed the former Eastern bloc conform itself. But depending on the country, Catholicism (or Orthodoxy), having served as a major means of withstanding Communism, retained more of its hold on society. For those so retained, Western immorality was anathema, as was the secularization, mass immigration, and all the rest of it. Moreover, those countries that had wholly lain within the boundaries of the old monarchy—Hungary, Czechia, Slovakia, Slovenia, and Croatia—were faced with a great paradox. Although their national annoyances with each other, exacerbated by a century of ill experiences and propaganda, were and are still very much in existence, they also still have a lot in common. (This phenomenon, incidentally, called the "Habsburg Effect" by researchers, extends into countries that encompass lands that were both inside and out of the old monarchy: things like voting patterns and attitudes toward government still follow the old frontiers in Poland, Romania, Ukraine, Serbia, and Montenegro.) Certainly, their basic attitudes toward life, religion, and culture were shared with one another far more than with Eurocratic elite, and of course, the misrule of that elite has given fuel to populist and nationalist groups all over Western Europe as well. For many, tearing up the EU seems easier than rescuing it and attempting to turn it to its original goal.

But the structures are in place, and as things stand, they do bring certain benefits. But how to reverse or alter the direction in which Brussels is going? None of the Central European nations within the EU separately are a match for the Franco-German axis of elites that dominates the union. But together, well, that is a different story. Already, due to shared perceptions and despite national antipathies, Poland, Czechia, Hungary, and Slovakia formed the Visegrad Group to further military, cultural, economic, and energy cooperation within the European Union; moreover, the latter three (with Poland as an observer) have joined with Slovenia, Croatia, and Austria (which in the past few years has looked much more toward her former partners) in the Central European Defense Cooperation (CEDC). This body is coordinating its members' defense and immigration policies regardless of Brussels.

Pragmatic as such measures are, how can they overcome the national antipathies which not only led to ill feeling in the past but sometimes atrocities? It is here that an unexpected byproduct of devotion to Blessed Emperor Charles is having an effect. The Gebetsliga is strictly non-political. But commemorating the peace emperor, studying his life, and assisting at Masses in his honor with members of nationalities you have been raised to dislike—but who as individuals love the blessed who loved them all—are a powerful experiences. This writer has been to the audience in Brandys, co-sponsored by the Czech Gebetsliga, the Georgsorden (of which more presently), and several other organizations. To stand on the platform at the train station filled with Czechs, Austrian Germans (some of Sudeten heritage), Hungarians, Slovaks, and others all cheering and waving double-eagle flags until the imperial train pulls in and the band strikes up the *Kaiserhymne* is quite an intoxicating experience. It is reenactment, but reenactment with a purpose, as the old feelings of joint loyalty are rekindled in hearts that could never have felt them at first hand. Then, in the later afternoon, as the reenactment units perform a marchpast by one of Charles's grandsons, the feeling is renewed, coming to a crescendo with the votive Mass in honor of Charles and the blessing with his relic. He said as he was dying that he was suffering that his peoples might come back together. Perhaps the annual event in the town he and his wife loved so much are a foretaste and exercise in "consciousness raising," as we said in my far-off youth.

Indeed, it must be said that there are those who are working for a concrete realization of that idea. There are of course many monarchists of sentiment through the old empire. But in terms of working actively for that goal, not perhaps that many, and they are often divided. Politically speaking, the most important of these is probably the political party in Czechia *Koruna Cesky*, which boasts two senators, two mayors, and one town councilor in 2019. Croatia has its

Kraljevina Hrvatska (Hrvatski monarhisti HKRV), Hungary its *Regnum*, and Austria its *Schwarz-Gelb Allianz*. There are, of course, in Austria as well a group of monarchist Catholic student fraternities, the *akademische Bund katholisch-österreichischer Landsmannschaften*. There are other groups and individuals who are certainly sympathetic.

Do such groups want to see Austria-Hungary restored as it was? No. Rather, although details differ, what is on offer is a vision not too far afield from what Franz Ferdinand and Blessed Charles wanted to see in their day: with the Habsburg heir as monarch individually of Austria, Hungary, Czechia, Slovakia, Slovenia, and Croatia, and the whole bound together in a federal structure strong enough to act as a counterweight to other influences in European affairs but loose enough to allow for subsidiarity. Certainly, if it ever came to pass, such an imperial federation would be both an example to and a catalyst for change for the whole of Europe.

But what of Blessed Charles's descendants and relations in all of this? Well, as is customary for members of non-reigning houses, they take no direct role in monarchist politics, while attempting to safeguard to the best of their ability cultural traditions and to act as a voice of sanity—all too often a thankless task, as we have seen. So a number of Habsburgs are involved with the work of the Gebetsliga (one of whom decides which churches shall be graced with a relic of Blessed Charles). Archduke Michael, head of the "Palatinal" branch of the family, established in Hungary for almost two centuries, heads the association seeking the beatification of Cardinal Mindszenty (fittingly, given the loyalty of the saintly cardinal to the Habsburgs); his son Eduard is Hungary's ambassador to the Holy See. Other branches are established in Belgium, Mexico, Poland, Romania, and elsewhere.

As for Archduke Otto's children, they too are quite hard-working, in common with the rest of their far-flung clan. The archdukes Karl and Georg work with a number of organizations in attempting to further the goals their grandfather and father set them. First, of course, is the work with the Paneuropa Union, in attempting to return the European Union to its original vision. Karl is president of the Blue Shield, an international organization that works to safeguard monuments and heritage threatened by warfare. He is also the head of the student fraternities earlier referred to. As grand master of the Order of the Golden Fleece, Karl presides over a nobiliary body over five hundred years old. He is also grand master of the European Order of St. George (which describes itself as having the goal "to fight for a Christian-Western Europe, which is in danger of losing its Christian and historical roots more and more, and to strengthen the historical ties of the countries of Central Europe under the auspices of the House of Habsburg-Lorraine"). He has the same title with the Order of St. Sebastian which "was founded in 1985 in Eupen, Belgium during a European rifle festival held there. The Knighthood is a community dedicated to the peaceful development of a united, Christian Europe, and to promote this development to the best of its ability. The knighthood came under the motto PRO DEO—PRO CHRISTIANAE EUROPE UNITATE—PRO VITA (For God—For a United, Christian Europe—For Life). The members of the knighthood are ready to stand up for the faith and to preserve and develop the Christian virtues." Its parent organization made up of historic European shooting brotherhoods (over which the archduke also presides) form EGS shooters associations from Belgium, Germany, France, Italy, Croatia, Liechtenstein, Netherlands, Austria, Poland, Sweden, Switzerland, Czechia, and Ukraine. He and his brother Archduke Georg work with these and many other organizations that share roughly the same ends.

A fairly unique institution in Central Europe today, but one with which Blessed Charles would have been familiar, is Archduke Karl's *Generaladjutantur* (General Adjutancy). A revival of the body which in imperial times assisted the emperor in setting up ceremonies and so on, currently, "The Adjutant General today has a wealth of tasks. He is loyal to Karl von Habsburg, takes care of the protocol, the protocol procedures at major events and is the first point of contact for the traditional regiments and shooters." As has been noted, these gentlemen are key to such events as the audience at Brandys, the funerals of Empress Zita and Archduke Otto, and the beatification of Emperor Charles, as well as innumerable other commemorative ceremonies, often in accord with the Gebetsliga. There is a central body for these as well, with which the Generaladjutantur often works: the *Militärkanzlei Wien* (the Vienna Military Chancellery). This group "was founded in Vienna in 1989 and constituted in 1993 in Regau as an association. Named after the junction between the emperor and the [imperial and royal] army leadership, the new military chancellery was launched as a reaction to the re-establishment of numerous citizen corps and traditional regiments in the successor states of the Danube monarchy after the fall of communism. The military office currently has 38 members from Austria, the Czech Republic, Hungary, Poland and Italy—for the most part members of existing traditional units." This may seem like play-acting, but it certainly has a symbolic importance, and it reminds people of the Habsburg legacy, which even today the small-minded attack.

It is terribly important for the future of the old Habsburg lands and Europe as a whole that this hatred be overcome. While it is, of course, convenient as a justification for holding on to the properties the Nazis pilfered and for maintaining the status quo, that very maintenance is ultimately an impossible goal. The only real question is whether the Mother Continent shall regain her Faith and so her soul, to bloom again, in perhaps better wise than ever she has before, or to fall beneath a new wave of domestic or foreign savagery. It was to the first vision that Charles and Zita, and Otto and his sons, were and are dedicated—a vision as true now as it was more than a hundred years ago. In the end, that is Charles's political legacy to the Continent of Europe, almost all of which, at one point or another, his and his wife's Habsburg and Bourbon ancestors ruled. Nor is it a vision that those of us of Christian Faith and European culture beyond the seas can safely ignore.

ENVOI

O Lórien! The Winter comes, the bare and leafless Day;
The leaves are falling in the stream, the River flows away.
O Lórien! Too long I have dwelt upon this Hither Shore
And in a fading crown have twined the golden elanor.
But if of ships I now should sing, what ship would come to me,
What ship would bear me ever back across so wide a Sea?

—J. R. R. Tolkien, *The Lord of the Rings*

So it is that we come to the end of our story. I have spent the last year in the lands of the old empire: in Vienna, in Budapest, in Prague and Zagreb, and in Bratislava and Krakow. I have visited the castles and palaces where so much of the drama I have written about took place. I have prayed by the tombs of Franz Ferdinand and his Sophie at Schloss Artstetten, for Rudolph at Mayerling, and for Franz Josef, doomed Elizabeth, and Otto—with whom I corresponded for years and met twice—at the Kaisergruft. In truth, the story of the House of Habsburg is, thus far, a tragedy.

But it is not really their tragedy, for all the pain it cost them; Charles and Zita are triumphs in themselves, as St. Joan of Arc is for France. No, the tragedy is all ours, and continues to be. For you see, with Charles in heaven and Zita quite possibly there, their victory is assured; we have to live with the dire results of their earthly defeat. Imagine had Franz Ferdinand not been killed, and World War I avoided, and the brightest and best of a whole generation of Europeans not butchered or maimed! Or if either he or Charles had succeeded in federalizing the empire! Or even if Charles had simply been able to end the war two or three years earlier!

So what are we to take back to our own time and place, after this voyage over those twin seas? That, as with Charles and Zita, the present is simply the historical stage against which we must work our salvation in fear and trembling. If we keep our Catholic faith—its practice and profession—as our dearest treasure and attempt to mold everything in our personal, professional, and public lives after its precepts and persevere to the end in doing so, we shall win the crown. That is true regardless of what is going on around us, and whomever may be emperor, pope, or president, even if it is oneself. Keeping the Faith and doing one's duty. It is a formula that won Blessed Charles heaven, and shall do so for us if we let it.

Charles A. Coulombe
Trumau, Lower Austria
July 16, 2019
Feast of Our Lady of Mount Carmel

BIBLIOGRAPHY

Bassett, Richard, *For God and Kaiser: The Imperial Austrian Army, 1619-1918* (Yale University Press, 2015).

Bogle, Joanna and James, *A Heart for Europe: The Lives of Emperor Charles and Empress Zita of Austria-Hungary* (Gracewing Publishing, 2000).

Brook-Shepherd, Gordon, *The Last Habsburg* (Weidenfeld & Nicolson Ltd., 1968).

———, *Uncrowned Emperor: The Life and Times of Otto von Habsburg* (Bloomsbury, 2007).

Bryce, James, *The Holy Roman Empire* (MacMillan and Co., 1871).

Coudenhove-Kalergi, Richard von, *Pan Europe* (Knopf, 1926).

Demmerle, Eva, *Kaiser Karl, Mythos & Wirklichkeit* (Amalthea Signum Verlag, 2016).

———, *Das Haus Habsburg* (HF Ullmann Verlag, 2011 und 2014).

———, *Otto von Habsburg* (Amalthea, 2007).

———, *Der Habsburg-Faktor: Visionen für das neue Jahrtausend. Eva Demmerle im Gespräch mit Otto von Habsburg* (REDLINE, 2007).

———, *Kaiser Karl I. "Selig, die Frieden stiften ..."* (Amalthea, 2004).

Harding, Bertita, *Imperial Twilight: The Story of Karl and Zita of Hungary* (The Bobbs-Merrill Company, Inc., 1939).

Habsburg, Otto von, *Charles V* (Weidenfeld and Nicolson, 1967).

———, *Die Reichsidee. Geschichte und Zukunft einer übernationalen Ordnung* (Amalthea, 1991).

———, *The Social Order of Tomorrow: State and Society in the Atomic Age* (Newman Press, 1959).

Hammerschmid, Leo, *Zita: The Last Empress of Austria* (Meridian Press, 1989).

Heer, Friedrich, *The Holy Roman Empire* (Phoenix, 2002).

Holborn, Hajo, *A History of Modern Germany, 1840-1945* (Princeton University Press, 1982).

Judson, Pieter, *The Habsburg Empire: A New History* (Harvard University Press, 2016).

Lichem, Heinz von, *Karl I: ein Kaiser sucht den Frieden* (Tyrolia, 1996).

Nichols, Aidan, *Christendom Awake!* (T. & T. Clark, 1999).

Polzer-Hoditz, Arthur, *The Emperor Karl* (Putnam, 1930).

Unterreiner, Katrin, *Emperor Franz Josef, 1830-1916: Myth and Truth* (Brandstätter Verlag, 2015).

Vivian, Herbert, *The life of the emperor Charles of Austria* (Grayson and Grayson, 1932).

Walsh, William S., *Curiosities of Popular Customs* (J.B. Lippincott, 1897).

Wassensteiner, Friedrich, *Franz Ferdinand – Der verhinderte Herrsher* (Verlag Kremayr & Scheriau GmbH & Co. KG, 2014).

Wiesinger, Alois, *Occult Phenomena in the Light of Theology* (The Newman Press, 1957).

Winkelhofer, Martina, *The Everyday Life of the Emperor: Francis Joseph and his Imperial Court* (Haymon, 2012).

Online Resources

Fletcher, Zita Ballinger, "Blessed Karl: A True Soldier," June 29, 2019, http://www.emperorcharles.org/blog/2019/6/29/blessed-karl-a-true-soldier.

Fux, Ildefons Maria, "Der selige Karl von Österreich und seine Beziehung zum Heiligsten Herzen Jesu," January 22, 2005, https://www.stjosef.at/artikel/sel_karl_v_oesterreich_herzjesu.htm.

Kovács, Elisabeth, "Kaiser Karl Research," https://www.elisabethkovacs.com/neue-forschungen-zu-kaiser-karl/.

Gebtsliga Central Site: https://www.gebetsliga.com.

Gebetsliga Worldwide: https://www.gebetsliga.com/home/wander-reliquie/weltweit/.

Gebetsliga North America: http://www.emperorcharles.org/.

Friends of Empress Zita: http://associationimperatricezita.com/2340-2/.

Archduke Karl von Habsburg: https://www.karlvonhabsburg.at/.

Finis Austriae: https://finisaustriae.it/.

World of the Habsburgs: https://www.habsburger.net/en.

GAZETTEER

Austria

Vienna

Vienna Hofburg: http://www.burghauptmannschaft.at/php/detail.php?ukatnr=21196&parent=21187.
Michaelerkirche: https://www.michaelerkirche.at/en/.
Augustinerkirche: https://augustinerkirche.augustiner.at/.
Kapuzinerkirche: https://www.kapuziner.at/kapuziner/wo-wir-sind/wien/.
Kaisergruft: https://www.kapuzinergruft.com/site/en/home.
Stephansdom: https://www.stephanskirche.at/.
Schottenstift (Charles's School): http://www.schotten.wien/schottengymnasium/schulgeschichte/.
Teutonic Order: http://www.deutscher-orden.at/site/home.
Imperial Chancellery: https://www.bundeskanzleramt.gv.at/en/federal-chancellery/visit-us.html?lang=en.
Austrian Parliament Building: https://www.parlament.gv.at/ENGL/PERK/HIS/MON/index.shtml.
Votivkirche: https://www.votivkirche.at/.
Karlskirche: http://www.pfarre-karlskirche.at/.
Palais Augarten (Charles's childhood home): http://www.burgen-austria.com/archive.php?id=90.

Belvedere Palais (Franz Ferdinand's town house): https://www.belvedere.at/das-museum.

Schoenbrunn: https://www.schoenbrunn.at/en/.

Schlosskapelle Schoenbrunn: http://www.schlosskapelle.at/.

Hofmobiliendepot (Imperial Furniture Collection): https://www.hofmobiliendepot.at/en/.

Military Chancery (Headquarters for reenactment units): http://www.militaerkanzlei-wien.org/.

Schloss Hetzendorf: https://www.wien.gv.at/bildung/schulen/modeschule/schloss/architektur.html.

Schlosskirche Hetzendorf: https://www.schlosskirche.at/.

Hermesvilla: https://www.wienmuseum.at/de/standorte/hermesvilla.html.

Canisiuskirche: https://www.pfarre-canisius.at/.

Lower Austria

The Castles at Laxenburg: https://www.schloss-laxenburg.at.

Kaiserhaus Baden: http://kaiserhaus-baden.at/.

Schloss Frohsdorf: http://petit-versailles.com/.

Schloss Shwarzau: https://www.justiz.gv.at/web2013/ja_schwarzau/justizanstalt-schwarzau~2c94848542ec4981014449659e7c401f.de.html.

Schloss Persenbeug: http://www.persenbeug.at/.

Villa Wartholtz: https://schloss-wartholz.at/.

Schloss Artstetten: https://www.schloss-artstetten.at/en/.

Schloss Eckartsau: https://www.schlosseckartsau.at/.

Upper Austria

Kaiservilla, Bad Ischl: https://www.kaiservilla.at/index.php/en/2-uncategorised/1-welcome-en.

Styria

Basilica of Mariazell: https://www.basilika-mariazell.at/.
Gasthaus Orthofer, Sankt Jakob in Walde: https://www.orthofer.at/.

Tyrol

Basilica of the Sacred Heart, Tyrol: https://www.herzjesukloster-hall.at/.

Hungary

Budapest

Royal Castle: http://budacastlebudapest.com/.
Coronation Church: https://www.matyas-templom.hu/main.php?Lang=EN.
St. Stephen's Basilica: http://en.bazilika.biz/.

Pest

Royal Castle, Godollo: http://www.kiralyikastely.hu/main_page.

Vas

Bishop's Palace, Szombathely: http://www.latogatokozpont.martinus.hu/angol.html.

Komárom-Esztergom

Esterhazy Palace, Tata: http://www.museum.hu/museum/1634/Esterhazy_Palace/actual?f.
Esztergom Basilica: https://www.bazilika-esztergom.hu/hu/?nyelv=2&oldal=28.

Veszprem

Tihany Abbey: http://www.tihanyiapatsag.hu/Tihanyi_Bences_Apatsag.html.
Bl. Charles IV Chapel, Ajka: https://plebaniaajka.wordpress.com/miserend/boldog-iv-karoly-kapolna-csinger/.

Győr-Moson-Sopron

Pejachevich Palace, Sopron: https://sopronanno.hu/bejegyzes/a-pejacsevich-palota.
Charles IV Chapel, Denesfa: http://denesfa.hu/kiralykapolna/a-kiralykapolna.html.
Abbey of Pannonhalma: https://bences.hu/lang/en./

Czechia

Prague

Prague Castle: https://www.hrad.cz/en/prague-castle-for-visitors.

St. Vitus Cathedral: https://www.katedralasvatehovita.cz/en.

Charles-Ferdinand University: https://cuni.cz/UKEN-106.html.

Central Bohemia

Chateau Brandýs nad Labem: http://www.brandyszamek.cz/.

Basilica of St. Wenceslaus, Stara Boleslav: https://www.staraboleslav.com/indexAJ.php.

Karlstejn Castle: https://www.hrad-karlstejn.cz/en.

Konopiste Castle: https://www.zamek-konopiste.cz/en.

Chlum Castle: https://www.chlumutrebone.cz/zamek.

North Bohemia

Zakupy Castle: https://www.zamek-zakupy.cz/en.

Karlovy Vary

Imperial Kurhaus, Františkovy Lázně: https://www.imperialfrantiskovylazne.cz/en

Croatia

Dubrovnik – Neretva

Lokrum Island: http://www.lokrum.hr/eng.

Poland

Silesia

Habsburg Palace, Cieszyn: http://www.zamekcieszyn.pl/.

Italy

South Tyrol

Karlspromenade, Brixen: https://www.hiwio.com/de/Artikel/Karlspromenade-bei-Brixen-114.

Hotel Elephant, Brixen: https://www.hotelelephant.com.

Friuli-Venezia Giulia

Miramare Castle, Trieste: http://www.miramare.beniculturali.it.

San Giusto Cathedral, Trieste: http://www.sangiustomartire.it/.

Tuscany

Villa Borbone, Pianore: http://www.comune.camaiore.lu.it/it/arte-cultura/villa-le-pianore.

Switzerland

Aargau

Muri Monastery: https://www.murikultur.ch/habsburger.

Habsburg Castle: https://www.ag.ch/de/bks/kultur/museen_schloesser/schloss_habsburg/schloss_habsburg.jsp.

Sankt Gallen

Schloss Wartegg: https://wartegg.ch/en/.

Geneve

Villa Prangins: https://www.golfdomaineimperial.com/en/page-history-p3.php.

Grisons

Sankt Johanns Stift, Zizers: https://www.suedostschweiz.ch/ereignisse/2019-08-30/eine-neue-schlossherrin-in-graubuenden.

France

Pays de La Loire

Abbaye Sainte Cecle de Solesmes: http://www.saintececiledesolesmes.org/.

Centre-Val de Loire

Chateau de Chambord: https://www.chambord.org/en/.

Auvergne

Chateau de Bostz: https://presence-bourbon.com/presentation-vieux-bostz/.

Belgium

Brabant

Castle Ter Ham, Steenokkerzeel: https://www.kasteelter-ham.be/en.

Germany

Bavaria

Kloster Zangberg: http://www.kloster-zangberg.de/.

England

Isle of Wight

St. Cecilia's Abbey, Ryde: https://www.stceciliasabbey.org.uk/.

Nottinghamshire

Wellbeck Abbey: https://www.welbeck.co.uk/.

St. Mary's Catholic Church, Worksop: https://worksop-catholicchurches.weebly.com/st-marys-worksop.html.

Spain

Madrid

Palacio El Pardo: https://www.patrimonionacional.es/real-sitio/palacio-real-de-el-pardo.

Vasconadas

Uribarren Palace, Lekeitio: https://www.hoteles-silken.com/en/hotel-palacio-uribarren-lekeitio/.
Basilica, Lekeitio: http://basilicalekeitio.blogspot.com/.

Madeira

Funchal

Our Lady of Monte Church: https://en.wikipedia.org/wiki/Church_of_Our_Lady_of_Monte.
Reid's Palace Hotel: https://cosmopolis.ch/reids-palace/.
Quinta do Monte: https://ifcn.madeira.gov.pt/quintas-e-jardins/quintas/quinta-do-imperador.html.

United States of America

Massachusetts

La Bastille House, Royalston: https://www.nehomemag.com/all-is-calm/.

New York

The Empress' Palace, Tuxedo Park: http://www.tuxedopark-realestate.com/propertydetails.aspx?propertyid=77.

Canada

Quebec

Spencer Grange Villa, Sillery: https://www.ville.quebec.qc.ca/citoyens/patrimoine/bati/fiche.aspx?fiche=2159.